D0763780

Catholic Mission and Culture in Colleges and Universities

Defining Documents: 1965–2014

Catholic Mission and Culture in Colleges and Universities

Defining Documents: 1965–2014

Committee on Catholic Education
United States Conference of Catholic Bishops

Washington, DC

Contents

III. CURIAL DOCUMENTS

IV. UNITED STATES CONFERENCE OF CATHOLIC BISHOPS' DOCUMENTS

Introduction to *Catholic Mission and Culture in Colleges and Universities*

April 2, 2014

The Apostolic Constitution, *Ex Corde Ecclesiae*, has described the Catholic University as a "privileged place for a *fruitful dialogue between the Gospel and culture*" (ECE, I, 43.). This remains true today. In completing the 2011 ten year review of *The Application of Ex Corde Ecclesiae for the United States*, the bishops of the United States spoke of progress in advancing Catholic identity. The bishops characterized their relationships with college and university presidents as positive and engaged. Clarity about Catholic identity among institutional leaders has fostered dialogue and cultivated greater mission driven practices across campuses. In acknowledging that much progress has been made, the bishops have recognized there is still work to be done.

Pope Francis articulated the importance of Catholic education and the cultural challenges that exist in his February 2014 address to the Congregation for Catholic Education. "Catholic education is one of the most important challenges for the Church, engaged as she is today in implementing the new evangelization in a historical and cultural context which is in constant flux." These remarks come as we prepare for two significant anniversaries that will take place in 2015: the 50th anniversary of the Conciliar Declaration *Gravissimum Educationis* and the 25th anniversary of the Apostolic Constitution *Ex Corde Ecclesiae*.

This volume expands upon a 2006 text entitled *Catholic Identity in Our Colleges and Universities*. In celebration of the 50th anniversary, the full text of *Gravissimum Educationis* is included in this compendium of defining documents. In addition, Apostolic Constitutions on education, *Sapientia Christiana* and *Ex Corde Ecclesiae*, provide a rich and textured vision for the Church's mission in higher education. Papal addresses give voice to the mission and purpose of the Church in the context of higher education as an expression of a living presence of the Gospel in the field of education, of science, and of culture. The growing global context of education becomes apparent through curial documents that address the pastoral care of international students and the engagement of the Church in the university and university culture. On a national level, education documents from the United States Conference of Catholic Bishops highlight the principle achievements, challenges, and aims of Catholic mission and culture in American higher education. The reflection of the bishops on the essential roles of education and formation grounded in pastoral care and evangelization provide direction and guidance to the work of higher education.

In these pages we explore the privileged place of higher education where faith and culture meet. Acknowledging the harmony of faith and reason provides a foundation for the Church's participation in the formation and preparation of men and women in search of truth and in service to the Church and to society. Whether you are a faculty member or an administrator, a campus minister or a mission officer, a student or a parent, you will find within these pages the conviction and commitment of the bishops and, indeed, the Catholic Church to education that stems from the eternal search for truth within the Catholic intellectual tradition.

+ Most Rev. George J. Lucas, Archbishop of Omaha
Chairman, Committee on Catholic Education
United States Conference of Catholic Bishops

Introduction to *Catholic Identity in Our Colleges and Universities*

March 2006

Today Catholic universities in the United States often face the question, What is a Catholic university? Reflection on the rich guidance offered by the Church is useful to answer this question and to strengthen institutional identity in the process. The purpose of this compilation is to present key guiding documents provided by the Magisterium of the Church (the teaching office of the Holy Father) and the United States Conference of Catholic Bishops for the community of Catholic colleges and universities in the United States.

The Second Vatican Council's *Gravissimum Educationis* (*Declaration on Christian Education*, 1965) provides the vision for all Catholic education and specifically addresses Catholic higher education. This declaration is an important reminder of the continued responsibility that Catholic colleges and universities have in contributing to society through the influence and training of the Christian mind.

Specific guiding canons of the *Code of Canon Law* pertain to those working in Catholic higher education. By consulting these canons, one may gain a more complete understanding of other documents in this compilation; they provide the foundation upon which Pope John Paul II promulgated *Sapientia Christiana* and *Ex corde Ecclesiae*.

Pope John Paul II was instrumental in providing clarity of vision on the purpose and mission of the Catholic college/university. Promulgated early in his pontificate, *Sapientia Christiana* (*On Ecclesiastical Universities and Faculties*, 1979) was addressed specifically to ecclesiastical universities whose degrees are bestowed by pontifical authority. The pope maintained that certain basic norms must be followed by all such institutions to ensure that universal value is attached to pontifical degrees awarded by these institutions.

Pope John Paul II's apostolic constitution *Ex corde Ecclesiae* (*On Catholic Colleges and Universities*, 1990) is the most noteworthy recent document affecting the non-ecclesiastical Catholic university, published after lengthy discourse with the nine hundred Catholic institutions of higher learning throughout the world. It identified certain norms and expectations that Catholic colleges or universities must meet to be in accordance with the teachings of the Church on Catholic higher education. In this constitution, the Holy Father John Paul II declares the essential characteristics and elements of a Catholic college or university.

Ex corde Ecclesiae required that each country develop local and regional applications of the apostolic constitution, which were subject to approval by the local ecclesiastical authority. In 2000, seven bishops and eleven advisors in the United States created *The Application of "Ex corde Ecclesiae" for the United States* to develop the system for implementing *Ex corde Ecclesiae* in the United States. The *Application* was promulgated in May 2001.

Three additional documents in this volume provide specific guidance to the unique roles and responsibilities of the theologian in the Catholic academy: *Instruction on the Ecclesial Vocation of the Theologian; Guidelines Concerning the Academic Mandatum in Catholic Universities;* and *Doctrinal Responsibilities: Approaches to Promoting Cooperation and Resolving Misunderstandings Between Bishops and Theologians.* These documents are offered herein for all those involved in Catholic higher education, and in particular for bishops and theologians to use in their ongoing conversations as called for in *Ex corde Ecclesiae*.

Finally, the translations of the Profession of Faith and Oath of Fidelity are beneficial for readers to consider and reflect upon. These documents will be familiar for those in leadership positions in Catholic higher education and inspiring for those who may be unaware of the commitments made by those in such positions. These two texts embody the deep obligations and submission to the Magisterium of those who assume offices in the name of the Church.

The members of the Committee on Education of the United States Conference of Catholic Bishops echo the Holy Father in promoting Catholic mission and identity in Catholic colleges and universities. Therefore, the members of the committee take this opportunity to call attention to these significant documents and guidelines with the publication of this compilation, *Catholic Identity in Our Colleges and Universities*.

The official documents of the Church brought together in this volume provide rich teachings and offer the practical and theological foundations for the tradition of Catholic higher education. While all documents in this collection were previously published separately, they are now combined in one volume to allow for simple access and regular reference.

> Most Rev. Bishop Bernard J. Harrington, Bishop of
> Winona
> Chairman, Committee on Education
> United States Conference of Catholic Bishops

I. Conciliar and Canonical Documents

Declaration *Gravissimum Educationis*

On Christian Education

Pope Paul VI

October 28, 1965

Introduction

The Sacred Ecumenical Council has considered with care how extremely important education is in the life of man and how its influence ever grows in the social progress of this age.[1]

Indeed, the circumstances of our time have made it easier and at once more urgent to educate young people and, what is more, to continue the education of adults. Men are more aware of their own dignity and position; more and more they want to take an active part in social and especially in economic and political life.[2] Enjoying more leisure, as they sometimes do, men find that the remarkable development of technology and scientific investigation and the new means of communication offer them an opportunity of attaining more easily their cultural and spiritual inheritance and of fulfilling one another in the closer ties between groups and even between peoples.

Consequently, attempts are being made everywhere to promote more education. The rights of men to an education, particularly the primary rights of children and parents, are being proclaimed and recognized in public documents.[3] As the number of pupils rapidly increases, schools are multiplied and expanded far and wide and other educational institutions are established. New experiments are conducted in methods of education and teaching. Mighty attempts are being made to

---

1   Among many documents illustrating the importance of education, above all see: Apostolic Letter of Benedict XV, *Communes Litteras*, April 10, 1919: AAS 11 (1919) 172. Pius XI's Apostolic Encyclical, *Divini Illius Magistri*, Dec. 31, 1929: AAS 22 (1930) 49-86. Pius XII's allocution to the youths of Italian Catholic Action, April 20, 1946: *Discourses and Radio Messages*, vol. 8, 53-57. Allocution to fathers of French families, Sept. 18, 1951: *Discourses and Radio Messages*, vol. 13, 241-245. John XXIII's 30th anniversary message on the publication of the Encyclical Letter, *Divini Illius Magistri*, Dec. 30, 1959: AAS 52 (1960) 57-59. Paul VI's allocution to members of Federated Institutes Dependent on Ecclesiastic Authority, Dec. 30, 1963: *Encyclicals and Discourses of His Holiness Paul VI*, Rome, 1964, 601-603. Above all are to be consulted the Acts and Documents of the Second Vatican Council appearing in the first series of the ante-preparatory phase. vol. 3. 363-364; 370-371; 373-374.

2   Cf. John XXIII's Encyclical Letter *Mater et Magistra*, May 15, 1961: AAS 53 (1961) 413-415; 417-424; Encyclical Letter, *Pacem in Terris*, April 11, 1963: AAS 55 (1963) 278 ff.

3   *Declaration on the Rights of Man* of Dec. 10, 1948, adopted by the General Assembly of the United Nations, and also cf. the *Declaration of the Rights of Children* of Nov. 20 1959; additional protocol to the Convention Safeguarding the Rights of Men and Fundamental Liberties, Paris, March 20, 1952; regarding that universal profession of the character of human laws cf. apostolic letter *Pacem in Terris*, of John XXIII of April 11, 1963: AAS 55 (1963) 295 ff.

obtain education for all, even though vast numbers of children and young people are still deprived of even rudimentary training and so many others lack a suitable education in which truth and love are developed together.

To fulfill the mandate she has received from her divine founder of proclaiming the mystery of salvation to all men and of restoring all things in Christ, Holy Mother the Church must be concerned with the whole of man's life, even the secular part of it insofar as it has a bearing on his heavenly calling.[4] Therefore she has a role in the progress and development of education. Hence this sacred synod declares certain fundamental principles of Christian education especially in schools. These principles will have to be developed at greater length by a special post-conciliar commission and applied by episcopal conferences to varying local situations.

1. THE MEANING OF THE UNIVERSAL RIGHT TO AN EDUCATION

All men of every race, condition and age, since they enjoy the dignity of a human being, have an inalienable right to an education[5] that is in keeping with their ultimate goal,[6] their ability, their sex, and the culture and tradition of their country, and also in harmony with their fraternal association with other peoples in the fostering of true unity and peace on earth. For a true education aims at the formation of the human person in the pursuit of his ultimate end and of the good of the societies of which, as man, he is a member, and in whose obligations, as an adult, he will share.

Therefore children and young people must be helped, with the aid of the latest advances in psychology and the arts and science of teaching, to develop harmoniously their physical, moral and intellectual endowments so that they may gradually acquire a mature sense of responsibility in striving endlessly to form their own lives properly and in pursuing true freedom as they surmount the vicissitudes of life with courage and constancy. Let them be given also, as they advance in years, a positive and prudent sexual education. Moreover they should be so trained to take their part in social life that properly instructed in the necessary and opportune skills they can become actively involved in various community organizations, open to discourse with others and willing to do their best to promote the common good.

This sacred synod likewise declares that children and young people have a right to be motivated to appraise moral values with a right conscience, to embrace them with a personal adherence, together with a deeper knowledge and love of God. Consequently it earnestly entreats all those who hold a position of public authority or who are in charge of education to see to it that youth is never deprived of this sacred right. It further exhorts the sons of the Church to give their attention with generosity to the entire field of education, having especially in mind the need of

---

4   Cf. John XXIII's Encyclical Letter, *Mater et Magistra*, May 15, 1961: AAS 53 (1961) 402. Cf. Second Vatican Council's *Dogmatic Constitution on the Church*, no. 17: AAS 57 (1965) 21, and schema on the *Pastoral Constitution on the Church in the Modern World*, 1965.

5   Pius XII's radio message of Dec. 24, 1942: AAS 35 (1943) 12-19, and John XXIII's Encyclical Letter, *Pacem in Terris* April 11, 1963: AAS 55 (1963) 259 ff. Also cf. Declaration cited on the rights of man in footnote 3.

6   Cf. Pius XI's Encyclical Letter, *Divini Illius Magistri*, Dec. 31, 1929: AAS 22 (1930) 50 ff.

extending very soon the benefits of a suitable education and training to everyone in all parts of the world.[7]

2. CHRISTIAN EDUCATION

Since all Christians have become by rebirth of water and the Holy Spirit a new creature[8] so that they should be called and should be children of God, they have a right to a Christian education. A Christian education does not merely strive for the maturing of a human person as just now described, but has as its principal purpose this goal: that the baptized, while they are gradually introduced the knowledge of the mystery of salvation, become ever more aware of the gift of Faith they have received, and that they learn in addition how to worship God the Father in spirit and truth (cf. Jn 4:23) especially in liturgical action, and be conformed in their personal lives according to the new man created in justice and holiness of truth (Eph 4:22-24); also that they develop into perfect manhood, to the mature measure of the fullness of Christ (cf. Eph 4:13) and strive for the growth of the Mystical Body; moreover, that aware of their calling, they learn not only how to bear witness to the hope that is in them (cf. Pt 3:15) but also how to help in the Christian formation of the world that takes place when natural powers viewed in the full consideration of man redeemed by Christ contribute to the good of the whole society.[9] Wherefore this sacred synod recalls to pastors of souls their most serious obligation to see to it that all the faithful, but especially the youth who are the hope of the Church, enjoy this Christian education.[10]

3. THE AUTHORS OF EDUCATION

Since parents have given children their life, they are bound by the most serious obligation to educate their offspring and therefore must be recognized as the primary and principal educators.[11] This role in education is so important that only with difficulty can it be supplied where it is lacking. Parents are the ones who must create a family atmosphere animated by love and respect for God and man, in which the well-rounded personal and social education of children is fostered. Hence the family is the first school of the social virtues that every society needs. It is particularly in the Christian family, enriched by the grace and office of the sacrament of matrimony, that children should be taught from their early years to have a knowledge of God according to the faith received in Baptism, to worship Him, and to love their neighbor. Here, too, they find their first experience of a wholesome human society and of the Church. Finally, it is through the family that they are gradually led to

---

7   Cf. John XXIII's Encyclical Letter, *Mater et Magistra*, May 15 1961: AAS 53 (1961) 441 ff.

8   Cf. Pius XI's Encyclical Letter, *Divini Illius Magistri* 1, 83.

9   Cf. Second Vatican Council's *Dogmatic Constitution on the Church*, no. 36: AAS 57 (1965) 41 ff.

10   Cf. Second Vatican Council's schema on the *Decree on the Lay Apostolate* (1965), no. 12.

11   Cf. Pius XI's Encyclical Letter *Divini Illius Magistri*, 1, 59 ff., Encyclical Letter *Mit Brennender Sorge*, March 14, 1937: AAS 29; Pius XII's allocution to the first national congress of the Italian Catholic Teachers' Association, Sept. 8, 1946: *Discourses and Radio Messages*, vol. 8, 218.

a companionship with their fellowmen and with the people of God. Let parents, then, recognize the inestimable importance a truly Christian family has for the life and progress of God's own people.[12]

The family which has the primary duty of imparting education needs help of the whole community. In addition, therefore, to the rights of parents and others to whom the parents entrust a share in the work of education, certain rights and duties belong indeed to civil society, whose role is to direct what is required for the common temporal good. Its function is to promote the education of youth in many ways, namely: to protect the duties and rights of parents and others who share in education and to give them aid; according to the principle of subsidiarity, when the endeavors of parents and other societies are lacking, to carry out the work of education in accordance with the wishes of the parents; and, moreover, as the common good demands, to build schools and institutions.[13]

Finally, in a special way, the duty of educating belongs to the Church, not merely because she must be recognized as a human society capable of educating, but especially because she has the responsibility of announcing the way of salvation to all men, of communicating the life of Christ to those who believe, and, in her unfailing solicitude, of assisting men to be able to come to the fullness of this life.[14] The Church is bound as a mother to give to these children of hers an education by which their whole life can be imbued with the spirit of Christ and at the same time do all she can to promote for all peoples the complete perfection of the human person, the good of earthly society and the building of a world that is more human.[15]

4. VARIOUS AIDS TO CHRISTIAN EDUCATION

In fulfilling its educational role, the Church, eager to employ all suitable aids, is concerned especially about those which are her very own. Foremost among these is catechetical instruction,[16] which enlightens and strengthens the faith, nourishes life according to the spirit of Christ, leads to intelligent and active participation in the

---

12   Cf. Second Vatican Council's *Dogmatic Constitution on the Church*, nos. 11 and 35: AAS 57 (1965) 16, 40 ff.

13   Cf. Pius XI's Encyclical Letter *Divini Illius Magistri*, 1, 63 ff. Pius XII's radio message of June 1, 1941: AAS 33 (1941) 200; Allocution to the first national congress of the Association of Italian Catholic Teachers, Sept 8, 1946: *Discourses and Radio Messages*, vol. 8, 1946: *Discourses and Radio Messages*, vol. 8 218. Regarding the principle of subsidiarity, cf. John XXIII's Encyclical Letter, *Pacem in Terris*, April 11, 1963: AAS 55 (1963) 294.

14   Cf. Pius XI's Encyclical Letter, *Divini Illius Magistri*, 1, 53 ff. and 56 ff.; Encyclical Letter, *Non Abbiamo Bisogno* June 29, 1931: AAS 23 (1931) 311 ff. Pius XII's letter from Secretariat of State to 28th Italian Social Week, Sept. 20, 1955; *L'Osservatore Romano*, Sept. 29, 1955.

15   The Church praises those local, national and international civic authorities who, conscious of the urgent necessity in these times, expend all their energy so that all peoples may benefit from more education and human culture. Cf. Paul VI's allocution to the United Nations General Assembly, Oct. 4, 1965: *L'Osservatore Romano*, Oct. 6, 1965.

16   Cf. Pius XI's Motu Proprio *Orbem Catholicum*, June 29 1923: AAS 15 (1923) 327-329; Decree, *Provide Sane*, Jan. 12, 1935: AAS 27 (1935) 145-152. Second Vatican Council's *Decree on Bishops and Pastoral Duties*, nos. 13 and 14.

liturgical mystery[17] and gives motivation for apostolic activity. The Church esteems highly and seeks to penetrate and ennoble with her own spirit also other aids which belong to the general heritage of man and which are of great influence in forming souls and molding men, such as the media of communication,[18] various groups for mental and physical development, youth associations, and, in particular, schools.

5. THE IMPORTANCE OF SCHOOLS

Among all educational instruments the school has a special importance.[19] It is designed not only to develop with special care the intellectual faculties but also to form the ability to judge rightly, to hand on the cultural legacy of previous generations, to foster a sense of values, to prepare for professional life. Between pupils of different talents and backgrounds it promotes friendly relations and fosters a spirit of mutual understanding; and it establishes as it were a center whose work and progress must be shared together by families, teachers, associations of various types that foster cultural, civic, and religious life, as well as by civil society and the entire human community.

Beautiful indeed and of great importance is the vocation of all those who aid parents in fulfilling their duties and who, as representatives of the human community, undertake the task of education in schools. This vocation demands special qualities of mind and heart, very careful preparation, and continuing readiness to renew and to adapt.

6. THE DUTIES AND RIGHTS OF PARENTS

Parents who have the primary and inalienable right and duty to educate their children must enjoy true liberty in their choice of schools. Consequently, the public power, which has the obligation to protect and defend the rights of citizens, must see to it, in its concern for distributive justice, that public subsidies are paid out in such a way that parents are truly free to choose according to their conscience the schools they want for their children.[20]

In addition it is the task of the state to see to it that all citizens are able to come to a suitable share in culture and are properly prepared to exercise their civic duties and rights. Therefore the state must protect the right of children to an adequate school education, check on the ability of teachers and the excellence of their training, look after the health of the pupils and in general, promote the whole school project. But it must always keep in mind the principle of subsidiarity so that there is no kind of school monopoly, for this is opposed to the native rights of the human

---

17   Cf. Second Vatican Council's *Constitution on the Sacred Liturgy*, no. 14: AAS 56 (1964) 104.

18   Cf. Second Vatican Council's *Decree on Communications Media*, nos. 13 and 14: AAS 56 (1964) 149 ff.

19   Cf. Pius XI's Encyclical Letter, *Divini Illius Magistri*, 1, 76; Pius XII's allocution to Bavarian Association of Catholic Teachers, Dec. 31, 1956: *Discourses and Radio Messages*, vol. 18, 746.

20   Cf. Provincial Council of Cincinnati III, a. 1861: *Collatio Lacensis*, III, col. 1240, c/d; Pius XI's Encyclical Letter, *Divini Illius Magistri*, 1, 60, 63 ff.

person, to the development and spread of culture, to the peaceful association of citizens and to the pluralism that exists today in ever so many societies.[21]

Therefore this sacred synod exhorts the faithful to assist to their utmost in finding suitable methods of education and programs of study and in forming teachers who can give youth a true education. Through the associations of parents in particular they should further with their assistance all the work of the school but especially the moral education it must impart.[22]

7. MORAL AND RELIGIOUS EDUCATION IN ALL SCHOOLS

Feeling very keenly the weighty responsibility of diligently caring for the moral and religious education of all her children, the Church must be present with her own special affection and help for the great number who are being trained in schools that are not Catholic. This is possible by the witness of the lives of those who teach and direct them, by the apostolic action of their fellow-students,[23] but especially by the ministry of priests and laymen who give them the doctrine of salvation in a way suited to their age and circumstances and provide spiritual aid in every way the times and conditions allow.

The Church reminds parents of the duty that is theirs to arrange and even demand that their children be able to enjoy these aids and advance in their Christian formation to a degree that is abreast of their development in secular subjects. Therefore the Church esteems highly those civil authorities and societies which, bearing in mind the pluralism of contemporary society and respecting religious freedom, assist families so that the education of their children can be imparted in all schools according to the individual moral and religious principles of the families.[24]

8. CATHOLIC SCHOOLS

The influence of the Church in the field of education is shown in a special manner by the Catholic school. No less than other schools does the Catholic school pursue cultural goals and the human formation of youth. But its proper function is to create for the school community a special atmosphere animated by the Gospel spirit of freedom and charity, to help youth grow according to the new creatures they were made through baptism as they develop their own personalities, and finally to order the whole of human culture to the news of salvation so that the knowledge

---

21   Cf. Pius XI's Encyclical Letter, *Divini Illius Magistri*, 1, 63; Encyclical Letter, *Non Abbiamo Bisogno*, June 29, 1931: AAS 23 (1931) 305, Pius XII's letter from the Secretary of State to the 28th Italian Social Week, Sept. 20, 1955: *L'Osservatore Romano*, Sept. 29, 1955. Paul VI's allocution to the Association of Italian Christian Workers, Oct. 6, 1963: *Encyclicals and Discourses of Paul VI*, vol. 1, Rome, 1964, 230.

22   Cf. John XXIII's message on the 30th anniversary of the Encyclical Letter, *Divini Illius Magistri*, Dec. 30, 1959: AAS 52 (1960) 57.

23   The Church considers it as apostolic action of great worth also when Catholic teachers and associates work in these schools. Cf. Second Vatican Council's schema of the *Decree on the Lay Apostolate* (1965), nos. 12 and 16.

24   Cf. Second Vatican Council's schema on the *Declaration on Religious Liberty* (1965), no. 5.

the students gradually acquire of the world, life and man is illumined by faith.[25] So indeed the Catholic school, while it is open, as it must be, to the situation of the contemporary world, leads its students to promote efficaciously the good of the earthly city and also prepares them for service in the spread of the Kingdom of God, so that by leading an exemplary apostolic life they become, as it were, a saving leaven in the human community.

Since, therefore, the Catholic school can be such an aid to the fulfillment of the mission of the People of God and to the fostering of the dialogue between the Church and mankind, to the benefit of both, it retains even in our present circumstances the utmost importance. Consequently this sacred synod proclaims anew what has already been taught in several documents of the magisterium,[26] namely: the right of the Church freely to establish and to conduct schools of every type and level. And the council calls to mind that the exercise of a right of this kind contributes in the highest degree to the protection of freedom of conscience, the rights of parents, as well as to the betterment of culture itself.

But let teachers recognize that the Catholic school depends upon them almost entirely for the accomplishment of its goals and programs.[27] They should therefore be very carefully prepared so that both in secular and religious knowledge they are equipped with suitable qualifications and also with a pedagogical skill that is in keeping with the findings of the contemporary world. Intimately linked in charity to one another and to their students and endowed with an apostolic spirit, may teachers by their life as much as by their instruction bear witness to Christ, the unique Teacher. Let them work as partners with parents and together with them in every phase of education give due consideration to the difference of sex and the proper ends Divine Providence assigns to each sex in the family and in society. Let them do all they can to stimulate their students to act for themselves and even after graduation to continue to assist them with advice, friendship and by establishing special associations imbued with the true spirit of the Church. The work of these teachers, this sacred synod declares, is in the real sense of the word an apostolate most suited to and necessary for our times and at once a true service offered to society. The Council also reminds Catholic parents of the duty of entrusting their children to Catholic schools wherever and whenever it is possible and of supporting these

---

25 Cf. Provincial Council of Westminster I, a. 1852: *Collatio Lacensis* III, col. 1334, a/b; Pius XI's Encyclical Letter, *Divini Illius Magistri*, 1, 77 ff.; Pius XII's allocution to the Bavarian Association of Catholic Teachers, Dec. 31, 1956: *Discourses and Radio Messages*, vol. 18, 746; Paul VI's allocution to the members of Federated Institutes Dependent on Ecclesiastic Authority, Dec. 30, 1963: *Encyclicals and Discourses of Paul VI*, 1, Rome, 1964, 602 ff.

26 Cf. especially the document mentioned in the first note; moreover this law of the Church is proclaimed by many provincial councils and in the most recent declarations of very many of the episcopal conferences.

27 Cf. Pius XI's Encyclical Letter, *Divini Illius Magistri*, 1, 80 ff.; Pius XII's allocution to the Catholic Association of Italian Teachers in Secondary Schools, Jan. 5, 1954: *Discourses and Radio Messages*, 15, 551-55B; John XXIII's allocution to the 6th Congress of the Associations of Catholic Italian Teachers Sept. 5, 1959: *Discourses, Messages, Conversations*, 1, Rome,1960, 427-431.

schools to the best of their ability and of cooperating with them for the education of their children.[28]

9. DIFFERENT TYPES OF CATHOLIC SCHOOLS

To this concept of a Catholic school all schools that are in any way dependent on the Church must conform as far as possible, though the Catholic school is to take on different forms in keeping with local circumstances.[29] Thus the Church considers very dear to her heart those Catholic schools, found especially in the areas of the new churches, which are attended also by students who are not Catholics.

Attention should be paid to the needs of today in establishing and directing Catholic schools. Therefore, though primary and secondary schools, the foundation of education, must still be fostered, great importance is to be attached to those which are required in a particular way by contemporary conditions, such as: professional[30] and technical schools, centers for educating adults and promoting social welfare, or for the retarded in need of special care, and also schools for preparing teachers for religious instruction and other types of education.

This Sacred Council of the Church earnestly entreats pastors and all the faithful to spare no sacrifice in helping Catholic schools fulfill their function in a continually more perfect way, and especially in caring for the needs of those who are poor in the goods of this world or who are deprived of the assistance and affection of a family or who are strangers to the gift of Faith.

10. CATHOLIC COLLEGES AND UNIVERSITIES

The Church is concerned also with schools of a higher level, especially colleges and universities. In those schools dependent on her she intends that by their very constitution individual subjects be pursued according to their own principles, method, and liberty of scientific inquiry, in such a way that an ever deeper understanding in these fields may be obtained and that, as questions that are new and current are raised and investigations carefully made according to the example of the doctors of the Church and especially of St. Thomas Aquinas,[31] there may be a deeper realization of the harmony of faith and science. Thus there is accomplished a public, enduring and pervasive influence of the Christian mind in the furtherance of culture and the students of these institutions are molded into men truly outstanding in

---

28   Cf. Pius XII's allocution to the Catholic Association of Italian Teachers in Secondary Schools, Jan. 5, 1954, 1, 555.

29   Cf. Paul VI's allocution to the International Office of Catholic Education, Feb. 25, 1964: *Encyclicals and Discourses of Paul VI*, 2, Rome, 1964, 232.

30   Cf. Paul VI's allocution to the Christian Association of Italian Workers, Oct. 6, 1963: *Encyclicals and Discourses of Paul VI*, 1, Rome, 1964, 229.

31   Cf. Paul VI's allocution to the International Thomistic Congress, Sept. 10, 1965: *L'Osservatore Romano*, Sept. 13-14, 1965.

their training, ready to undertake weighty responsibilities in society and witness to the faith in the world.[32]

In Catholic universities where there is no faculty of sacred theology there should be established an institute or chair of sacred theology in which there should be lectures suited to lay students. Since science advances by means of the investigations peculiar to higher scientific studies, special attention should be given in Catholic universities and colleges to institutes that serve primarily the development of scientific research.

The sacred synod heartily recommends that Catholic colleges and universities be conveniently located in different parts of the world, but in such a way that they are outstanding not for their numbers but for their pursuit of knowledge. Matriculation should be readily available to students of real promise, even though they be of slender means, especially to students from the newly emerging nations.

Since the destiny of society and of the Church itself is intimately linked with the progress of young people pursuing higher studies,[33] the pastors of the Church are to expend their energies not only on the spiritual life of students who attend Catholic universities, but, solicitous for the spiritual formation of all their children, they must see to it, after consultations between bishops, that even at universities that are not Catholic there should be associations and university centers under Catholic auspices in which priests, religious and laity, carefully selected and prepared, should give abiding spiritual and intellectual assistance to the youth of the university. Whether in Catholic universities or others, young people of greater ability who seem suited for teaching or research should be specially helped and encouraged to undertake a teaching career.

11. FACULTIES OF SACRED SCIENCES

The Church expects much from the zealous endeavors of the faculties of the sacred sciences.[34] For to them she entrusts the very serious responsibility of preparing her own students not only for the priestly ministry, but especially for teaching in the seats of higher ecclesiastical studies or for promoting learning on their own or for undertaking the work of a more rigorous intellectual apostolate. Likewise it is the role of these very faculties to make more penetrating inquiry into the various aspects of the sacred sciences so that an ever deepening understanding of sacred Revelation is obtained, the legacy of Christian wisdom handed down by our forefathers is more

---

32 Cf. Pius XII's allocution to teachers and students of French Institutes of Higher Catholic Education, Sept. 21, 1950: *Discourses and Radio Messages*, 12, 219-221; Letters to the 22nd Congress of Pax Romana, Aug. 12, 1952: *Discourses and Radio Messages*, 14, 567-569; John XXIII's allocution to the Federation of Catholic Universities, April 1, 1959: *Discourses, Messages and Conversations*, 1, Rome, 1960, 226-229; Paul VI's allocution to the Academic Senate of the Catholic University of Milan, April 5, 1964: *Encyclicals and Discourses of Paul VI*, 2, Rome, 1964, 438-443.

33 Cf. Pius XII's allocution to the academic senate and students of the University of Rome, June 15, 1952: *Discourses and Radio Messages*, 14, 208: "The direction of today's society principally is placed in the mentality and hearts of the universities of today."

34 Cf. Pius XII's Apostolic Constitution, *Deus Scientiarum Dominus*, May 24, 1931: AAS 23 (1931) 245-247.

fully developed, the dialogue with our separated brethren and with non-Christians is fostered, and answers are given to questions arising from the development of doctrine.[35]

Therefore ecclesiastical faculties should reappraise their own laws so that they can better promote the sacred sciences and those linked with them and, by employing up-to-date methods and aids, lead their students to more penetrating inquiry.

12. COORDINATION TO BE FOSTERED IN SCHOLASTIC MATTERS

Cooperation is the order of the day. It increases more and more to supply the demand on a diocesan, national and international level. Since it is altogether necessary in scholastic matters, every means should be employed to foster suitable cooperation between Catholic schools, and between these and other schools that collaboration should be developed which the good of all mankind requires.[36] From greater coordination and cooperative endeavor greater fruits will be derived particularly in the area of academic institutions. Therefore in every university let the various faculties work mutually to this end, insofar as their goal will permit. In addition, let the universities also endeavor to work together by promoting international gatherings, by sharing scientific inquiries with one another, by communicating their discoveries to one another, by having exchange of professors for a time and by promoting all else that is conducive to greater assistance.

Conclusion

The sacred synod earnestly entreats young people themselves to become aware of the importance of the work of education and to prepare themselves to take it up, especially where because of a shortage of teachers the education of youth is in jeopardy. This same sacred synod, while professing its gratitude to priests, Religious men and women, and the laity who by their evangelical self-dedication are devoted to the noble work of education and of schools of every type and level, exhorts them to persevere generously in the work they have undertaken and, imbuing their students with the spirit of Christ, to strive to excel in pedagogy and the pursuit of knowledge in such a way that they not merely advance the internal renewal of the Church but preserve and enhance its beneficent influence upon today's world, especially the intellectual world.

---

35   Cf. Pius XII's Encyclical Letter, *Humani Generis* Aug. 12, 1950 AAS 42 (1950) 568 ff. and 578; Paul VI's Encyclical Letter, *Ecclesiam Suam*, part III Aug. 6, 1964; AAS 56 (1964) 637-659; Second Vatican Council's *Decree on Ecumenism*: AAS 57 (1965) 90-107.

36   Cf. John XXIII's Encyclical Letter, *Pacem in Terris*, April 11, 1963: AAS 55 (1963) 284 and elsewhere.

Canons Pertinent to Catholic Higher Education

Code of Canon Law (1998)

CHAPTER II
Catholic Universities and Other Institutes of Higher Studies

Can. 807 The Church has the right to erect and direct universities, which contribute to a more profound human culture, the fuller development of the human person, and the fulfillment of the teaching function of the Church.

Can. 808 Even if it is in fact Catholic, no university is to bear the title or name of *Catholic university* without the consent of competent ecclesiastical authority.

Can. 809 If it is possible and expedient, conferences of bishops are to take care that there are universities or at least faculties suitably spread through their territory, in which the various disciplines are studied and taught, with their academic autonomy preserved and in light of Catholic doctrine.

Can. 810 §1. The authority competent according to the statutes has the duty to make provision so that teachers are appointed in Catholic universities who besides their scientific and pedagogical qualifications are outstanding in integrity of doctrine and probity of life and that they are removed from their function when they lack these requirements; the manner of proceeding defined in the statutes is to be observed.

§2. The conferences of bishops and diocesan bishops concerned have the duty and right of being watchful so that the principles of Catholic doctrine are observed faithfully in these same universities.

Can. 811 §1. The competent ecclesiastical authority is to take care that in Catholic universities a faculty or institute or at least a chair of theology is erected in which classes are also given for lay students.

§2. In individual Catholic universities, there are to be classes which especially treat those theological questions which are connected to the disciplines of their faculties.

Can. 812 Those who teach theological disciplines in any institutes of higher studies whatsoever must have a mandate from the competent ecclesiastical authority.

Can. 813 The diocesan bishop is to have earnest pastoral care for students, even by erecting a parish or at least by designating priests stably for this, and is to make provision that at universities, even non-Catholic ones, there are Catholic university centers which give assistance, especially spiritual assistance, to youth.

Can. 814 The prescripts established for universities apply equally to other institutes of higher learning.

CHAPTER III
Ecclesiastical Universities and Faculties

Can. 815 Ecclesiastical universities or faculties, which are to investigate the sacred disciplines or those connected to the sacred and to instruct students scientifically in the same disciplines, are proper to the Church by virtue of its function to announce the revealed truth.

Can. 816 §1. Ecclesiastical universities and faculties can be established only through erection by the Apostolic See or with its approval; their higher direction also pertains to it.

§2. Individual ecclesiastical universities and faculties must have their own statutes and plan of studies approved by the Apostolic See.

Can. 817 No university or faculty which has not been erected or approved by the Apostolic See is able to confer academic degrees which have canonical effects in the Church.

Can. 818 The prescripts established for Catholic universities in cann. 810, 812, and 813 are also valid for ecclesiastical universities and faculties.

Can. 819 To the extent that the good of a diocese, a religious institute, or even the universal Church itself requires it, diocesan bishops or the competent superiors of the institutes must send to ecclesiastical universities or faculties youth, clerics, and members, who are outstanding in character, virtue, and talent.

Can. 820 The moderators and professors of ecclesiastical universities and faculties are to take care that the various faculties of the university offer mutual assistance as their subject matter allows and that there is mutual cooperation between their own university or faculty and other universities and faculties, even non-ecclesiastical ones, by which they work together for the greater advance of knowledge through common effort, meetings, coordinated scientific research, and other means.

Can. 821 The conference of bishops and the diocesan bishop are to make provision so that where possible, higher institutes of the religious sciences are established, namely, those which teach the theological disciplines and other disciplines which pertain to Christian culture.

TITLE V
The Profession of Faith (Can. 833)

Can. 833 The following are obliged personally to make a profession of faith according to the formula approved by the Apostolic See:

6° in the presence of the local ordinary or his delegate and at the beginning of their function, pastors, the rector of a seminary, and teachers of theology and philosophy in seminaries; those to be promoted to the order of the diaconate;

7° in the presence of the grand chancellor or, in his absence, in the presence of the local ordinary or their delegates, the rector of an ecclesiastical or Catholic university, when the rector's function begins; in the presence of the rector if he is a priest or in the presence of the local ordinary or their delegates, teachers in any universities whatsoever who teach disciplines pertaining to faith or morals, when they begin their function.

II. Papal Documents

Speech to the International Meeting of the Representatives of Catholic Universities*

Pope Paul VI

May 6, 1971

Your Eminence and My Dear Sons,

We are happy to welcome you at the very time when, preparing a new international meeting of the representatives of Catholic universities, you touch on themes that while sensitive, are of great importance for the future of these universities: their relationship with the Magisterium of the Church, their coordination, and their permanent representation with the Holy See. We leave it to you to examine carefully these problems. As a way of exploring them in depth, all we want—if there is need of it—is to sharpen the awareness that you already possess of the ongoing mission of the Catholic university within the Church and in today's world. We are not speaking only of the "ecclesiastical faculties" dedicated to the sacred sciences: the importance of their choice and their close tie to the Church are obvious. We are thinking also of the scientific and natural disciplines: how, even in these fields can and must a university remain "Catholic"? (See, for example, N.A. Luyten, OP: *Pourquoi une Université catholique?* in *Recherches et Culture Tâches d'une université catholique*, Fribourg, Editions universitaires 1965, 1-22).

Even at the level of research, a Catholic university should first of all bear witness to the homage that the Church wants to pay to culture, by a material and teaching that seek to include the good, the true, and the beautiful, at every scientific, literary, artistic or philosophic level, using the correct and fitting method, and without being distracted by predetermined methods that dispense with the authentic forms of analysis and synthesis that people have such need of (See Vatican II, *Gaudium et Spes*, no. 59, para. II). Culture understood in this way stimulates the believer in his belief: it is the study of the work of the Creator, of God's wisdom spread through the cosmos and in the heart of humankind (Cf. ibid. no. 57, para. 3). Just as culture lends itself to these thoughts, it contributes also to human development, to our use of nature and to the development of society. Finally, by a more and more universal knowledge of the natural truth into which it brings us, culture opens the ways leading to a fruitful encounter with revealed truth. The believer would be unable to arrive at anything less at a harmonious synthesis between these two domains (Cf. ibid. no. 62). And so the Council has spoken plainly of the good done in this regard by the Catholic universities: "[The Church intends] that an ever deeper

---

* Unofficial translation of Pope Paul VI's Speech of May 6, 1971, "*Discours Du Pape Paul VI Au Congrès International Des Représentants Des Universités Catholiques.*"

understanding in these fields may be obtained and that . . . there may be a deeper realization of the harmony of faith and science" (*Gravissimum Educationis*, no. 10).

The Catholic mission of these universities can be found also at the level of the cultural education that they seek to instill in their students. Students should learn there how intellectual research can be lived out in a Christian way: they will hear in it the call of faith and be initiated into work that is marked by an active and fraternal participation. They will take it to heart to be ready to put at the service of civil society the human competences they have acquired as well as the witness of a deep and lively faith. It is such people that the Catholic universities are trying to form, without claiming any monopoly on them. Who would dare to say, even if conditions between countries are quite different, that this work has lost any of its value or its urgency? You are aware of it; it is of importance for the whole Church, and so it is a matter of deep concern for her caring shepherds.

Setting you before the major outlines of this project, we encourage your council and your committee to set for it strong, realistic and efficacious bases, in union with the Congregation for Catholic Education to whom we express, your Eminence, our loving esteem and all our trust.

With these feelings, and praying that God may give you strength and light in your work for the Church, we bless you with our whole heart.

Apostolic Constitution
Sapientia Christiana

On Ecclesiastical Universities and Faculties

Pope John Paul II
April 29, 1979

Foreword

I

Christian wisdom, which the Church teaches by divine authority, continuously inspires the faithful of Christ zealously to endeavor to relate human affairs and activities with religious values in a single living synthesis. Under the direction of these values all things are mutually connected for the glory of God and the integral development of the human person, a development that includes both corporal and spiritual well-being.[1]

Indeed, the Church's mission of spreading the Gospel not only demands that the Good News be preached ever more widely and to ever greater numbers of men and women, but that the very power of the Gospel should permeate thought patterns, standards of judgment, and norms of behavior; in a word, it is necessary that the whole of human culture be steeped in the Gospel.[2]

The cultural atmosphere in which a human being lives has a great influence upon his or her way of thinking and, thus, of acting. Therefore, a division between faith and culture is more than a small impediment to evangelization, while a culture penetrated with the Christian spirit is an instrument that favors the spreading of the Good News.

Furthermore, the Gospel is intended for all peoples of every age and land and is not bound exclusively to any particular culture. It is valid for pervading all cultures so as to illumine them with the light of divine revelation and to purify human conduct, renewing them in Christ.

For this reason, the Church of Christ strives to bring the Good News to every sector of humanity so as to be able to convert the consciences of human beings, both individually and collectively, and to fill with the light of the Gospel their works and undertakings, their entire lives, and, indeed, the whole of the social environment

---

1   Cf. Second Vatican Ecumenical Council, Pastoral Constitution on the Church in the Modern World *Gaudium et Spes*, no. 43 ff.: AAS 58 (1966) 1061 ff.

2   Cf. Apostolic Exhortation *Evangelii Nuntiandi*, nos. 19-20: AAS 68 (1976) 18 ff.

in which they are engaged. In this way the Church carries out her mission of evangelizing also by advancing human culture.[3]

II

In this activity of the Church with regard to culture, Catholic universities have had and still have special importance. By their nature they aim to secure that "the Christian outlook should acquire a public, stable and universal influence in the whole process of the promotion of higher culture."[4]

In fact, as my Predecessor Pope Pius XI recalled in the preface to the Apostolic Constitution *Deus Scientiarum Dominus*,[5] there arose within the Church, from her earliest period, didascaleia for imparting instruction in Christian wisdom so that people's lives and conduct might be formed. From these houses of Christian wisdom the most illustrious Fathers and Doctors of the Church, teachers, and ecclesiastical writers drew their knowledge.

With the passing of centuries schools were established in the neighborhood of cathedrals and monasteries, thanks especially to the zealous initiatives of bishops and monks. These schools imparted both ecclesiastical doctrine and secular culture, forming them into one whole. From these schools arose the universities, those glorious institutions of the Middle Ages which, from their beginning, had the Church as their most bountiful mother and patroness.

Subsequently, when civil authorities, to promote the common good, began and developed their own universities, the Church, loyal to her very nature, did not desist from founding and favoring such kinds of centers of learning and institutions of instruction. This is shown by the considerable number of Catholic universities established in recent times in nearly all parts of the world. Conscious of her worldwide salvific mission, the Church wishes to be especially joined to these centers of higher learning and she desires that they flourish everywhere and work effectively to make Christ's true message present in the field of human culture and to make it advance in that field.

In order that Catholic universities might better achieve this goal, my Predecessor Pope Pius XII sought to stimulate their united activity when, by his Apostolic Brief of July 27, 1949, he formally established the International Federation of Catholic Universities. It was "to include all Athenaea which the Holy See either has canonically erected or will in the future erect in the world, or will have explicitly recognized as following the norms of Catholic teaching and as completely in conformity with that teaching."[6]

The Second Vatican Council, for this reason, did not hesitate to affirm that "the Church devotes considerable care to schools of higher learning," and it strongly recommended that Catholic universities should "be established in suitable locations

---

3   Cf. ibid., no. 18: AAS 68 (1976) 17 f. and also Pastoral Constitution on the Church in the Modern World *Gaudium et Spes*, no. 58: AAS 58 (1966) 1079.

4   Cf. Second Vatican Ecumenical Council Declaration on Christian Education *Gravissimum Educationis*, no. 10: AAS 58 (1966) 737.

5   AAS 23 (1931) 241.

6   AAS 42 (1950) 387.

throughout the world" and that "the students of these institutions should be truly outstanding in learning, ready to shoulder duties of major responsibility in society and to witness to the faith before the world."[7] As the Church well knows, "the future of society and of the Church herself is closely bound up with the development of young people engaged in higher studies."[8]

III

It is not surprising, however, that among Catholic universities the Church has always promoted with special care Ecclesiastical Faculties and Universities, which is to say those concerned particularly with Christian revelation and questions connected therewith and which are therefore more closely connected with her mission of evangelization.

In the first place, the Church has entrusted to these Faculties the task of preparing with special care students for the priestly ministry, for teaching the sacred sciences, and for the more arduous tasks of the apostolate. It is also the task of these Faculties "to explore more profoundly the various areas of the sacred disciplines so that day by day a deeper understanding of sacred revelation will be developed, the heritage of Christian wisdom handed down by our ancestors will be more plainly brought into view, dialogue will be fostered with our separated brothers and sisters and with non-Christians, and solutions will be found for problems raised by doctrinal progress."[9]

In fact, new sciences and new discoveries pose new problems that involve the sacred disciplines and demand an answer. While carrying out their primary duty of attaining through theological research a deeper grasp of revealed truth, those engaged in the sacred sciences should therefore maintain contact with scholars of other disciplines, whether these are believers or not, and should try to evaluate and interpret the latters' affirmations and judge them in the light of revealed truth.[10]

From this assiduous contact with reality, theologians are also encouraged to seek a more suitable way of communicating doctrine to their contemporaries working in other various fields of knowledge, for "the deposit of faith, or the truths contained in our venerable doctrine, is one thing; quite another is the way in which these truths are formulated, while preserving the same sense and meaning."[11] This will be very useful so that among the People of God religious practice and uprightness of soul may proceed at an equal pace with the progress of science and technology, and so that, in pastoral work, the faithful may be gradually led to a purer and more mature life of faith.

The possibility of a connection with the mission of evangelization also exists in Faculties of other sciences which, although lacking a special link with Christian revelation, can still help considerably in the work of evangelizing. These are looked

---

7   Declaration on Christian Education *Gravissimum Educationis*, no. 10: AAS 58 (1966) 737.

8   Ibid.

9   Ibid. no. 11: AAS 58 (1966) 738.

10   Pastoral Constitution on the Church in the Modern World *Gaudium et Spes*, no. 62: AAS 58 (1966) 1083.

11   Cf. Pope John XXIII, Allocution at the opening of the Second Vatican Ecumenical Council: AAS 54 (1962) 792 and also the Pastoral Constitution on the Church in the Modern World *Gaudium et Spes*, no. 62: AAS 58 (1966) 1083.

at by the Church precisely under this aspect when they are erected as Ecclesiastical Faculties. They therefore have a particular relationship with the Church's Hierarchy.

Thus, the Apostolic See, in carrying out its mission, is clearly aware of its right and duty to erect and promote Ecclesiastical Faculties dependent on itself, either with a separate existence or as parts of universities, Faculties destined for the education of both ecclesiastical and lay students. This See is very desirous that the whole People of God, under the guidance of their Shepherds, should cooperate to ensure that these centers of learning contribute effectively to the growth of the faith and of Christian life.

IV

Ecclesiastical Faculties—which are ordered to the common good of the Church and have a valuable relationship with the whole ecclesial community—ought to be conscious of their importance in the Church and of their participation in the ministry of the Church. Indeed, those Faculties which treat of matters that are close to Christian revelation should also be mindful of the orders which Christ, the Supreme Teacher, gave to His Church regarding this ministry: "Go therefore and make disciples of all nations, baptizing them in the name of the Father and of the Son and of the Holy Spirit, teaching them to observe all that I have commanded you" (Mt 28:19-20). From this it follows that there must be in these Faculties that adherence by which they are joined to the full doctrine of Christ, whose authentic guardian and interpreter has always been through the ages the Magisterium of the Church.

Bishops' Conferences in the individual nations and regions where these Faculties exist must diligently see to their care and progress, at the same time that they ceaselessly promote their fidelity to the Church's doctrine, so that these Faculties may bear witness before the whole community of the faithful to their wholehearted following of the above-mentioned command of Christ. This witness must always be borne both by the Faculty as such and by each and every member of the Faculty. Ecclesiastical Universities and Faculties have been constituted in the Church for the building up and perfecting of Christ's faithful, and they must always bear this in mind as a criterion in the carrying out of their work.

Teachers are invested with very weighty responsibility in fulfilling a special ministry of the word of God and in being instructors of the faith for the young. Let them, above all, therefore be for their students, and for the rest of the faithful, witnesses of the living truth of the Gospel and examples of fidelity to the Church. It is fitting to recall the serious words of Pope Paul VI: "The task of the theologian is carried out with a view to building up ecclesial communion so that the People of God may grow in the experience of faith."[12]

---

12   Pope Paul VI, Letter to the Rector of the Catholic University of Louvain regarding the transfer to Louvain-la-Neuve, September 13, 1975 (cf. *L'Osservatore Romano*, September 22-23, 1975). Also cf. Pope John Paul II, Encyclical Letter *Redemptor Hominis*, no. 19: AAS 71 (1979) 305 ff.

V

To attain these purposes, Ecclesiastical Faculties should be organized in such a way as to respond to the new demands of the present day. For this reason, the Second Vatican Council stated that their laws should be subjected to revision.[13]

In fact, the Apostolic Constitution *Deus Scientiarum Dominus*, promulgated by my Predecessor Pope Pius XI on May 24, 1931, did much in its time to renew higher ecclesiastical studies. However, as a result of changed circumstances, it now needs to be suitably adapted and altered.

In the course of nearly fifty years great changes have taken place not only in civil society but also in the Church herself. Important events, especially the Second Vatican Council, have occurred, events which have affected both the internal life of the Church and her external relationships with Christians of other churches, with non-Christians, and with non-believers, as well as with all those in favor of a more human civilization.

In addition, there is a steadily growing interest being shown in the theological sciences, not only among the clergy but also by lay people, who are attending theological schools in increasing numbers. These schools have, as a consequence, greatly multiplied in recent times.

Finally, a new attitude has arisen about the structure of universities and Faculties, both civil and ecclesiastical. This is a result of the justified desire for a university life open to greater participation, a desire felt by all those in any way involved in university life.

Nor can one ignore the great evolution that has taken place in pedagogical and didactic methods, which call for new ways of organizing studies. Then too there is the closer connection that is being felt more and more between various sciences and disciplines, as well as the desire for greater cooperation in the whole university environment.

To meet these new demands, the Sacred Congregation for Catholic Education, responding to the mandate received from the Council, already in 1967 began to study the question of renewal along the lines indicated by the Council. On May 20, 1968, it promulgated the *Normae quaedam ad Constitutionem Apostolicam "Deus Scientiarum Dominus" de studies academicis ecclesiasticis recognoscendam*, which has exercised a beneficial influence during recent years.

VI

Now, however, this work needs to be completed and perfected with a new law. This law, abrogating the Apostolic Constitution *Deus Scientiarum Dominus* and the Norms of Application attached to it, as well as the *Normae quaedam* published on May 20, 1968, by the Sacred Congregation for Catholic Education, includes some still valid elements from these documents, while laying down new norms whereby the renewal that has already successfully begun can be developed and completed.

Nobody is unaware of the difficulties that appear to impede the promulgation of a new Apostolic Constitution. In the first place, there is the "passage of time" which

---

13   Declaration on Christian Education *Gravissimum Educationis*, no. 11: AAS 58 (1966) 738.

brings changes so rapidly that it seems impossible to lay down anything stable and permanent. Then there is the "diversity of places" which seems to call for a pluralism which would make it appear almost impossible to issue common norms, valid for all parts of the world.

Since however there exist Ecclesiastical Faculties throughout the world, which are erected and approved by the Holy See and which grant academic degrees in its name, it is necessary that a certain substantial unity be respected and that the requisites for gaining academic degrees be clearly laid down and have universal value. Things which are necessary and which are foreseen as being relatively stable must be set down by law, while at the same time a proper freedom must be left for introducing into the Statutes of the individual Faculties further specifications, taking into account varying local conditions and the university customs obtaining in each region. In this way, legitimate progress in academic studies is neither hindered nor restricted, but rather is directed through right channels towards obtaining better results. Moreover, together with the legitimate differentiation of the Faculties, the unity of the Catholic Church in these centers of education will also be clear to everyone.

Therefore, the Sacred Congregation for Catholic Education, by command of my Predecessor Pope Paul VI, has consulted first of all, the Ecclesiastical Universities and Faculties themselves, then, the departments of the Roman Curia and the other bodies interested. After this, it established a commission of experts who, under the direction of the same Congregation, have carefully reviewed the legislation covering ecclesiastical academic studies.

This work has now been successfully completed, and Pope Paul VI was about to promulgate this Constitution, as he so ardently desired to do, when he died; likewise Pope John Paul I was prevented by sudden death from doing so. After long and careful consideration of the matter, I decree and lay down, by my apostolic authority, the following laws and norms.

Part One: General Norms

SECTION I
Nature and Purpose of Ecclesiastical Universities and Faculties

Article 1. To carry out the ministry of evangelization given to the Church by Christ, the Church has the right and duty to erect and promote Universities and Faculties which depend upon herself.

Article 2. In this Constitution the terms Ecclesiastical Universities and Faculties mean those which have been canonically erected or approved by the Apostolic See, which foster and teach sacred doctrine and the sciences connected therewith, and which have the right to confer academic degrees by the authority of the Holy See.

Article 3. The purpose of Ecclesiastical Faculties are:

no. 1. through scientific research to cultivate and promote their own disciplines, and especially to deepen knowledge of Christian revelation and of matters connected with it, to enunciate systematically the truths contained therein, to consider in the light of revelation the most recent progress of the sciences, and to present them to the people of the present day in a manner adapted to various cultures;

no. 2. to train the students to a level of high qualification in their own disciplines, according to Catholic doctrine, to prepare them properly to face their tasks, and to promote the continuing permanent education of the ministers of the Church;

no. 3. to collaborate intensely, in accordance with their own nature and in close communion with the Hierarchy, with the local and the universal Church the whole work of evangelization.

Article 4. It is the duty of Bishops' Conferences to follow carefully the life and progress of Ecclesiastical Universities and Faculties, because of their special ecclesial importance.

Article 5. The canonical erection or approval of Ecclesiastical Universities and Faculties is reserved to the Sacred Congregation for Catholic Education, which governs them according to law.[14]

Article 6. Only Universities and Faculties canonically erected or approved by the Holy See and ordered according to the norms of this present Constitution have the right to confer academic degrees which have canonical value, with the exception of the special right of the Pontifical Biblical Commission.[15]

Article 7. The Statutes of each University or Faculty, which must be drawn up in accordance with the present Constitution, require approval by the Sacred Congregation for Catholic Education.

Article 8. Ecclesiastical Faculties erected or approved by the Holy See in non-ecclesiastical universities, which confer both canonical and civil academic degrees, must observe the prescriptions of the present Constitution, account being taken of the conventions signed by the Holy See with various nations or with the universities themselves.

Article 9. no. 1. Faculties which have not been canonically erected or approved by the Holy See may not confer academic degrees having canonical value.

no. 2. Academic degrees conferred by such Faculties, if they are to have value for some canonical effects only, require the recognition of the Sacred Congregation for Catholic Education.

no. 3. For this recognition to be given for individual degrees for a special reason, the conditions laid down by the Sacred Congregation must be fulfilled.

Article 10. For the correct carrying out of the present Constitution, the Norms of application issued by the Sacred Congregation for Catholic Education must be observed.

SECTION II
The Academic Community and Its Government

Article 11. no. 1. Since the University or Faculty forms a sort of community, all the people in it, either as individuals or as members of councils, must feel, each according to his or her own status, co-responsible for the common good and must strive to work for the institution's goals.

---

14   Cf. Apostolic Constitution *Regimini Ecclesiae Universae*, no. 78: AAS 59 (1967) 914.

15   Cf. Motu Proprio *Sedula Cura*: AAS 63 (1971) 665 ff. and also the Decree of the Pontifical Biblical Commission *Ratio periclitandae doctrinae*: AAS 67 (1975) 153 ff.

no. 2. Therefore, their rights and duties within the academic community must be accurately set down in the Statutes, to ensure that they are properly exercised within correctly established limits.

Article 12. The Chancellor represents the Holy See to the University or Faculty and equally the University or Faculty to the Holy See. He promotes the continuation and progress of the University or Faculty and he fosters its communion with the local and universal Church.

Article 13. no. 1. The Chancellor is the Prelate Ordinary on whom the University or Faculty legally depends, unless the Holy See established otherwise.

no. 2. Where conditions favor such a post, it is also possible to have a Vice-Chancellor, whose authority is determined in the Statutes.

Article 14. If the Chancellor is someone other than the local Ordinary, the statutory norms are to establish how the Ordinary and the Chancellor carry out their respective offices in mutual accord.

Article 15. The academic authorities are personal and collegial. Personal authorities are, in the first place, the Rector or President and the Dean. The collegial authorities are the various directive organisms or councils of the University or Faculty.

Article 16. The Statute of the University Faculty must very carefully set out the names and offices of the academic authorities, determining the way they are designated and their term of office, taking into account both the canonical nature of the individual University or Faculty and the university practice in the local area.

Article 17. Those designed as academic authorities are to be people who are truly knowledgeable about university life and, usually, who come from among the teachers of some Faculty.

Article 18. The Rector and the President are named, or at least confirmed, by the Sacred Congregation for Catholic Education.

Article 19. no. 1. The Statutes determine how the personal and the collegial authorities are to collaborate with each other, so that, carefully observing the principle of collegiality, especially in more serious matters and above all in those of an academic nature, the persons in authority will enjoy that exercise of power which really corresponds to their office.

no. 2. This applies, in the first place, to the Rector, who has the duty to govern the entire University and to promote, in a suitable way, its unity, cooperation, and progress.

Article 20. no. 1. When Faculties are parts of an Ecclesiastical University, their governance must be coordinated through the Statutes with the governance of the entire University in such a way that the good of the single Faculties is assured, at the same time that the good of the whole University is promoted and the cooperation of all the Faculties with each other is favored.

no. 2. The canonical exigencies of Ecclesiastical Faculties must be safeguarded even when such Faculties are inserted into non-Ecclesiastical universities.

Article 21. When a Faculty is joined to a seminary or college, the Statutes, while always having due concern for cooperation in everything pertaining to the students' good, must clearly and effectively provide that the academic direction and administration of the Faculty is correctly distinct from the governance and administration of the seminary or college.

SECTION III
Teachers

Article 22. In each Faculty there must be a number of teachers, especially permanent ones, which corresponds to the importance and development of the individual disciplines as well as to the proper care and profit of the students.

Article 23. There must be various ranks of teachers, determined in the Statutes, according to their measure of preparation, their insertion into the Faculty, their permanence, and their responsibility to the Faculty, taking into account the university practice of the local area.

Article 24. The Statutes are to define which authorities are responsible for hiring, naming, and promoting teachers, especially when it is a question of giving them a permanent position.

Article 25. no. 1. To be legitimately hired as a permanent teacher in a Faculty, a person must:

1) be distinguished by wealth of knowledge, witness of life, and a sense of responsibility;
2) have a suitable doctorate or equivalent title or exceptional and singular scientific accomplishment;
3) show documentary proof of suitability for doing scientific research, especially by a published dissertation;
4) demonstrate teaching ability.

no. 2. These requirements for taking on permanent teachers must be applied also, in proportionate measure, for hiring non-permanent ones.

no. 3. In hiring teachers, the scientific requirements in current force in the university practice of the local area should be taken into account.

Article 26. no. 1. All teachers of every rank must be marked by an upright life, integrity of doctrine, and devotion to duty, so that they can effectively contribute to the proper goals of an Ecclesiastical Faculty.

no. 2. Those who teach matters touching on faith and morals are to be conscious of their duty to carry out their work in full communion with the authentic Magisterium of the Church, above all, with that of the Roman Pontiff.[16]

Article 27. no. 1. Those who teach disciplines concerning faith or morals must receive, after making their profession of faith, a canonical mission from the Chancellor or his delegate, for they do not teach on their own authority but by virtue of the mission they have received from the Church. The other teachers must receive permission to teach from the Chancellor or his delegate.

no. 2. All teachers, before they are given a permanent post or before they are promoted to the highest category of teacher, or else in both cases, as the Statutes are to state, must receive a declaration of *nihil obstat* from the Holy See.

Article 28. Promotion to the higher ranks of teachers is to take place only after a suitable interval of time and with due reference to teaching skill, to research

---

16   Cf. Second Vatican Ecumenical Council, Dogmatic Constitution on the Church *Lumen Gentium*, no. 25: AAS 57 (1965) 29-31.

accomplished, to the publication of scientific works, to the spirit of cooperation in teaching and in research, and to commitment to the Faculty.

Article 29. The teachers, in order to carry out their tasks satisfactorily, must be free from other employment which cannot be reconciled with their duty to do research and to instruct, according to what the Statutes require for each rank of teacher.

Article 30. The Statutes must state:

a) when and under which conditions a teaching post ends;
b) for what reasons and in which ways a teacher can be suspended, or even deprived of his post, so as to safeguard suitably the rights of the teachers, of the Faculty or University, and, above all, of the students and also of the ecclesial community.

SECTION IV
Students

Article 31. Ecclesiastical Faculties are open to all, whether ecclesiastics or laity, who can legally give testimony to leading a moral life and to having completed the previous studies appropriate to enrolling in the Faculty.

Article 32. no. 1. To enroll in a Faculty in order to obtain an academic degree, one must present that kind of study title which would be necessary to permit enrollment in a civil university of one's own country or of the country where the Faculty is located.

no. 2. The Faculty, in its own Statutes, should determine what, besides what is contained in no. 1 above, is needed for entrance into its course of study, including ancient and modern language requirements.

Article 33. Students must faithfully observe the laws of the Faculty about the general program and about discipline—in the first place about the study program, class attendance, and examinations—as well as all that pertains to the life of the Faculty.

Article 34. The Statutes should define how the students, either individually or collectively, take part in the university community life in those aspects which can contribute to the common good of the Faculty or University.

Article 35. The Statutes should equally determine how the students can for serious reasons be suspended from certain rights or be deprived of them or even be expelled from the Faculty, in such a way that the rights of the student, of the Faculty or University, and also of the ecclesial community are appropriately protected.

SECTION V
Officials and Staff Assistants

Article 36. no. 1. In governing and administering a University or Faculty, the authorities are to be assisted by officials trained for various tasks.

no. 2. The officials are, first of all, the Secretary, the Librarian, and the Financial Procurator.

Article 37. There should also be other staff assistants who have the task of vigilance, order, and other duties, according to the needs of the University or Faculty.

SECTION VI
Study Program

Article 38. no. 1. In arranging the studies, the principles and norms which for different matters are contained in ecclesiastical documents, especially those of the Second Vatican Council, must be carefully observed. At the same time account must be taken of sound advances coming from scientific progress which can contribute to answering the questions being currently asked.

no. 2. In the single Faculties let that scientific method be used which corresponds to the needs of the individual sciences. Up-to-date didactic and teaching methods should be applied in an appropriate way, in order to bring about the personal involvement of the students and their suitable, active participation in their studies.

Article 39. no. 1. Following the norm of the Second Vatican Council, according to the nature of each Faculty:

1) just freedom[17] should be acknowledged in research and teaching so that true progress can be obtained in learning and understanding divine truth;

2) at the same time it is clear that:

    a) true freedom in teaching is necessarily contained within the limits of God's Word, as this is constantly taught by the Church's Magisterium,

    b) likewise, true freedom in research is necessarily based upon firm adherence to God's Word and deference to the Church's Magisterium, whose duty it is to interpret authentically the Word of God.

no. 2. Therefore, in such a weighty matter one must proceed with prudence, with trust, and without suspicion, at the same time with judgment and without rashness, especially in teaching, while working to harmonize studiously the necessities of science with the pastoral needs of the People of God.

Article 40. In each Faculty a curriculum of studies is to be suitably organized in steps or cycles, adapted to the material. They are usually as follows:

    a) first, a general instruction is imparted, covering a coordinated presentation of all the disciplines, along with an introduction into scientific methodology;

    b) next, one section of the disciplines is studied more profoundly, at the same time that the students practice scientific research more fully;

---

17 Second Vatican Ecumenical Council, Pastoral Constitution on the Church in the Modern World *Gaudium et Spes*, no. 59: AAS 58 (1966) 1080.

c) finally, there is progress toward scientific maturity, especially through a written work which truly makes a contribution to the advance of the science.

Article 41. no. 1. The disciplines which are absolutely necessary for the Faculty to achieve its purposes should be determined. Those also should be set out which in a different way are helpful to these purposes and, therefore, how these are suitably distinguished one from another.

no. 2. In each Faculty the disciplines should be arranged in such a way that they form an organic body, so as to serve the solid and coherent formation of the students and to facilitate collaboration by the teachers.

Article 42. Lectures, especially in the basic cycle, must be given, and the students must attend them, according to the norms to be determined in the Statutes.

Article 43. Practical exercises and seminars, mainly in the specialization cycle, must be assiduously carried on under the direction of the teachers. These ought to be constantly complemented by private study and frequent discussions with the teachers.

Article 44. The Statutes of the Faculty are to define which examinations or which equivalent tests the students are to take, whether written or oral, at the end of the semester, of the year, and especially of the cycle, so that their ability can be verified in regard to continuing in the Faculty and in regard to receiving academic degrees.

Article 45. Likewise the Statutes are to determine what value is to given for studies taken elsewhere, especially in regard to being dispensed from some disciplines or examinations or even in regard to reducing the curriculum, always, however, respecting the prescriptions of the Sacred Congregation for Catholic Education.

SECTION VII
Academic Degrees

Article 46. no. 1. After each cycle of the curriculum of studies, the suitable academic degree can be conferred, which must be established for each Faculty, with attention given to the duration of the cycle and to the disciplines taught in it.

no. 2. Therefore, according to the general and special norms of this Constitution, all degrees conferred and the conditions under which they are conferred are to be determined in the Statutes of the individual Faculties.

Article 47. no. 1. The academic degrees conferred by an Ecclesiastical Faculty are: Baccalaureate, Licentiate, and Doctorate.

no. 2. Special qualifications can be added to the names of these degrees according to the diversity of Faculties and the order of studies in the individual Faculties.

Article 48. Academic degrees can be given different names in the Statutes of the individual Faculties, taking account of the university practice in the local area, indicating, however, with clarity the equivalence these have with the names of the academic degrees above and maintaining uniformity among the Ecclesiastical Faculties of the same area.

Article 49. no. 1. Nobody can obtain an academic degree unless properly enrolled in a Faculty, completing the course of studies prescribed by the Statutes, and successfully passing the examinations or tests.

no. 2. Nobody can be admitted to the doctorate unless first having obtained the licentiate.

no. 3. A requisite for obtaining a doctorate, furthermore, is a doctoral dissertation that makes a real contribution to the progress of science, written under the direction of a teacher, publicly defended and collegially approved; the principal part, at least, must be published.

Article 50. no. 1. The doctorate is the academic degree which enables one to teach in a Faculty and which is therefore required for this purpose, the licentiate is the academic degree which enables one to teach in a major seminary or equivalent school and which is therefore required for this purpose.

no. 2. The academic degrees which are required for filling various ecclesiastical posts are to be stated by the competent ecclesiastical authority.

Article 51. An honorary doctorate can be conferred for special scientific merit or cultural accomplishment in promoting the ecclesiastical sciences.

SECTION VIII
Matters Related to Teaching

Article 52. In order to achieve its proper purposes, especially in regard to scientific research, each University or Faculty must have an adequate library, in keeping with the needs of the staff and students. It must be correctly organized and equipped with an appropriate catalogue.

Article 53. Through an annual allotment of money, the library must continually acquire books, old and new, as well as the principal reviews, so as to be able effectively to serve research, teaching of the disciplines, instructional needs, and the practical exercises and seminars.

Article 54. The library must be headed by a trained librarian, assisted by a suitable council. The librarian participates opportunely in the Council of the University or Faculty.

Article 55. no. 1. The Faculty must also have technical equipment, audio-visual materials, etc., to assist its didactic work.

no. 2. In relationship to the special nature and purpose of a University or Faculty, research institutions and scientific laboratories should also be available, as well as other apparatus needed for the accomplishment of its ends.

SECTION IX
Economic Matters

Article 56. A University or Faculty must have enough money to achieve its purposes properly. Its financial endowments and its property rights are to be carefully described.

Article 57. The Statutes are to determine the duty of the Financial Procurator as well as the part the Rector or President and the University or Faculty Council play in money matters, according to the norms of good economics and so as to preserve healthy administration.

Article 58. Teachers, officials, and staff assistants are to be paid a suitable remuneration, taking account of the customs of the local area, and also taking into consideration social security and insurance protection.

Article 59. Likewise, the Statutes are to determinate the general norms that will indicate the ways the students are to contribute to the expenses of the University or Faculty, by paying admission fees, yearly tuition, examination fees, and diploma fees.

SECTION X
Planning and Cooperation of Faculties

Article 60. no. 1. Great care must be given to the distribution, or as it is called, the planning of Universities and Faculties, so as to provide for their conservation, their progress, and their suitable distribution in different parts of the world.

no. 2. To accomplish this end, the Sacred Congregation for Catholic Education is to be helped by advice from the Bishops' Conferences and from a commission of experts.

Article 61. The erection or approval of a new University or Faculty is decided upon by the Sacred Congregation for Catholic Education when all the requirements are fulfilled. In this the Congregation listens to the local Ordinaries, the Bishops' Conference, and experts, especially from neighboring Faculties.

Article 62. no. 1. Affiliation of some institution with a Faculty for the purpose of being able to grant the bachelor's degree is approved by the Sacred Congregation for Catholic Education, after the conditions established by that same Sacred Congregation are fulfilled.

no. 2. It is highly desirable that theological study centers, whether diocesan or religious, be affiliated to a Faculty of Sacred Theology.

Article 63. Aggregation to a Faculty and incorporation into a Faculty by an institution for the purposes of also granting higher academic degrees is decided upon by the Sacred Congregation for Catholic Education, after the conditions established by that same Sacred Congregation are fulfilled.

Article 64. Cooperation between Faculties, whether of the same University or of the same region or of a wider territorial area, is to be diligently striven for. For this cooperation is of great help to the scientific research of the teachers and to the better formation of the students. It also fosters the advance of interdisciplinary collaboration, which appears ever more necessary in current times, as well as contributing to the development of complementarity among Faculties. It also helps to bring about the penetration by Christian wisdom of all culture.

Part Two: Special Norms

Article 65. Besides the norms common to all Ecclesiastical Faculties, which are established in the first part of this Constitution, special norms are given here-under for certain of those Faculties, because of their particular nature and importance for the Church.

SECTION I
Faculty of Sacred Theology

Article 66. A Faculty of Sacred Theology has the aim of profoundly studying and systematically explaining, according to the scientific method proper to it, Catholic doctrine, derived with the greatest care from divine revelation. It has the further aim of carefully seeking the solution to human problems in the light of that same revelation.

Article 67. no. 1. The study of Sacred Scripture is, as it were, the soul of Sacred Theology, which rests upon the written Word of God together with living Tradition, as its perpetual foundation.[18]

no. 2. The individual theological disciplines are to be taught in such a way that, from their internal structure and from the proper object of each as well as from their connection with other disciplines, including philosophical ones and the sciences of man, the basic unity of theological instruction is quite clear, and in such a way that all the disciplines converge in a profound understanding of the mystery of Christ, so that this can be announced with greater effectiveness to the People of God and to all nations.

Article 68. no. 1. Revealed truth must be considered also in connection with contemporary, evolving, scientific accomplishments, so that it can be seen "how faith and reason give harmonious witness to the unity of all truth."[19] Also, its exposition is to be such that, without any change of the truth, there is adaptation to the nature and character of every culture, taking special account of the philosophy and the wisdom of various peoples. However, all syncretism and every kind of false particularism are to be excluded.[20]

no. 2. The positive values in the various cultures and philosophies are to be sought out, carefully examined, and taken up. However, systems and methods incompatible with Christian faith must not be accepted.

Article 69. Ecumenical questions are to be carefully treated, according to the norms of competent Church authorities.[21] Also to be carefully considered are relationships with non-Christian religions; and problems arising from contemporary atheism are to be scrupulously studied.

Article 70. In studying and teaching the Catholic doctrine, fidelity to the Magisterium of the Church is always to be emphasized. In the carrying out of teaching duties, especially in the basic cycle, those things are, above all, to be imparted which belong to the received patrimony of the Church. Hypothetical or personal opinions which come from new research are to be modestly presented as such.

---

18 Second Vatican Ecumenical Council, Dogmatic Constitution on Divine Revelation *Dei Verbum* 24: AAS 58 (1966) 827.

19 Second Vatican Ecumenical Council, Declaration on Christian Education *Gravissimum Educationis*, no. 10: AAS 58 (1966) 737.

20 Second Vatican Ecumenical Council, Decree on the Missionary Activity of the Church *Ad Gentes*, no. 22: AAS 58 (1966) 973 ff.

21 See the Ecumenical Directory, Second Part: AAS 62 (1970) 705-724.

Article 71. In presenting doctrine, those norms are to be followed which are in the documents of the Second Vatican Council,[22] as well as those found in more recent documents of the Holy See[23] insofar as these pertain to academic studies.

Article 72. The curriculum of studies of a Faculty of Sacred Theology comprises:

a) the first cycle, fundamentals, which lasts for five years or ten semesters, or else, when a previous two-year philosophy course is an entrance requirement, for three years. Besides a solid philosophical formation, which is a necessary propaedeutic for theological studies, the theological disciplines must be taught in such a way that what is presented is an organic exposition of the whole of Catholic doctrine, together with an introduction to theological scientific methodology.

   The cycle ends with the academic degree of Baccalaureate or some other suitable degree as the Statutes of the Faculty determine.

b) the second cycle, specialization, which lasts for two years or four semesters. In this cycle the special disciplines are taught corresponding to the nature of the diverse specializations being undertaken. Also seminars and practical exercises are conducted for the acquisition of the ability to do scientific research.

   The cycle concludes with the academic degree of specialized Licentiate.

c) the third cycle, in which for a suitable period of time scientific formation is brought to completion, especially through the writing of a doctrinal dissertation.

   The cycle concludes with the academic degree of Doctorate.

Article 73. no. 1. To enroll in a Faculty of Sacred Theology, the student must have done the previous studies called for in accordance with article 32 of this Constitution.

no. 2. Where the first cycle of the Faculty lasts for only three years, the student must submit proof of having properly completed a two-year course in philosophy at a Faculty of Philosophy or at an approved institution.

Article 74. no. 1. A Faculty of Sacred Theology has the special duty of taking care of the scientific theological formation of those preparing for the priesthood or preparing to hold some ecclesiastical office.

no. 2. For this purpose, special courses suitable for seminarians should be offered. It is also appropriate for the Faculty itself to offer the "pastoral year" required for the

---

22 See especially Second Vatican Ecumenical Council, Dogmatic Constitution on Divine Revelation *Dei Verbum: AAS* 58 (1966) 713 ff.

23 See especially the Letter of Pope Paul VI *Lumen Ecclesiae,* about St. Thomas Aquinas, of November 20, 1974: *AAS* 66 (1974) 673 ff. Also see the circular letters of the Sacred Congregation for Catholic Education: on the Theological Formation of Future Priests, February 22, 1976, on Canon Law Studies in Seminaries, March 1, 1975; and on Philosophical Studies, January 20, 1972.

priesthood, in addition to the five-year basic cycle. At the end of this year, a special Diploma may be conferred.

SECTION II
Faculty of Canon Law

Article 75. A Faculty of Canon Law, whether Latin or Oriental, has the aim of cultivating and promoting the juridical disciplines in the light of the law of the Gospel and of deeply instructing the students in these, so as to form researchers, teachers, and others who will be trained to hold special ecclesiastical posts.

Article 76. The curriculum of studies of a Faculty of Canon Law comprises:

a) the first cycle, lasting at least one year or two semesters, in which are studied the general fundamentals of Canon Law and those disciplines which are required for higher juridical formation;

b) the second cycle, lasting two years or four semesters, during which the entire *Code of Canon Law* is studied in depth, along with other disciplines having an affinity with it;

c) the third cycle, lasting at least a year or two semesters, in which juridical formation is completed and a doctoral dissertation is written.

Article 77. no. 1. With regard to the studies prescribed for the first cycle, the Faculty may make use of the studies done in another Faculty and which it can acknowledge as responding to its needs.

no. 2. The second cycle concludes with the Licentiate and the third with the Doctorate.

no. 3. The Statutes of the Faculty are to define the special requirements for the conferring of the academic degrees, observing the Norms of Application of the Sacred Congregation for Catholic Education.

Article 78. To enroll in a Faculty of Canon Law, the student must have done the previous studies called for in accordance with Article 32 of this Constitution.

SECTION III
Faculty of Philosophy

Article 79. no. 1. An Ecclesiastical Faculty of Philosophy has the aim of investigating philosophical problems according to scientific methodology, basing itself on a heritage of perennially valid philosophy.[24] It has to search for solutions in the light of natural reason and, furthermore, it has to demonstrate their consistency with the Christian view of the world, of man, and of God, placing in a proper light the relationship between philosophy and theology.

---

24 See Second Vatican Ecumenical Council, Decree on Priestly Formation *Optatam Totius*, no. 15: AAS 58 (1966) 722.

no. 2. Then, the students are to be instructed so as to make them ready to teach and to fill other suitable intellectual posts as well as to prepare them to promote Christian culture and to undertake a fruitful dialogue with the people of our time.

Article 80. In the teaching of philosophy, the relevant norms should be observed which are contained in the documents of the Second Vatican Council[25] and in other recent documents of the Holy See concerning academic studies.[26]

Article 81. The curriculum of studies of a Faculty of Philosophy comprises:

a) the first cycle, basics, in which for two years or four semesters an organic exposition of the various parts of philosophy is imparted, which includes treating the world, man, and God. It also includes the history of philosophy, together with an introduction into the method of scientific research;

b) the second cycle, the beginning of specialization, in which for two years or four semesters through special disciplines and seminars a more profound consideration is imparted in some sector of philosophy;

c) the third cycle, in which for a suitable period of time philosophical maturity is promoted, especially by means of writing a doctoral dissertation.

Article 82. The first cycle ends with the degree of Baccalaureate, the second with the specialized Licentiate, and the third with the Doctorate.

Article 83. To enroll in a Faculty of Philosophy, the student must have done the previous studies called for in accordance with Article 32 of the Constitution.

SECTION IV
Other Faculties

Article 84. Besides the Faculties of Sacred Theology, Canon Law, and Philosophy, other Faculties have been or can be canonically erected, according to the needs of the Church and with a view to attaining certain goals, as for instance:

a) a more profound study of certain sciences which are of greater importance to the theological, juridical, and philosophical disciplines;

b) the promotion of other sciences, first of all the humanities, which have a close connection with the theological disciplines or with the work of evangelization;

---

25 Especially see the Second Vatican Council, Decree on Priestly Formation *Optatam Totius: AAS* 58 (1966) 713 ff. and the Declaration on Christian Education *Gravissimum Educationis: AAS* 58 (1966) 728 ff.

26 See especially the letter of Pope Paul VI on St. Thomas Aquinas *Lumen Ecclesiae* of November 20, 1974: *AAS* 66 (1974) 673 ff. and the Circular Letter of the Sacred Congregation for Catholic Education, On the Study of Philosophy in Seminaries, of January 20, 1972.

c) the cultivation of letters which provide a special help either to a better understanding of Christian revelation or else in carrying on the work of evangelizing;

d) finally, the more exacting preparation both of the clergy and laity for properly carrying out specialized apostolic tasks.

Article 85. In order to achieve the goals set down in the preceding article, the following Faculties or institutions *"ad instar Facultatis"* have already been erected and authorized to grant degrees by the Holy See itself:

- Christian archaeology
- Biblical studies and ancient Eastern studies
- Church history
- Christian and classical literature
- Liturgy
- Missiology
- Sacred Music
- Psychology
- Educational science or Pedagogy
- Religious science
- Social sciences
- Arabic studies and Islamology
- Mediaeval studies
- Oriental Ecclesiastical studies
- *"Utriusque Iuris"* (both canon and civil law)

Article 86. It belongs to the Sacred Congregation for Catholic Education to set out, in accordance with circumstances, special norms for these Faculties, just as has been done in the above sections for the Faculties of Sacred Theology, Canon Law, and Philosophy.

Article 87. The Faculties and Institutes for which special norms have not yet been set out must also draw up their own Statutes. These must conform to the General Norms established in the first part of this Constitution, and they must take into account the special nature and purpose proper to each of these Faculties or Institutes.

Transitional Norms

Article 88. This present Constitution comes into effect on the first day of the 1980-1981 academic year or of the 1981 academic year, according to the scholastic calendar in use in various places.

Article 89. Each University or Faculty must, before January 1, 1981, present its proper Statutes, revised according to this Constitution, to the Sacred Congregation for Catholic Education. If this is not done, its power to give academic degrees is, by this very fact, suspended.

Article 90. In each Faculty the studies must be arranged so that the students can acquire academic degrees according to the norms of this Constitution, immediately upon this Constitution coming into effect, preserving the students' previously acquired rights.

Article 91. The Statutes are to be approved experimentally for three years so that, when this period is completed, they may be perfected and approved definitively.

Article 92. Those Faculties which have a juridical connection with civil authorities may be given a longer period of time to revise their Statutes, providing that this is approved by the Sacred Congregation for Catholic Education.

Article 93. It is the task of the Sacred Congregation for Catholic Education, when, with the passage of time, circumstances shall require it, to propose changes to be introduced into this Constitution, so that this same Constitution may be continuously adapted to the needs of Ecclesiastical Faculties.

Article 94. All laws and customs presently obtaining which are in contradiction to this Constitution are abrogated, whether these are universal or local, even if they are worthy of special or individual mention. Likewise completely abrogated are all privileges hitherto granted by the Holy See to any person, whether physical or moral, if these are contrary to the prescriptions of this Constitution.

It is my will, finally, that this my Constitution be established, be valid, and be efficacious always and everywhere, fully and integrally in all its effects, that it be religiously observed by all to whom it pertains, anything to the contrary notwithstanding. If anyone, knowingly or unknowingly, acts otherwise than I have decreed, I order that this action is to be considered null and void.

Given at St. Peter's in Rome, the fifteenth day of April, the Solemnity of the Resurrection of our Lord Jesus Christ, in the year 1979, the first of my Pontificate.

Norms of Application

Of the Sacred Congregation for Catholic Education for the Correct Implementation of the Apostolic Constitution Sapientia Christiana

The Sacred Congregation for Catholic Education, according to article 10 of the Apostolic Constitution *Sapientia Christiana*, presents to the Ecclesiastical Universities and Faculties the following Norms of Application and orders that they be faithfully observed.

Part One: General Norms

SECTION I
Nature and Purpose of Ecclesiastical Universities and Faculties
(Apostolic Constitution, articles 1-10)

Article 1. By the term University or Faculty is understood also those Athenaea, Institutes, or Academic Centers which have been canonically erected or approved by the Holy See with the right to confer academic degrees by the authority of the same See.

Article 2. With a view to promoting scientific research, a strong recommendation is given for specialized research centers, scientific periodicals and collections, and meetings of learned societies.

Article 3. The tasks for which students can be prepared can be either strictly scientific, such as research or teaching, or else pastoral. Account must be taken of this diversity in the ordering of the studies and in the determining of the academic degrees, while always preserving the scientific nature of the studies for both.

Article 4. Active participation in the ministry of evangelization concerns the action of the Church in pastoral work, in ecumenism, and in missionary undertakings. It also extends to the understanding, defense, and diffusion of the faith. At the same time it extends to the whole context of culture and human society.

Article 5. Bishops' Conferences, joined to the Apostolic See in these matters also, are thus to follow carefully the Universities and Faculties:

1.   together with the Chancellor they are to foster their progress and, while of course respecting the autonomy of science according to the mind of the Second Vatican Council, they are to be solicitous for their scientific and ecclesial condition;

2.   with regard to common problems which occur within the boundaries of their own region, they are to help, inspire, and harmonize the activity of the Faculties;

3. bearing in mind the needs of the Church and the cultural progress of their own area, they are to take care that there exist an adequate number of such Faculties;

4. to do all this, they are to constitute among themselves a commission for this purpose, which should be helped by a committee of experts.

Article 6. In preparing the Statutes and Study Program, the norms in Appendix I of these directives must be kept in mind.

Article 7. no. 1. The canonical value of an academic degree means that such a degree enables one to assume an office in the Church for which a degree is required. This is, first of all, for teaching sacred sciences in Faculties, major seminaries, or equivalent schools.

no. 2. The condition to be fulfilled for the recognition of individual degrees mentioned in article 9 of the Apostolic Constitution, concern, first of all, besides the consent of the local or regional ecclesiastical authorities, the college of teachers, the study program, and the scientific helps used.

no. 3. Degrees thus recognized, for certain canonical effects only may never be considered simply as equal to canonical degrees.

SECTION II
The Academic Community and Its Government
(Apostolic Constitution, articles 11-21)

Article 8. The duty of the Chancellor is:

1. to promote continually the progress of the University or Faculty, to advance scientific progress, to ensure that Catholic doctrine is integrally followed, and to enforce the faithful implementation of the Statutes and the prescriptions of the Holy See;

2. to help ensure close relationships between all the different ranks and members of the community;

3. to propose to the Sacred Congregation for Catholic Education the names of those who are to be nominated or confirmed as Rector and President, as well as the names of the teachers for whom a nihil obstat is to be requested;

4. to receive the profession of faith of the Rector and President;

5. to give to or take away from the teachers the canonical mission or permission to teach, according to the norms of the Constitution;

6. to inform the Sacred Congregation for Catholic Education about more important matters and to send to that Congregation every three years a detailed report on the academic, moral, and economic condition of the University or Faculty.

Article 9. If the University or Faculty depends upon a collegial entity (for instance, on an Episcopal Conference), one designated member of the group is to exercise the office of Chancellor.

Article 10. The local Ordinary, if he is not the Chancellor, since he has the pastoral responsibility for his Diocese, is, whenever something in the University or Faculty is known to be contrary to doctrine, morals, or ecclesiastical discipline, to take the matter to the Chancellor so that the latter may take action. In case the Chancellor does nothing, the Ordinary may have recourse to the Holy See, without prejudice to his own obligation to provide personally for action in those cases which are more serious or urgent and which carry danger for his Diocese.

Article 11. What is contained in article 19 of the Constitution must be explained further in the proper Statutes of the individual Faculties, giving more weight, as the case may require, either to collegial or else to personal government, while always preserving both forms. Account should be taken of the university practice of the region where the Faculty is located or of the Religious Institute on which the Faculty may depend.

Article 12. Besides the University Council (Academic Senate) and the Faculty Council, both of which must everywhere exist even if under different names, the Statutes can suitably establish other special councils or commissions for scientific learning, teaching, discipline, finances, etc.

Article 13. no. 1. According to the Constitution, a Rector is one who presides over a University; a President is one who presides over an Institute or a Faculty which exists separately; a Dean is one who presides over a Faculty which is a part of a University.

no. 2. The Statutes are to fix a term of office for these persons (for instance, three years) and are to determine how and how many times their term can be renewed.

Article 14. The office of the Rector or President is:

1. to direct, promote, and coordinate all the activity of the academic community;
2. to be the representative of the University or of the Institute or Faculty existing separately;
3. to convoke the Council of the University or of the Institute or Faculty existing separately and preside over the same according to the norms of the Statutes;
4. to watch over the administration of temporalities;
5. to refer more important matters to the Chancellor;
6. to send, every year, a statistical summary to the Sacred Congregation for Catholic Education, according to the outline provided by that same Congregation.

Article 15. The Dean of the Faculty is:

1. to promote and coordinate all the activity of the Faculty, especially matters regarding studies, and to see to providing with due speed for their needs;
2. to convoke the Faculty Council and preside over it;
3. to admit or exclude students in the name of the Rector according to the norms of the Statutes;

4. to refer to the Rector what is done or proposed by the Faculty;

5. to see that the instructions of higher authorities are carried out.

SECTION III
Teachers
(Apostolic Constitution, articles 22-30)

Article 16. no. 1. Teachers who are permanently attached to a Faculty are, in the first place, those who are assumed in full and firm right and who are called Ordinary Professors; next come Extraordinary Professors. It can also be useful to have others according to university practice.

no. 2. Besides permanent teachers, there are other teachers who are designated by various titles, in the first place, those invited from other Faculties.

no. 3. Finally, it is also opportune to have Teaching Assistants to carry out certain academic functions.

Article 17. By a suitable doctorate is meant one that corresponds to the discipline that is being taught. If the discipline is sacred or connected with the sacred, the doctorate must be canonical. In the event that the doctorate is not canonical, the teacher will usually be required to have at least a canonical licentiate.

Article 18. Non-Catholic teachers, co-opted according to the norms of competent ecclesiastical authority,[1] require permission to teach from the Chancellor.

Article 19. no. 1. The Statutes must establish when a permanent status is conferred in relationship with the obtaining of the nihil obstat that must be procured in accordance with article 27 of the Constitution.

no. 2. The nihil obstat of the Holy See is the declaration that, in accordance with the Constitution and the special Statutes, there is nothing to impede a nomination which is proposed. If some impediment should exist, this will be communicated to the Chancellor who will listen to the teacher in regard to the matter.

no. 3. If particular circumstances of time or place impede the requesting of the nihil obstat from the Holy See, the Chancellor is to take counsel with the Sacred Congregation for Catholic Education to find a suitable solution.

no. 4. In Faculties which are under special concordat law the established norms are to be followed.

Article 20. The time interval between promotions, which must be at least three years, is to be set down in the Statutes.

Article 21. no. 1. Teachers, first of all the permanent ones, are to seek to collaborate with each other. It is also recommended that there be collaboration with the teachers of other Faculties, especially those with subjects that have an affinity or some connection with those of the Faculty.

no. 2. One cannot be at one and the same time a permanent teacher in more than one Faculty.

Article 22. no. 1. The Statutes are to set out with care the procedure in regard to the suspension or dismissal of a teacher, especially in matters concerning doctrine.

---

1   See the Ecumenical Directory, Second Part: AAS 62 (1970), 705 ff.

no. 2. Care must be taken that, first of all, these matters be settled between the Rector or President or Dean and the teacher himself. If they are not settled there, the matters should be dealt with by an appropriate Council or committee, so that the first examination of the facts be carried out within the University or Faculty itself. If this is not sufficient, the matters are to be referred to the Chancellor, who, with the help of experts, either of the University or the Faculty or from other places, must consider the matter and provide for a solution. The possibility remains open for recourse to the Holy See for a definitive solution, always allowing the teacher to explain and defend himself.

no. 3. However, in more grave or urgent cases for the good of the students and the faithful, the Chancellor can suspend the teacher for the duration of the regular procedure.

Article 23. Diocesan priests and Religious or those equivalent to Religious from whatever Institute, in order to be teachers in a Faculty or to remain as such, must have the consent of their proper Ordinary or Religious Superior, following the norms established in these matters by competent Church authority.

SECTION IV
Students
(Apostolic Constitution, articles 31-35)

Article 24. no. 1. Legal testimony, according to the norm of article 31 of the Constitution:

1) about a moral life is to be given, for clergy and seminarians, by their own Ordinary or his delegate; for all other persons by some ecclesiastic;

2) about previous studies in the study title required in accordance with article 32 of the Constitution.

no. 2. Since the studies required before entry into a University differ from one country to another, the Faculty has the right and duty to investigate whether all the disciplines have been studied which the Faculty itself considers necessary.

no. 3. A suitable knowledge of the Latin language is required for the Faculties of the sacred sciences, so that the students can understand and use the sources and the documents of the Church.[2]

no. 4. If one of the disciplines has been found not to have been studied or to have been studied in an insufficient way, the Faculty is to require that this be made up at a suitable time and verified by an examination.

Article 25. no. 1. Besides ordinary students, that is, those studying for academic degrees, extraordinary students can be admitted according to the norms determined in the Statutes.

no. 2. A person can be enrolled as an ordinary student in only one Faculty at a time.

Article 26. The transfer of a student from one Faculty to another can take place only at the beginning of the academic year or semester, after a careful examination

---

2   The Second Vatican Ecumenical Council, Decree on Priestly Formation *Optatam Totius*, 13: AAS 58 (1966), 721 and the Chirograph of Pope Paul VI *Romani Sermonis*: AAS 68 (1976), 481 ff.

of his academic and disciplinary situation. But in any event nobody can be given an academic degree unless all the requirements for the degree are fulfilled as the Statutes of the Faculty demand.

Article 27. In the norms which determine the suspension or the expulsion of a student from a Faculty, the student's right to defend himself must be safeguarded.

SECTION V
Officials and Staff Assistants
(Apostolic Constitution, articles 36-37)

Article 28. In the Statutes or in some other suitable document of the University or Faculty, the rights and duties of the Officials and Staff Assistants should be determined, as well as their participation in the community life of the University.

SECTION VI
Study Program
(Apostolic Constitution, articles 38-45)

Article 29. The Statutes of each Faculty must define which disciplines (principal and auxiliary) are obligatory and must be followed by all, and which are free or optional.

Article 30. Equally, the Statutes are to determine the practical exercises and seminars in which the students must not only be present but also actively work together with their colleagues and produce their own expositions.

Article 31. The lectures and practical exercises are to be suitably distributed so as to foster private study and personal work under the guidance of the teachers.

Article 32. no. 1. The Statutes are also to determine in what way the examiners are to make their judgments about candidates.

no. 2. In the final judgment about the candidates for the individual academic degrees, account is to be taken of all the marks received in the various tests in the same cycle, whether written or oral.

no. 3. In the examinations for the giving of degrees, especially the doctorate, it is also useful to invite examiners from outside the Faculty.

Article 33. The Statutes are to indicate the permanent curricula of studies which are to be instituted in a Faculty for special purposes and indicate the diplomas which are conferred at their conclusion.

SECTION VII
Academic Degrees
(Apostolic Constitution, articles 46-51)

Article 34. In Ecclesiastical Universities or Faculties which are canonically erected or approved, the academic degrees are given in the name of the Supreme Pontiff.

Article 35. The Statutes are to establish the necessary requisites for the preparation of the doctrinal dissertation and the norms for their public defense and publication.

Article 36. A copy of the published dissertation must be sent to the Sacred Congregation for Catholic Education. It is recommended that copies also be sent to other Ecclesiastical Faculties, at least those of the same region, which deal with the same science.

Article 37. Authentic documents regarding the conferring of degrees are to be signed by the Academic Authorities, according to the Statutes, and then are to be countersigned by the Secretary of the University or Faculty and have the appropriate seal affixed.

Article 38. Honorary doctorates are not to be conferred except with the consent of the Chancellor, who, having listened to the opinion of the University or Faculty Council, has obtained the *nihil obstat* of the Holy See.

SECTION VIII
Matters Relating to Teaching
(Apostolic Constitution, articles 52-55)

Article 39. The University or Faculty must have lecture halls which are truly functional and worthy and suited to the teaching of the disciplines and to the number of students.

Article 40. There must be a library open for consultation, in which the principle works for the scientific work of the teachers and students are available.

Article 41. Library norms are to be established in such a way that access and use is made easy for the students and teachers.

Article 42. Cooperation and coordination between libraries of the same city and region should be fostered.

SECTION IX
Economic Matters
(Apostolic Constitution, articles 56-59)

Article 43. To provide for continuous good administration, the authorities must inform themselves at set times about the financial situation and they must provide for careful, periodic audits.

Article 44. no. 1. Suitable ways should be found so that tuition fees do not keep from academic degrees gifted students who give good hope of one day being useful to the Church.

no. 2. Therefore care must be taken to set up forms of assistance for scholars, whatever their various names (scholarships, study burses, student subsidies, etc.), to be given to needy students.

SECTION X
Planning and Cooperation of Faculties
(Apostolic Constitution, articles 60-64)

Article 45. no. 1. In order to undertake the erection of a new University or Faculty, it is necessary that:

a) a true need or usefulness can be demonstrated, which cannot be satisfied either by affiliation, aggregation, or incorporation,

b) the necessary prerequisites are present, which are mainly:

1) permanently engaged teachers who in number and quality respond to the nature and demands of a Faculty;
2) a suitable number of students;
3) a library with scientific apparatus and suitable buildings;
4) economic means really sufficient for a University or Faculty;

c) the Statutes, together with the Study Program, be exhibited, which are in conformity to the Constitution and to these Norms of Application.

no. 2. The Sacred Congregation for Catholic Education—after listening to the advice first of the Bishops' Conference, mainly from the pastoral viewpoint, and next of experts, principally from nearby Faculties, mainly from the scientific viewpoint—will decide about the suitability of a new erection. This is commonly conceded at first experimentally for a period of time before being definitely confirmed.

Article 46. When, on the other hand, the approval of a University or Faculty is undertaken, this is to be done:

a) after the consent of both the Episcopal Conference and the local diocesan authority is obtained;

b) after the conditions stated in article 45, no. 1, under b) and c) are fulfilled.

Article 47. The conditions for affiliation regard, above all, the number and qualification of teachers, the study program, the library, and the duty of the affiliating Faculty to help the institution being affiliated. Therefore, this is usually granted only when the affiliating Faculty and the affiliated institution are in the same country or cultural region.

Article 48. no. 1. Aggregation is the linking with a Faculty of some Institute which embraces only the first and second cycle, for the purpose of granting the degrees corresponding to those cycles through the Faculty.

no. 2. Incorporation is the insertion into a Faculty of some Institute which embraces either the second or third cycle or both, for the purpose of granting the corresponding degrees through the Faculty.

no. 3. Aggregation and incorporation cannot be granted unless the Institute is specially equipped to grant degrees in such a way that there is a well-founded hope that, through the connection with the Faculty, the desired ends will be achieved.

Article 49. no. 1. Cooperation is to be fostered among the Ecclesiastical Faculties themselves by means of teacher exchanges, mutual communication of scientific work, and the promoting of common research for the benefit of the People of God.

no. 2. Cooperation with other Faculties, even those of non-Catholics, should be promoted, care always however being taken to preserve one's own identity.

Part Two: Special Norms

SECTION I
Faculty of Sacred Theology
(Apostolic Constitution, articles 66-67)

Article 50. The theological disciplines are to be taught in such a way that their organic connection is made clear and that light be shed upon the various aspects or dimensions that pertain intrinsically to the nature of sacred doctrine. The chief ones are the biblical, patristic, historical, liturgical, and pastoral dimensions. The students are to be led to a deep grasp of the material, at the same time as they are led to form a personal synthesis, to acquire a mastery of the method of scientific research, and thus to become able to explain sacred doctrine appropriately.

Article 51. The obligatory disciplines are:

1. in the first cycle:

    a)   the philosophical disciplines needed for theology, which are above all systematic philosophy together with its main parts and its historical evolution;

    b)   the theological disciplines, namely:
Sacred Scripture, introduction and exegesis
fundamental theology, which also includes reference to ecumenism, non-Christian religions, and atheism
dogmatic theology
moral and spiritual theology
pastoral theology
liturgy
Church history, patrology, archaeology
Canon law

    c)   the auxiliary disciplines, namely, some of the sciences of man and, besides Latin, the biblical languages insofar as they are required for the following cycles.

2.   in the second cycle: the special disciplines established in various sections, according to the diverse specializations offered, along with the practical exercises and seminars, including written work.

3.   in the third cycle: the Statutes are to determine if special disciplines are to be taught and which ones, together with practical exercises and seminars.

Article 52. In the fifth-year basic cycle, diligent care must be exercised that all the disciplines are taught with order, fullness, and with correct method, so that the student receives harmoniously and effectively a solid, organic, and complete basic instruction in theology, which will enable him either to go on to the next cycle's higher studies or to exercise some office in the Church.

Article 53. Besides examinations or equivalent tests for each discipline, at the end of the first and of the second cycle there is to be a comprehensive examination or equivalent test, so that the student proves that he has received the full and scientific formation demanded by the respective cycle.

Article 54. It belongs to the Faculty to determine under which conditions students who have completed a normal six-year philosophy/theology course in an ordinary seminary or in some other approved institution of higher learning may be admitted into the second cycle, taking account of their previous studies and, where necessary, prescribing special courses and examinations.

SECTION II
Faculty of Canon Law
(Apostolic Constitution, articles 76-79)

Article 55. In a Faculty of Canon Law, whether Latin or Oriental, there must be a careful setting forth both of the history and texts of ecclesiastical laws and of their disposition and connection.

Article 56. The obligatory disciplines are:

1. in the first cycle:

    a) the general fundamentals of canon law;
    b) the elements of Sacred Theology (especially of ecclesiology and sacramental theology) and of philosophy (especially ethics and natural law) which by their very nature are prerequisites for the study of canon law. It is useful to add elements from the sciences of man which are connected with the juridical sciences.

2. in the second cycle:

    a) the Code of Canon Law with all its various parts and the other canonical laws;
    b) the connected disciplines, which are: the philosophy of law, the public law of the Church, fundamentals of Roman law, elements of civil law, the history of canon law. The student must also write a special dissertation.

3. in the third cycle: the Statutes are to determine which special disciplines and which practical exercises are to be prescribed, according to the nature of the Faculty and the needs of the students.

Article 57. no. 1. Whoever successfully completes the philosophy/theology curriculum in an ordinary seminary or in some other approved institution of higher learning, or who has already successfully completed the studies of the first cycle, may be admitted directly into the second cycle.

no. 2. A person who has already earned a doctorate in civil law, may be allowed, according to the judgment of the Faculty, to abbreviate the course, always maintaining however the obligation to pass all the examinations and tests required for receiving academic degrees.

Article 58. Besides examinations or equivalent tests for each discipline, at the end of the second cycle there is to be a comprehensive examination or equivalent test, whereby the student proves that he has received the full and scientific formation demanded by the cycle.

SECTION III
Faculty of Philosophy
(Apostolic Constitution, articles 79-83)

Article 59. no. 1. Philosophy is to be taught in such a way that the students in the basic cycle will come to a solid and coherent synthesis of doctrine, will learn to examine and judge the different systems of philosophy, and will also gradually become accustomed to personal philosophical reflection.

no. 2. All of the above is to be perfected in the second cycle, which begins specialization. In this cycle there is to be a deeper grasp of the determined object of philosophy and of the proper philosophical method.

Article 60. The obligatory disciplines are:

1. in the first cycle:

    a) systematic philosophy (preceded by a general introduction) with its principal parts: philosophy of knowledge, natural philosophy, philosophy of man, philosophy of being (including natural theology) and moral philosophy;
    b) history of philosophy, especially of modern philosophy, with a careful study of the systems which are exercising a major influence;
    c) the auxiliary disciplines, namely selected natural and human sciences.

2. in the second cycle: the special disciplines established in various sections, according to the diverse specializations offered, along with practical exercises and seminars, including written work.
3. in the third cycle: the Statutes are to determine if special disciplines are to be taught and which ones, together with the practical exercises and seminars.

Article 61. Besides examinations or equivalent tests for each discipline, at the end of the first and second cycle there is to be a comprehensive examination or equivalent test whereby the student proves that he has received the full and scientific formation demanded by the respective cycle.

Article 62. It belongs to the Faculty to determine under what conditions students who have done a biennium of philosophy in an approved institution, or who have done a six-year philosophy/theology course in an ordinary seminary or equivalent school, may be admitted to the second cycle, taking account of their previous studies and, where necessary, prescribing special courses and examinations.

SECTION IV
Other Faculties
(Apostolic Constitution, articles 84-87)

Article 63. In accordance with article 86 of the Constitution, the Sacred Congregation for Catholic Education will gradually give special norms for the other Faculties, taking account of the experience already gained in these Faculties and Institutes.

Article 64. In the meantime, in Appendix II there is a list of the areas or divisions of ecclesiastical studies—besides the theological, canonical, and philosophical ones treated of in the three previous sections of these Norms of Application—which at the present time in the Church are ordered academically and are in existence as Faculties, Institutes ad instar, or Specialization Sections. The Sacred Congregation for Catholic Education will add to the list of these Sections when appropriate, indicating for these Sections their special purposes and the more important disciplines to be taught and researched.

His Holiness John Paul II, by divine Providence Pope, has ratified, confirmed, and ordered to be published each and every one of these Norms of Application, anything to the contrary notwithstanding.

Given from the offices of the Sacred Congregation for Catholic Education in Rome, April 29, the Memorial of St. Catherine of Siena, Virgin and Doctor of the Church, in the year of our Lord 1979.

Gabriel-Marie Cardinal Garrone,
Prefect

Antonio Maria Javierre Ortas,
Titular Archbishop of Meta, Secretary

Appendix I: According to Article 6 of the Norms of Application

Norms for Drawing Up Statutes

Taking into account what is contained in the Apostolic Constitution and in the Norms of Application—and leaving to their own internal regulations what is of a particular or changeable nature—the Universities or Faculties must mainly deal with the following points in drawing up their Statutes:

1.   The name, nature and purpose of the University or Faculty (with a brief history in the foreword).

2. The government—the Chancellor, the personal and collegial academic authorities: what their exact functions are; how the personal authorities are chosen and how long their term of office is; how the collegial authorities or the members of the Councils are chosen and how long their term is.
3. The teachers—what the minimum number of teachers is in each Faculty; into which ranks the permanent and non-permanent are divided; what requisites they must have; how they are hired, named, promoted, and how they cease functioning; their duties and rights.
4. The students—requisites for enrollment and their duties and rights.
5. The officials and staff assistants—their duties and rights.
6. The study program—what the order of studies is in each Faculty; how many cycles it has; what disciplines are taught; which are obligatory, attendance at them; which seminars and practical exercises; which examinations and tests are to be given.
7. The academic degrees—which degrees are given in each Faculty and under what conditions.
8. Matters relating to teaching—the library; how its conservation and growth are provided for; other didactic helps and scientific laboratories, if required.
9. Economic matters—the financial endowment of the University or Faculty and its economic administration; norms for paying the staff assistants, teachers, and officials; student fees and payments, burses and scholarships.
10. Relationships with other Faculties and Institutes, etc.

Appendix II: According to Article 64 of the Norms of Application

Divisions of Ecclesiastical Studies as Now (1979) Existing in the Church

Note: These individual study Sectors are listed alphabetically (according to their Latin names) and in parenthesis is noted the academic organizational form (whether a Faculty or an Institute *ad instar* or a Sector of specialization) in which it now exists in some ecclesiastical academic center. Not listed are the studies of a theological, philosophical, or canonical kind which are treated in articles 51, 56, and 60 of the Norms of Application.

1. Arabic-Islamic studies (an Institute *ad instar*, a specialized Sector in a Theology Faculty)
2. Christian Archaeology studies (an Institute *ad instar*)
3. Studies in Atheism (a specialized Sector in a Theology and/or Philosophy Faculty)

4. Biblical studies (a Faculty of Biblical Science, a specialized Sector in a Theology Faculty)
5. Catechetical studies (a specialized Sector in a Theology or Education Faculty)
6. Ecclesiastical Oriental studies (a Faculty of Ecclesiastical Oriental Studies)
7. Education studies (a Faculty of Education).
8. Church History studies (a Faculty of Church History, a specialized Sector in a Theology Faculty)
9. Comparative Canonical-Civil Juridical studies (a Faculty of comparative civil law)
10. Classical and Christian Literary studies (a Faculty of Christian and Classical Letters)
11. Liturgical studies (a Faculty, a specialized Sector in a Theology Faculty)
12. Mariological studies (a specialized Sector in a Theology Faculty)
13. Medieval studies (an Institute *ad instar*, a specialized Sector in a Faculty of Theology or Canon Law or Philosophy)
14. Missiological studies (a Faculty of Missiology, a specialized Sector in a Theology Faculty)
15. Moral studies (a specialized Sector in a Theology Faculty)
16. Studies in Sacred Music (an Institute *ad instar*, a specialized Sector in a Theology Faculty)
17. Ecumenical studies (a specialized Sector in a Theology Faculty)
18. Ancient Oriental studies (a Faculty of Eastern Antiquity, a specialized Sector in a Theology or Philosophy Faculty)
19. Pedagogical studies (a Faculty of Pedagogy, a specialized Sector in a Philosophy or Education Faculty)
20. Pastoral studies (a specialized Sector in a Theology Faculty)
21. Patristic studies (a specialized Sector in a Theology Faculty)
22. Studies in Psychology (an Institute *ad instar*, a specialized Sector in a Faculty of Philosophy, or Pedagogy, or Education)
23. Studies in Religion and Religious Phenomenology (a specialized Sector in a Theology or Philosophy Faculty)
24. Catholic Religious studies (a Higher Institute of Religious Science)
25. Sociological studies (a Faculty of Social Science, a specialized Sector in a Faculty of Education)
26. Spirituality studies (a specialized Sector in a Theology Faculty)
27. Studies in the Theology of Religious Life (a specialized Sector in a Theology Faculty)

Address to the Council of the International Federation of Catholic Universities and Rectors of Catholic Universities of Europe

Pope John Paul II
February 24, 1979

Dear Brothers and Sons,

Is it necessary to say how happy I am to be again with you, members of the Council of the International Federation of Catholic Universities or Rectors of the Catholic Universities of Europe? The pontifical yearbook of 1978 still named me among the members of the Congregation for Catholic Education, where I became familiar with your problems. I have also kept an excellent memory of my participation in the meeting at Lublin, which you have just recalled so kindly. As for the work of University professor, I quite naturally gauge its interest and importance, after the years I myself spent teaching in the Theological Faculty of Krakow, the most ancient in Poland, at Lublin University

   1. You are certainly quite convinced, but I am anxious to stress again that the Catholic Universities have a select place in the Pope's heart, as they must have in the whole Church and in the concerns of her Pastors in the midst of the many activities of their ministry. Dedicated to a work of research and teaching, they have also thereby a sole of witness and an apostolate without which the Church could not fully and durably evangelize the vast world of culture, or simply the rising generations, more and more highly educated, who will also be increasingly demanding to face up to, in faith, the many questions raised by sciences and the various systems of thought. From the first centuries the Church has felt the importance of an apostolate of the intellect—let it be enough to recall St Justin, St Augustine—and her initiatives are numberless in this field. I do not need to quote the texts of the recent Council which you know by heart. For some time now, the attention of leaders of the Church has rightly been drawn by the spiritual needs of social environments that are quite dechristianized or little christianized: workers, peasants, migrants, poor people of every kind. It is certainly necessary, and the Gospel makes it a duty for us. But the University world also needs a Church presence more than ever. And, in the specific framework which is yours, you help to provide it.

   2. Addressing teachers and students in Mexico recently, I indicated three aims for Catholic University Institutes: to make a specific contribution to the Church and society—thanks to a really complete study of the different problems—with the concern to show the full significance of man regenerated in Christ and thus permit his complete development; to form pedagogically men who, having made a personal synthesis between faith and culture, will be capable both of keeping their place in

society and of bearing witness in it to their faith; to set up, among teachers and students, a real community which already bears witness visibly to a living Christianity.

3. I stress here some fundamental points. Research at the University level presupposes all the loyalty, the seriousness and, for that very reason, the freedom of scientific investigation. It is at this price that you bear witness to the truth, that you serve the Church and society, that you deserve the esteem of the University world; and this in all branches of knowledge.

But when it is a question of man, of the field of human sciences, it is necessary to add the following; if it is right to take advantage of the contribution of the different methodologies, it is not sufficient to choose one, or even make a synthesis of several, to determine what man is in depth. The Christian cannot let himself be hemmed in by them, all the more so in that he is not taken in by their premises. He knows that he must go beyond the purely natural perspective; his faith makes him approach anthropology in the perspective of man's full vocation and salvation; it is the light beneath which he works, the line that guides his research. In other words, a Catholic University is not only a field of religious research open in all directions. It presupposes in its teachers an anthropology enlightened by faith, consistent with faith, in particular with the Creation and with the Redemption of Christ. In the midst of the swarm of present-day approaches, which too often lead, moreover, to a minimizing of man, Christians have an original role to play, within research and teaching, precisely because they reject any partial vision of man.

As for theological research properly speaking, by definition it cannot exist without seeking its source and its regulation in Scripture and Tradition, in the experience and decisions of the Church handed down by the Magisterium throughout the course of the centuries. These brief reminders mark the specific exigencies of the responsibility of the teaching staff in Catholic Faculties. It is in this sense that Catholic Universities must safeguard their own character. It is in this framework that they bear witness not only before their students, but also before other Universities, to the seriousness with which the Church approaches the world of thought, and, at the same time, to a real understanding of faith.

4. Before this great and difficult mission, collaboration between Catholic Universities of the whole world is highly desirable, for themselves and for the development, in an opportune way, of their relations with the world of culture. This shows all the importance of your Federation. I warmly encourage its initiatives, and in particular the study of the subject of the next Assembly on the ethical problems of the modern technological society. A fundamental subject, to which I am very sensitive myself, and to which I hope to have the opportunity to return. May the Holy Spirit guide you with his light and give you the necessary strength! May the intercession of Mary keep you available for his action, for the will of God! You know that I remain very close to your concerns and to your work. I willingly give you my Apostolic Blessing.

Message to the National Catholic Educational Association of the United States

Pope John Paul II

April 16, 1979

Praised be Jesus Christ.

IT IS A JOY for me to address the members of the National Catholic Educational Association of the United States, as you assemble in the great cause of Catholic Education. Through you I would hope that my message of encouragement and blessing would also reach the numerous Catholic schools of your country, all the students and teachers of these institutions and all those generously committed Catholic education. With the Apostle Peter I send you my greeting in the faith of our Lord Jesus Christ: "Peace to all of you who are in Christ."[1]

As Catholic educators assembled in the communion of the universal Church and in prayer, you will certainly share with each other insights of value that will assist you in your important work, in your ecclesial mission. The Holy Spirit is with you and the Church is deeply grateful for your dedication. The Pope speaks to you in order to confirm you in your lofty role as Catholic educators, to assist you, to direct you, to support you.

Among the many reflections that could be made at this time there are three points in particular to which I would like to make a brief reference at the beginning of my pontificate. These are: the value of Catholic schools, the importance of Catholic teachers and educators, and the nature of Catholic education itself. These are themes that have been developed at length by my predecessors. At this time, however, it is important that I add my own testimony to theirs, in the special hope of giving a new impulse to Catholic education throughout the vast area of the United States of America.

With profound conviction I ratify and reaffirm the words that Paul VI spoke originally to the Bishops of your country: " Brethren, we know the difficulties involved in preserving Catholic schools, and the uncertainties of the future, and yet we rely on the help of God and on your own zealous collaboration and untiring efforts, so that Catholic schools can continue, despite grave obstacles, to fulfill their providential role at the service of genuine Catholic education, and at the service of your country."[2] Yes, the Catholic school must remain a privileged means of Catholic education in America. As an instrument of the apostolate it is worthy of the greatest sacrifices.

---

1   1 Pt. 5:14.

2   Address of September 15, 1975.

But no Catholic school can be effective without dedicated Catholic teachers, convinced of the great ideal of Catholic education. The Church needs men and women who are intent on teaching by word and example—intent on helping to permeate the whole educational milieu with the spirit of Christ. This is a great vocation, and the Lord himself will reward all who serve in it as educators in the cause of the word of God.

In order that the Catholic school and the Catholic teachers may truly make their irreplaceable contribution to the Church and to the world, the goal of Catholic education itself must be crystal clear. Beloved sons and daughters of the Catholic Church, brothers and sisters in the faith: Catholic education is above all a question of communicating Christ, of helping to form Christ in the lives of others.

In the expression of the Second Vatican Council, those who have been baptized must be made ever more aware of the gift of faith that they have received, they must learn to adore the Father in spirit and in truth, and they must be trained to live the newness of Christian life in justice and in the holiness of truth.[3]

These are indeed essential aims of Catholic education. To foster and promote them gives meaning to the Catholic school; it spells out the dignity of the vocation of Catholic educators.

Yes, it is above all a question of communicating Christ, and helping his uplifting Gospel to take root in the hearts of the faithful. Be strong, therefore, in pursuing these goals. The cause of Catholic education is the cause of Jesus Christ and of his Gospel at the service of man.

And be assured of the solidarity of the entire Church, and of the sustaining grace of our Lord Jesus Christ. In his name, I send you all my Apostolic Blessing: in the name of the Father, and of the Son, and of the Holy Spirit. Amen.

---

3   Cf. *Gravissimum Educationis*, no. 2.

Address to Presidents of Catholic Colleges and Universities

Pope John Paul II

October 7, 1979

Given at the Catholic University of America

Dear brothers and sisters in Christ.

1. Our meeting today gives me great pleasure, and I thank you sincerely for your cordial welcome. My own association with the university world, and more particularly with the Pontifical Theological Faculty of Cracow, makes our encounter all the more gratifying for me. I cannot but feel at home with you.

The sincere expressions with which the chancellor and the president of the Catholic University of America have confirmed, in the name of all of you, the faithful adherence to Christ and the generous commitment to the service of truth and charity of your Catholic associations and institutions of higher learning are appreciated.

Ninety-one years ago Cardinal Gibbons and the American bishops requested the foundation of the Catholic University of America, as a university "destined to provide the church with worthy ministers for the salvation of souls and the propagation of religion and to give the republic most worthy citizens." It seems appropriate to me on this occasion to address myself not only to this great institution, so irrevocably linked to the bishops of the United States, who have founded it and who generously support it, but also to all the Catholic universities, colleges and academies of post-secondary learning in your land, those with formal and sometimes juridical links with the Holy See, as well as all those who are "Catholic."

2. Before doing so, though, allow me first to mention the ecclesiastical faculties, three of which are established here at the Catholic University of America. I greet these faculties and all who dedicate their best talents in them.

I offer my prayers for the prosperous development and the unfailing fidelity and success of these faculties. In the apostolic constitution *Sapientia Christiana*, I have dealt directly with these institutions in order to provide guidance and to ensure that they fulfill their role in meeting the needs of the Christian community in today's rapidly changing circumstances.

I also wish to address a word of praise and admiration for the men and women, especially priests and religious, who dedicate themselves to all forms of campus ministry. Their sacrifices and efforts to bring the true message of Christ to the university world, whether secular or Catholic, cannot go unnoticed.

The church also greatly appreciates the work and witness of those of her sons and daughters whose vocation places them in non-Catholic universities in your country. I am sure that their Christian hope and Catholic patrimony bring an enriching and irreplaceable dimension to the world of higher studies.

A special word of gratitude and appreciation also goes to the parents and students who, sometimes at the price of great personal and financial sacrifice, look toward the Catholic universities and colleges for the training that unites faith and science, culture and the gospel values.

To all engaged in administration, teaching or study in Catholic colleges and universities I would apply the words of Daniel: "They who are learned shall shine like the brightness of the firmament and those that instruct many in justice as stars for all eternity" (Dn 12:3). Sacrifice and generosity have accomplished heroic results in the foundation and development of these institutions. Despite immense financial strain, enrollment problems and other obstacles, divine providence and the commitment of the whole people of God have allowed us to see these Catholic institutions flourish and advance.

3. I would repeat here before you what I told the professors and students of the Catholic universities in Mexico when I indicated three aims that are to be pursued. A Catholic university or college must make a specific contribution to the church and to society through high-quality scientific research, in-depth study of problems, and a just sense of history, together with the concern to show the full meaning of the human person regenerated in Christ, thus favoring the complete development of the person.

Furthermore, the Catholic university or college must train young men and women of outstanding knowledge who, having made a personal synthesis between faith and culture, will be both capable and willing to assume tasks in the service of the community and of society in general, and to bear witness to their faith before the world. And finally, to be what it ought to be, a Catholic college or university must set up, among its faculty and students, a real community which bears witness to a living and operative Christianity, a community where sincere commitment to scientific research and study goes together with a deep commitment to authentic Christian living.

This is your identity. This is your vocation. Every university or college is qualified by a specific mode of being. Yours is the qualification of being Catholic, of affirming God, his revelation and the Catholic Church as the guardian and interpreter of that revelation. The term "Catholic" will never be a mere label, either added or dropped according to the pressures of varying factors.

4. As one who for long years has been a university professor, I will never tire of insisting on the eminent role of the university, which is to instruct but also to be a place of scientific research. In both these fields, its activity is closely related to the deepest and noblest aspiration of the human person: the desire to come to the knowledge of truth.

No university can deserve the rightful esteem of the world of learning unless it applies the highest standards of scientific research, constantly updating its methods and working instruments, and unless it excels in seriousness and therefore in freedom of investigation. Truth and science are not gratuitous conquests, but the result of a surrender to objectivity and of the exploration of all aspects of nature and man.

Whenever man himself becomes the object of investigation, no single method or combination of methods can fail to take into account, beyond any purely natural approach, the full nature of man. Because he is bound by the total truth on man, the Christian will, in his research and in his teaching, reject any partial vision of human reality, but he will let himself be enlightened by his faith in the creation of God and the redemption of Christ.

The relationship to truth explains therefore the historical bond between the university and the church. Because she herself finds her origin and her growth in the words of Christ, which are the liberating truth (cf. Jn 8:32), the church has always tried to stand by the institutions that serve, and cannot but serve, the knowledge of truth.

The church can rightfully boast of being in a sense the mother of universities. The names of Bologna, Padua, Prague and Paris shine in the earliest history of intellectual endeavor and human progress. The continuity of the historic tradition in this field has come down to our day.

5. An undiminished dedication to intellectual honesty and academic excellence are seen, in a Catholic university, in the perspective of the church's mission of evangelization and service. This is why the church asks these institutions, your institutions, to set out without equivocation your Catholic nature. This is what I have desired to emphasize in my apostolic constitution *Sapientia Christiana*, where I stated:

"Indeed, the church's mission of spreading the Gospel not only demands that the good news be preached ever more widely and to ever greater numbers of men and women, but that the very power of the Gospel should permeate thought patterns, standards of judgment and the norms of behavior. In a word, it is necessary that the whole of human culture be steeped in the Gospel. The cultural atmosphere in which a human being lives has a great influence upon his or her way of thinking and, thus, of acting. Therefore, a division between faith and culture is more than a small impediment to evangelization, while a culture penetrated with the Christian spirit is an instrument that favors the spreading of the good news" (*Sapientia Christiana*, I).

The goals of Catholic higher education go beyond education for production, professional competence, technological and scientific competence. They aim at the ultimate destiny of the human person, at the full justice and holiness born of truth (cf. Eph 4:24).

6. If then your universities and colleges are institutionally committed to the Christian message, and if they are part of the Catholic community of evangelization, it follows that they have an essential relationship to the hierarchy of the church. And here I want to say a special word of gratitude, encouragement and guidance for the theologians.

The church needs her theologians, particularly in this time and age so profoundly marked by deep changes in all areas of life and society. The bishops of the church, to whom the Lord has entrusted the keeping of the unity of the faith and the preaching of the message - individual bishops for their dioceses, and bishops collegially with the successor of Peter for the universal church - we all need your work, your dedication and the fruits of your reflection. We desire to listen to you and we are eager to receive the valued assistance of your responsible scholarship.

But true theological scholarship, and by the same token theological teaching, cannot exist and be fruitful without seeking its inspiration and its source in the word of God as contained in sacred scripture and in the sacred tradition of the church, as interpreted by the authentic magisterium throughout history, (cf. *Dei Verbum*, no. 10). True academic freedom must be seen in relation to the finality of the academic enterprise which looks to the total truth of the human person.

The theologian's contribution will be enriching for the church only if it takes into account the proper function of the bishops and the rights of the faithful. It devolves upon the bishops of the church to safeguard the Christian authenticity and unity of faith and moral teaching, in accordance with the injunction of the Apostle Paul: "Proclaim the message and, welcome or unwelcome, insist on it. Refute falsehood, correct error, call to obedience . . . (2 Tim 4:2).

It is the right of the faithful not to be troubled by theories and hypotheses that they are not expert in judging or that are easily simplified or manipulated by public opinion for ends that are alien to the truth. On the day of his death, John Paul I stated: "Among the rights of the faithful, one of the greatest is the right to receive God's word in all its entirety and purity . . ." (Sept. 28, 1979).

It behooves the theologian to be free, but with the freedom that is openness to the truth and the light that comes from faith and from fidelity to the church.

In concluding I express to you once more my joy in being with you today. I remain very close to your work and your concerns. May the Holy Spirit guide you. May the intercession of Mary, seat of wisdom, sustain you always in your irreplaceable service of humanity and the church. God bless you.

Speech to Representatives of Catholic Universities

Pope John Paul II

September 12, 1987

Given at Xavier University

Dear Friends,
Dear Leaders in Catholic Higher Education,

1. At the end of this day dedicated to *the prayerful celebration of Catholic education in the United States*, I greet you and all those whom you represent, with esteem and with affection in our Lord Jesus Christ. I thank the Association of Catholic Colleges and Universities for having arranged this meeting. I express my gratitude to Dr. Norman Francis and to all at Xavier University for their hospitality at this institution, which, in so many ways, serves the cause of Catholic higher education.

"I will bless the Lord at all times;
his praise shall be ever in my mouth.
Glorify the Lord with me,
Let us together extol his name" (Ps 34 (33):2-4).

Yes, let us join *in thanking* God for the many good things that he, the Father of Wisdom, has accomplished through Catholic colleges and universities. In doing so, let us be thankful for the special strengths of your schools–for their Catholic identity, for their service of truth, and for their role in helping to make the Church's presence felt in the world of culture and science. And let us be thankful *above all for the men and women committed to this mission*, those of the past and those of today, who have made and are making Catholic higher education the great reality that it is.

2. The United States is unique in its *network of more than two hundred and thirty-five colleges and universities* which identify themselves as Catholic. The number and diversity of your institutions are in fact without parallel; they exercise an influence not only within the United States but also throughout the universal Church, and they bear a responsibility for her good.

Two years from now you will celebrate the two hundredth anniversary of the founding by John Carroll of Georgetown University, the first Catholic university in the United States. After Georgetown, through the leadership of religious congregations and farseeing bishops, and with the generous support of the Catholic people, other colleges and universities have been established in different parts of this vast country. For two centuries these institutions have contributed much to *the emergence of a Catholic laity*, which today is intimately and extensively involved in industry, government, the professions, arts and all forms of public and private endeavor—all those activities that constitute the characteristic dynamism and vitality of this land.

Amidst changing circumstances, Catholic universities and colleges are challenged to retain *a lively sense of their Catholic identity* and to fulfill their specific *responsibilities to the Church and to society*. It is precisely in doing so that they make their distinctive contribution to the wider field of higher education.

The Catholic identity of your institutions is a complex and vitally important matter. This identity depends upon *the explicit profession of Catholicity* on the part of the university as an institution and also upon *the personal conviction and sense of mission* on the part of its professors and administrators.

3. During my pastoral visit to this country in 1979, I spoke of various elements that contribute to the mission of Catholic higher education. It is useful once again to stress the importance of *research into questions vital for the Church and society*—a research carried out "with a just sense of history, together with the concern to show the full meaning of the human person regenerated in Christ"; to emphasize the need for *educating men and women of outstanding knowledge* who, "having made a personal synthesis between faith and culture, will be both capable and willing to assume tasks in the service of the community and of society in general, and to bear witness to their faith before the world"; and finally, to pursue the establishment of *a living community of faith*, "where sincere commitment to scientific research and study goes together with a deep commitment to authentic Christian living" (Pope John Paul II, *Allocutio ad moderatores et doctores Universitatis Catholicae Vashintoniensis et ad legatos Collegiorum Universitatumque catholicarum totius Nationis*, 3, Oct. 7, 1979: *Insegnamenti di Giovanni Paolo II*, II, 2 (1979) 687).

4. To appreciate fully the value of your heritage, we need to recall the origins of Catholic university life. The university as we know it began in close association with the Church. This was no accident. *Faith and love of learning have a close relationship.* For the Fathers of the Church and the thinkers and academics of the Middle Ages, the search for truth was associated with the search for God. According to Catholic teaching—as expressed also in the First Vatican Council—the mind is capable not only of searching for the truth but also of grasping it, however imperfectly.

Religious *faith itself calls for intellectual inquiry*; and the confidence that there can be no contradiction between faith and reason is a distinctive feature of the Catholic humanistic tradition, as it existed in the past and as it exists in our own day.

Catholic higher education is called to exercise, through the grace of God, an extraordinary "share in the work of truth" (3 Jn 8). The Catholic university is dedicated to the service of the truth, as is every university. In its research and teaching, however, it proceeds from the vision and perspective of faith and is thus enriched in a specific way.

From this point of view one sees that there is an intimate relationship between the Catholic university and the teaching office of the Church. The bishops of the Church, as *Doctores et Magistri Fidei*, should be seen not as external agents but as participants in the life of the Catholic university in its privileged role as protagonist in *the encounter between faith and science and between revealed truth and culture*.

Modern culture reflects many tensions and contradictions. We live in an age of great technological triumphs but also of great human anxieties. Too often, today, the individual's vision of reality is fragmented. At times experience is mediated by forces over which people have no control; sometimes there is not even an awareness of these forces. The temptation grows to relativize moral principles and to privilege process over truth. This has grave consequences for the moral life as well as for the intellectual life of individuals and of society. The Catholic university must address all these issues from the perspective of faith and out of its rich heritage.

5. Modern culture is marked by a pluralism of attitudes, points of view and insights. This situation rightly requires mutual understanding; it means that society and groups within society must respect those who have a different outlook from their own. But *pluralism does not exist for its own sake; it is directed to the fullness of truth.* In the academic context, the respect for persons which pluralism rightly envisions does not justify the view that ultimate questions about human life and destiny have no final answers or that all beliefs are of equal value, provided that none is asserted as absolutely true and normative. Truth is not served in this way.

It is true, of course, that the culture of every age contains certain ambiguities, which reflect the inner tensions of the human heart, the struggle between good and evil. Hence the Gospel, in its continuing encounter with culture, must always *challenge the accomplishments and assumptions of the age* (cf. Rom 12:2). Since, in our day, the implications of this ambiguity are often so destructive to the community, so hostile to human dignity, it is crucial that the Gospel should purify culture, uplift it, and orient it to the service of what is authentically human. Humanity's very survival may depend on it. And here, as leaders in Catholic education in the United States, you have an extremely important contribution to make.

Today there exists an increasingly evident need for philosophical reflection concerning the truth about the human person. A metaphysical approach is needed as an antidote to intellectual and moral relativism. But what is required even more is *fidelity to the word of God,* to ensure that human progress takes into account the entire revealed truth of the eternal act of love in which the universe and especially the human person acquire ultimate meaning. The more one seeks to unravel the mystery of the human person, the more open one becomes to the mystery of transcendence. The more deeply one penetrates the divine mystery, the more one discovers the true greatness and dignity of human beings.

6. In your institutions, which are privileged settings for the encounter between faith and culture, *theological science has a special role* and deserves a prominent place in the curriculum of studies and in the allocation of research resources. But theology, as the Church understands it, is much more than an academic discipline. Its data are the data of God's Revelation entrusted to the Church. The deeper understanding of the mystery of Christ, the understanding which theological reflection seeks, is ultimately *a gift of the Holy Spirit given for the common good of the whole Church.* Theology is truly a search to understand ever more clearly the heritage of faith preserved, transmitted and made explicit by the Church's teaching office. And theological instruction serves the community of faith by helping new generations to understand and to integrate into their lives the truth of God, which is so vital to the fundamental issues of the modern world.

7. *Theology is at the service of the whole ecclesial community.* The work of theology involves an interaction among the various members of the community of faith. The bishops, united with the Pope, have the mission of authentically teaching the message of Christ; as pastors, they are called to sustain the unity in faith and Christian

living of the entire People of God. In this they need the assistance of Catholic theologians, who perform an inestimable service to the Church. But theologians also need the charism entrusted by Christ to the bishops and, in the first place, to the Bishop of Rome. The fruits of their work, in order to enrich the life-stream of the ecclesial community, must ultimately be tested and validated by the Magisterium. In effect, therefore, *the ecclesial context of Catholic theology gives it a special character and value, even when theology exists in an academic setting.*

Here, the words of Saint Paul concerning the spiritual gifts should be a source of light and harmony for us all: "There are different gifts but the same Spirit; there are different ministries but the same Lord; there are different works but the same God who accomplishes all of them in everyone. To each person the manifestation of the Spirit is given for the common good" (1 Cor 12:4-7). In the different offices and functions in the Church, it is not some power and dominion that is being divided up, but rather *the same service of the Body of Christ that is shared according to the vocation of each.* It is a question of unity in the work of service. In this spirit I wish to express cordial support for the humble, generous and patient work of theological research and education being carried out in your universities and colleges in accordance with the Church's mission to proclaim and teach the saving wisdom of God (cf. ibid. 1:21).

8. My own university experience impels me to mention another related matter of supreme importance in the Catholic college and university, namely, *the religious and moral education of students and their pastoral care.* I am confident that you too take this special service very seriously, and that you count it among your most pressing and most satisfying responsibilities. One cannot meet college and university students anywhere in the world without hearing their questions and sensing their anxieties. In their hearts your students have many questions about faith, religious practice and holiness of life. Each one arrives on your campuses with a family background, a personal history, and an acquired culture. They all want to be accepted, loved and supported by *a Christian educational community* which shows friendship and authentic spiritual commitment.

It is your *privilege to serve your students in faith and love*; to help them deepen their friendship with Christ; to make available to them the opportunities for prayer and liturgical celebration, including the possibility to know the forgiveness and love of Jesus Christ in the Sacraments of Penance and the Eucharist. You are able, as Catholic educators, to introduce your students to *a powerful experience of community and to a very serious involvement in social concerns that will* enlarge their horizons, challenge their life styles and offer them authentic human fulfilment.

University students, for example, are in a splendid position to take to heart the Gospel invitation to go out of themselves, to reject introversion and to concentrate on the needs of others. Students with the opportunities of higher education can readily grasp *the relevance for today of Christ's parable of the rich man and Lazarus* (cf. Lk 16:19 ff.), with all of its consequences for humanity. What is at stake is not only the rectitude of individual human hearts but also the whole social order as it touches the spheres of economics, politics and human rights and relations.

Here in the Catholic university centers of this nation, vivified by the inspiration of the Gospel, must be drawn up *the blueprints for the reform of attitudes and structures* that will influence the whole dynamic of peace and justice in the world, as it affects East and West, North and South. It is not enough to offer to the disadvantaged of the world crumbs of freedom, crumbs of truth and crumbs of bread. The Gospel calls for much more. The parable of the rich man and the poor man is directed to the conscience of humanity, and, today in particular, to the conscience of America. But that conscience often passes through the halls of Academe, through nights of study and hours of prayer, finally to reach and embrace the whole prophetic message of the Gospel. "Keep your attention closely fixed on it," we are told in the Second Letter of Peter, "as you would on a lamp shining in a dark place until the first streaks of dawn appear and the morning star rises in your hearts" (2 Pt 1:19).

9. Dear brothers and sisters: as leaders in Catholic university and college education, you have inherited a tradition of service and academic excellence, the cumulative effort of so many who have worked so hard and sacrificed to much for Catholic education in this country. Now there lies before you the wide horizon of the third century of the nation's constitutional existence, and the third century of Catholic institutions of higher learning serving the people of this land. The challenges that confront you are just as testing as those your forefathers faced in establishing the network of institutions over which you now preside. Undoubtedly, the greatest challenge is, and will remain, that of *preserving and strengthening the Catholic character of your colleges and universities*—that institutional commitment to the word of God as proclaimed by the Catholic Church. This commitment is both an expression of spiritual consistency and a specific contribution to the cultural dialogue proper to American life. As you strive to make the presence of the Church in the world of modern culture more luminous, may you listen once again to Christ's prayer to his Father for his disciples: "*Consecrate them by means of truth—'Your word is truth'*" (Jn 17:17).

May the Holy Spirit, the Counsellor and Spirit of Truth, who has enlivened and enlightened the Church of Christ from the beginning, give you great confidence in the Father's word, and sustain you in the service that you render to the truth through Catholic higher education in the United States of America.

Apostolic Constitution
Ex corde Ecclesiae

On Catholic Universities

Pope John Paul II
August 15, 1990

INTRODUCTION

1. BORN FROM THE HEART of the Church, a Catholic University is located in that course of tradition which may be traced back to the very origin of the University as an institution. It has always been recognized as an incomparable center of creativity and dissemination of knowledge for the good of humanity. By vocation, the *Universitas magistrorum et scholarium* is dedicated to research, to teaching and to the education of students who freely associate with their teachers in a common love of knowledge.[1] With every other University it shares that *gaudium de veritate*, so precious to Saint Augustine, which is that joy of searching for, discovering, and communicating truth[2] in every field of knowledge. A Catholic University's privileged task is "to unite existentially by intellectual effort two orders of reality that too frequently tend to be placed in opposition as though they were antithetical: the search for truth and the certainty of already knowing the fount of truth."[3]

2. For many years I myself was deeply enriched by the beneficial experience of university life: the ardent search for truth and its unselfish transmission to youth and to all those learning to think rigorously, so as to act rightly and to serve humanity better.

Therefore, I desire to share with everyone my profound respect for Catholic Universities, and to express my great appreciation for the work that is being done in them in the various spheres of knowledge. In a particular way, I wish to manifest my joy at the numerous meetings which the Lord has permitted me to have in the course of my apostolic journeys with the Catholic University communities of various continents. They are for me a lively and promising sign of the fecundity of the Christian mind in the heart of every culture. They give me a well-founded hope for a new flowering of Christian culture in the rich and varied context of our changing times, which certainly face serious challenges but which also bear so much promise under the action of the Spirit of truth and of love.

---

1   Cf. the letter of Pope Alexander IV to the University of Paris, 14 April 1255, Introduction: *Bullarium Diplomatum* . . . , vol. III, Turin 1858, 602.

2   Saint Augustine, *Confes.* X, xxiii, 33: "In fact, the blessed life consists in *the joy that comes from the truth*, since this joy comes from You who are Truth, God my light, salvation of my face, my God." PL 32, 793-794. Cf. Saint Thomas Aquinas, *De Malo*, IX, 1: "It is actually natural to man to strive for knowledge of the truth."

3   John Paul II, Discourse to the "Institut Catholique de Paris," 1 June 1980: *Insegnamenti di Giovanni Paolo II*, Vol. III/1 (1980), 1581.

It is also my desire to express my pleasure and gratitude to the very many Catholic scholars engaged in teaching and research in non-Catholic Universities. Their task as academics and scientists, lived out in the light of the Christian faith, is to be considered precious for the good of the Universities in which they teach. Their presence, in fact, is a continuous stimulus to the selfless search for truth and for the wisdom that comes from above.

3. Since the beginning of this Pontificate, I have shared these ideas and sentiments with my closest collaborators, the Cardinals, with the Congregation for Catholic Education, and with men and women of culture throughout the world. In fact, the dialogue of the Church with the cultures of our times is that vital area where "the future of the Church and of the world is being played out as we conclude the twentieth century."[4] There is only one culture: that of man, by man, and for man.[5] And thanks to her Catholic Universities and their humanistic and scientific inheritance, the Church, expert in humanity, as my predecessor, Paul VI, expressed it at the United Nations,[6] explores the mysteries of humanity and of the world, clarifying them in the light of Revelation.

4. It is the honor and responsibility of a Catholic University to consecrate itself without reserve to *the cause of truth*. This is its way of serving at one and the same time both the dignity of man and the good of the Church, which has "an intimate conviction that truth is (its) real ally . . . and that knowledge and reason are sure ministers to faith."[7] Without in any way neglecting the acquisition of useful knowledge, a Catholic University is distinguished by its free search for the whole truth about nature, man, and God. The present age is in urgent need of this kind of disinterested service, namely of *proclaiming the meaning of truth*, that fundamental value without which freedom, justice and human dignity are extinguished. By means of a kind of universal humanism a Catholic University is completely dedicated to the research of all aspects of truth in their essential connection with the supreme Truth, who is God. It does this without fear but rather with enthusiasm, dedicating itself to every path of knowledge, aware of being preceded by him who is "the Way, the Truth, and the Life,"[8] the *Logos*, whose Spirit of intelligence and love enables the human person with his or her own intelligence to find the ultimate reality of which he is the source and end and who alone is capable of giving fully that Wisdom without which the future of the world would be in danger.

5. It is in the context of the impartial search for truth that the relationship between faith and reason is brought to light and meaning. The invitation of

---

4   John Paul II, Discourse to the Cardinals, 10 November 1979: *Insegnamenti di Giovanni Paolo II*, Vol. II/2 (1979), 1096; cf. Discourse to UNESCO, Paris, 2 June 1980: AAS 72 (1980), 735-752.

5   Cf. John Paul II, Discourse to the University of Coimbra, 15 May 1982: *Insegnamenti di Giovanni Paolo II*, Vol. V/2 (1982), 1692.

6   Paul VI, Allocution to Representatives of States, 4 October 1965: *Insegnamenti di Paolo VI*, Vol. III (1965), 508.

7   John Henry Cardinal Newman, *The Idea of a University*, London, Longmans, Green and Company, 1931, XI.

8   Jn 14:6.

Saint Augustine, "*Intellege ut credas; crede ut intellegas*,"[9] is relevant to Catholic Universities that are called to explore courageously the riches of Revelation and of nature so that the united endeavor of intelligence and faith will enable people to come to the full measure of their humanity, created in the image and likeness of God, renewed even more marvelously, after sin, in Christ, and called to shine forth in the light of the Spirit.

6. Through the encounter which it establishes between the unfathomable richness of the salvific message of the Gospel and the variety and immensity of the fields of knowledge in which that richness is incarnated by it, a Catholic University enables the Church to institute an incomparably fertile dialogue with people of every culture. Man's life is given dignity by culture, and, while he finds his fullness in Christ, there can be no doubt that the Gospel which reaches and renews him in every dimension is also fruitful for the culture in which he lives.

7. In the world today, characterized by such rapid developments in science and technology, the tasks of a Catholic University assume an ever greater importance and urgency. Scientific and technological discoveries create an enormous economic and industrial growth, but they also inescapably require the correspondingly necessary *search for meaning* in order to guarantee that the new discoveries be used for the authentic good of individuals and of human society as a whole. If it is the responsibility of every University to search for such meaning, a Catholic University is called in a particular way to respond to this need: its Christian inspiration enables it to include the moral, spiritual, and religious dimension in its research, and to evaluate the attainments of science and technology in the perspective of the totality of the human person.

In this context, Catholic Universities are called to a continuous renewal, both as "Universities" and as "Catholic." For, "What is at stake is the *very meaning of scientific and technological research, of social life and of culture*, but, on an even more profound level, what is at stake is *the very meaning of the human person*."[10] Such renewal requires a clear awareness that, by its Catholic character, a University is made more capable of conducting an *impartial* search for truth, a search that is neither subordinated to nor conditioned by particular interests of any kind.

8. Having already dedicated the Apostolic Constitution *Sapientia Christiana* to Ecclesiastical Faculties and Universities,[11] I then felt obliged to propose an analogous Document for Catholic Universities as a sort of "magna carta," enriched by the long and fruitful experience of the Church in the realm of Universities and open to the promise of future achievements that will require courageous creativity and rigorous fidelity.

9. The present Document is addressed especially to those who conduct Catholic Universities, to the respective academic communities, to all those who have an interest in them, particularly the Bishops, Religious Congregations, and ecclesial

---

9   Cf. Saint Augustine, *Serm.* 43, 9: PL 38, 258. Cf. also Saint Anselm, *Proslogion*, chap. I: PL 158, 227.

10   Cf. John Paul II, *Allocution to the International Congress on Catholic Universities*, 25 April 1989, no. 3: AAS 18 (1989), 1218.

11   John Paul II, Apostolic Constitution *Sapientia Christiana* concerning the Ecclesiastical Universities and Faculties, 15 April 1979: AAS 71 (1979), 469-521.

Institutions, and to the numerous laity who are committed to the great mission of higher education. Its purpose is that "the Christian mind may achieve, as it were, a public, persistent, and universal presence in the whole enterprise of advancing higher culture and that the students of these institutions become people outstanding in learning, ready to shoulder society's heavier burdens and to witness the faith to the world."[12]

10. In addition to Catholic Universities, I also turn to the many Catholic Institutions of higher education. According to their nature and proper objectives, they share some or all of the characteristics of a University and they offer their own contribution to the Church and to society, whether through research, education or professional training. While this Document specifically concerns Catholic Universities, it is also meant to include all Catholic Institutions of higher education engaged in instilling the Gospel message of Christ in souls and cultures.

Therefore, it is with great trust and hope that I invite all Catholic Universities to pursue their irreplaceable task. Their mission appears increasingly necessary for the encounter of the Church with the development of the sciences and with the cultures of our age.

Together with all my brother Bishops who share pastoral responsibility with me, I would like to manifest my deep conviction that a Catholic University is without any doubt one of the best instruments that the Church offers to our age which is searching for certainty and wisdom. Having the mission of bringing the Good News to everyone, the Church should never fail to interest herself in this Institution. By research and teaching, Catholic Universities assist the Church in the manner most appropriate to modern times to find cultural treasures both old and new, "*nova et vetera*," according to the words of Jesus.[13]

11. Finally, I turn to the whole Church, convinced that Catholic Universities are essential to her growth and to the development of Christian culture and human progress. For this reason, the entire ecclesial Community is invited to give its support to Catholic Institutions of higher education and to assist them in their process of development and renewal. It is invited in a special way to guard the rights and freedom of these Institutions in civil society, and to offer them economic aid, especially in those countries where they have more urgent need of it, and to furnish assistance in founding new Catholic Universities wherever this might be necessary.

My hope is that these prescriptions, based on the teaching of Vatican Council II and the directives of the *Code of Canon Law*, will enable Catholic Universities and other Institutes of higher studies to fulfill their indispensable mission in the new advent of grace that is opening up to the new Millennium.

---

12   Vatican Council II, Declaration on Catholic Education *Gravissimum Educationis*, no. 10: AAS 58 (1966), 737.

13   Mt 13:52.

PART I
IDENTITY AND MISSION

A. The Identity of a Catholic University

1. NATURE AND OBJECTIVES

12. Every Catholic University, *as a university*, is an academic community which, in a rigorous and critical fashion, assists in the protection and advancement of human dignity and of a cultural heritage through research, teaching, and various services offered to the local, national, and international communities.[14] It possesses that institutional autonomy necessary to perform its functions effectively and guarantees its members academic freedom, so long as the rights of the individual person and of the community are preserved within the confines of the truth and the common good.[15]

13. Since the objective of a Catholic University is to assure in an institutional manner a Christian presence in the university world confronting the great problems of society and culture,[16] every Catholic University, as *Catholic*, must have the following *essential characteristics*:

> "1.   a Christian inspiration not only of individuals but of the university community as such;
>
> 2.   a continuing reflection in the light of the Catholic faith upon the growing treasury of human knowledge, to which it seeks to contribute by its own research;
>
> 3.   fidelity to the Christian message as it comes to us through the Church;

---

14   Cf. *The Magna Carta of the European Universities*, Bologna, Italy, 18 September 1988, "Fundamental Principles."

15   Cf. Vatican Council II, Pastoral Constitution on the Church in the Modern World *Gaudium et Spes*, no. 59: AAS 58 (1966), 1080; Declaration on Catholic Education *Gravissimum Educationis*, no. 10: AAS 58 (1966), 737. "Institutional autonomy" means that the governance of an academic institution is and remains internal to the institution; "academic freedom" is the guarantee given to those involved in teaching and research that, within their specific specialized branch of knowledge, and according to the methods proper to that specific area, they may search for the truth wherever analysis and evidence leads them, and may teach and publish the results of this search, keeping in mind the cited criteria, that is, safeguarding the rights of the individual and of society within the confines of the truth and the common good.

16   There is a two-fold notion of *culture* used in this document: the *humanistic* and the *socio-historical*. "The word 'culture' in its general sense indicates all those factors by which man refines and unfolds his manifold spiritual and bodily qualities. It means his effort to bring the world itself under his control by his knowledge and his labor. It includes the fact that by improving customs and institutions he renders social life more human both within the family and in the civic community. Finally, it is a feature of culture that throughout the course of time man expresses, communicates, and conserves in his works great spiritual experiences and desires, so that these may be of advantage to the progress of many, even of the whole human family. Hence it follows that human culture necessarily has a historical and social aspect and that the word 'culture' often takes on a sociological and ethnological sense." Vatican Council II, Pastoral Constitution on the Church in the Modern World *Gaudium et Spes*, no. 53: AAS 58 (1966), 1075.

4. an *institutional commitment* to the service of the people of God and of the human family in their pilgrimage to the transcendent goal which gives meaning to life."[17]

14. "In the light of these four characteristics, it is evident that besides the teaching, research, and services common to all Universities, a Catholic University, by *institutional commitment*, brings to its task the inspiration and light of the *Christian message*. In a Catholic University, therefore, Catholic ideals, attitudes, and principles penetrate and inform university activities in accordance with the proper nature and autonomy of these activities. In a word, being both a University and Catholic, it must be both a community of scholars representing various branches of human knowledge, and an academic institution in which Catholicism is vitally present and operative."[18]

15. A Catholic University, therefore, is a place of research, where scholars *scrutinize reality* with the methods proper to each academic discipline, and so contribute to the treasury of human knowledge. Each individual discipline is studied in a systematic manner; moreover, the various disciplines are brought into dialogue for their mutual enhancement.

In addition to assisting men and women in their continuing quest for the truth, this research provides an effective witness, especially necessary today, to the Church's belief in the intrinsic value of knowledge and research.

In a Catholic University, research necessarily includes (a) the search for an *integration of knowledge*, (b) a *dialogue between faith and reason*, (c) an *ethical concern*, and (d) a *theological perspective*.

16. *Integration of knowledge* is a process, one which will always remain incomplete; moreover, the explosion of knowledge in recent decades, together with the rigid compartmentalization of knowledge within individual academic disciplines, makes the task increasingly difficult. But a University, and especially a Catholic University, "*has to be a 'living union' of individual organisms* dedicated to the search for truth. . . . It is necessary *to work towards a higher synthesis* of knowledge, in which alone lies the possibility of satisfying that thirst for truth which is profoundly inscribed on the heart of the human person."[19] Aided by the specific contributions of philosophy and theology, university scholars will be engaged in a constant effort to determine the relative place and meaning of each of the various disciplines within the context of a vision of the human person and the world that is enlightened by the Gospel, and therefore by a faith in Christ, the *Logos*, as the center of creation and of human history.

---

17   *L'Université Catholique dans le monde moderne*. Document final du 2ème Congrès des Délégués des Universités Catholiques, Rome, 20-29 November 1972, § 1.

18   Ibid.

19   John Paul II, Allocution to the International Congress on Catholic Universities, 25 April 1989, no. 4: AAS 81 (1989), 1219. Cf. also Vatican Council II, Pastoral Constitution on the Church in the Modern World *Gaudium et Spes*, no. 61: AAS 58 (1966), 1081-1082. Cardinal Newman observes that a University "professes to assign to each study which it receives, its proper place and its just boundaries; to define the rights, to establish the mutual relations, and to effect the intercommunion of one and all." (*Op. cit.*, 457).

17. In promoting this integration of knowledge, a specific part of a Catholic University's task is to promote *dialogue between faith and reason*, so that it can be seen more profoundly how faith and reason bear harmonious witness to the unity of all truth. While each academic discipline retains its own integrity and has its own methods, this dialogue demonstrates that "methodical research within every branch of learning, when carried out in a truly scientific manner and in accord with moral norms, can never truly conflict with faith. For the things of the earth and the concerns of faith derive from the same God."[20] A vital interaction of two distinct levels of coming to know the one truth leads to a greater love for truth itself, and contributes to a more comprehensive understanding of the meaning of human life and of the purpose of God's creation.

18. Because knowledge is meant to serve the human person, research in a Catholic University is always carried out with a concern for the *ethical* and *moral implications* both of its methods and of its discoveries. This concern, while it must be present in all research, is particularly important in the areas of science and technology. "It is essential that we be convinced of the priority of the ethical over the technical, of the primacy of the person over things, of the superiority of the spirit over matter. The cause of the human person will only be served if knowledge is joined to conscience. Men and women of science will truly aid humanity only if they preserve 'the sense of the transcendence of the human person over the world and of God over the human person.'"[21]

19. *Theology* plays a particularly important role in the search for a synthesis of knowledge as well as in the dialogue between faith and reason. It serves all other disciplines in their search for meaning, not only by helping them to investigate how their discoveries will affect individuals and society but also by bringing a perspective and an orientation not contained within their own methodologies. In turn, interaction with these other disciplines and their discoveries enriches theology, offering it a better understanding of the world today, and making theological research more relevant to current needs. Because of its specific importance among the academic disciplines, every Catholic University should have a faculty, or at least a chair, of theology.[22]

20. Given the close connection between research and teaching, the research qualities indicated above will have their influence on all teaching. While each discipline is taught systematically and according to its own methods, *interdisciplinary studies*, assisted by a careful and thorough study of philosophy and theology, enable students to acquire an organic vision of reality and to develop a continuing desire

---

20 Vatican Council II, Pastoral Constitution on the Church in the Modern World *Gaudium et Spes*, no. 36: AAS 58 (1966), 1054. To a group of scientists I pointed out that "while reason and faith surely represent two distinct orders of knowledge, each autonomous with regard to its own methods, the two must finally converge in the discovery of a single whole reality which has its origin in God." (John Paul II, Address at the Meeting on Galileo, 9 May 1983, no. 3: AAS 75 [1983], 690).

21 John Paul II, Address at UNESCO, 2 June 1980, no. 22: AAS 72 (1980), 750. The last part of the quotation uses words directed to the Pontifical Academy of Sciences, 10 November 1979: *Insegnamenti di Giovanni Paolo II*, Vol. II/2 (1979), 1109.

22 Cf. Vatican Council II, Declaration on Catholic Education *Gravissimum Educationis*, no. 10: AAS 58 (1966), 737.

for intellectual progress. In the communication of knowledge, emphasis is then placed on how *human reason in its reflection* opens to increasingly broader questions, and how the complete answer to them can only come from above through faith. Furthermore, the *moral implications* that are present in each discipline are examined as an integral part of the teaching of that discipline so that the entire educative process be directed towards the whole development of the person. Finally, Catholic theology, taught in a manner faithful to Scripture, Tradition, and the Church's Magisterium, provides an awareness of the Gospel principles which will enrich the meaning of human life and give it a new dignity.

Through research and teaching the students are educated in the various disciplines so as to become truly competent in the specific sectors in which they will devote themselves to the service of society and of the Church, but at the same time prepared to give the witness of their faith to the world.

2. THE UNIVERSITY COMMUNITY

21. A Catholic University pursues its objectives through its formation of an authentic human community animated by the spirit of Christ. The source of its unity springs from a common dedication to the truth, a common vision of the dignity of the human person and, ultimately, the person and message of Christ which gives the Institution its distinctive character. As a result of this inspiration, the community is animated by a spirit of freedom and charity; it is characterized by mutual respect, sincere dialogue, and protection of the rights of individuals. It assists each of its members to achieve wholeness as human persons; in turn, everyone in the community helps in promoting unity, and each one, according to his or her role and capacity, contributes towards decisions which affect the community, and also towards maintaining and strengthening the distinctive Catholic character of the Institution.

22. *University teachers* should seek to improve their competence and endeavor to set the content, objectives, methods, and results of research in an individual discipline within the framework of a coherent world vision. Christians among the teachers are called to be witnesses and educators of authentic Christian life, which evidences attained integration between faith and life, and between professional competence and Christian wisdom. All teachers are to be inspired by academic ideals and by the principles of an authentically human life.

23. *Students* are challenged to pursue an education that combines excellence in humanistic and cultural development with specialized professional training. Most especially, they are challenged to continue the search for truth and for meaning throughout their lives, since "the human spirit must be cultivated in such a way that there results a growth in its ability to wonder, to understand, to contemplate, to make personal judgments, and to develop a religious, moral, and social sense."[23] This enables them to acquire or, if they have already done so, to deepen a Christian way of life that is authentic. They should realize the responsibility of their professional

---

23   Vatican Council II, Pastoral Constitution on the Church in the Modern World *Gaudium et Spes*, no. 59: AAS 58 (1966), 1080. Cardinal Newman describes the ideal to be sought in this way: "A habit of mind is formed which lasts through life, of which the attributes are freedom, equitableness, calmness, moderation, and wisdom." (*Op. cit.*, 101-102).

life, the enthusiasm of being the trained 'leaders' of tomorrow, of being witnesses to Christ in whatever place they may exercise their profession.

24. *Directors* and *administrators* in a Catholic University promote the constant growth of the University and its community through a leadership of service; the dedication and witness of the *non-academic staff* are vital for the identity and life of the University.

25. Many Catholic Universities were founded by Religious Congregations, and continue to depend on their support; those Religious Congregations dedicated to the apostolate of higher education are urged to assist these Institutions in the renewal of their commitment, and to continue to prepare religious men and women who can positively contribute to the mission of a Catholic University.

Lay people have found in university activities a means by which they too could exercise an important apostolic role in the Church and, in most Catholic Universities today, the academic community is largely composed of laity; in increasing numbers, lay men and women are assuming important functions and responsibilities for the direction of these Institutions. These lay Catholics are responding to the Church's call "to be present, as signs of courage and intellectual creativity, in the privileged places of culture, that is, the world of education—school and university."[24] The future of Catholic Universities depends to a great extent on the competent and dedicated service of lay Catholics. The Church sees their developing presence in these institutions both as a sign of hope and as a confirmation of the irreplaceable lay vocation in the Church and in the world, confident that lay people will, in the exercise of their own distinctive role, "illumine and organize these (temporal) affairs in such a way that they always start out, develop, and continue according to Christ's mind, to the praise of the Creator and the Redeemer."[25]

26. The university community of many Catholic institutions includes members of other Churches, ecclesial communities and religions, and also those who profess no religious belief. These men and women offer their training and experience in furthering the various academic disciplines or other university tasks.

3. THE CATHOLIC UNIVERSITY IN THE CHURCH

27. Every Catholic University, without ceasing to be a University, has a relationship to the Church that is essential to its institutional identity. As such, it participates most directly in the life of the local Church in which it is situated; at the same time, because it is an academic institution and therefore a part of the international community of scholarship and inquiry, each institution participates in and contributes to the life and the mission of the universal Church, assuming consequently a special bond with the Holy See by reason of the service to unity which it is called to render to the whole Church. One consequence of its essential relationship to the Church is that the *institutional* fidelity of the University to the Christian message

---

24 John Paul II, Post-Synodal Apostolic Exhortation *Christifideles Laici*, 30 December 1988, no. 44: AAS 81 (1989), 479.

25 Vatican Council II, Dogmatic Constitution on the Church *Lumen Gentium*, no. 31: AAS 57 (1965), 37-38. Cf. Decree on the Apostolate of the Laity *Apostolicam Actuositatem*, passim: AAS 58 (1966), 837ff. Cf. also *Gaudium et Spes*, no. 43: AAS 58 (1966), 1061-1064.

includes a recognition of and adherence to the teaching authority of the Church in matters of faith and morals. Catholic members of the university community are also called to a personal fidelity to the Church with all that this implies. Non-Catholic members are required to respect the Catholic character of the University, while the University in turn respects their religious liberty.[26]

28. Bishops have a particular responsibility to promote Catholic Universities, and especially to promote and assist in the preservation and strengthening of their Catholic identity, including the protection of their Catholic identity in relation to civil authorities. This will be achieved more effectively if close personal and pastoral relationships exist between University and Church authorities, characterized by mutual trust, close and consistent cooperation, and continuing dialogue. Even when they do not enter directly into the internal governance of the University, Bishops "should be seen not as external agents but as participants in the life of the Catholic University."[27]

29. The Church, accepting "the legitimate autonomy of human culture and especially of the sciences," recognizes the academic freedom of scholars in each discipline in accordance with its own principles and proper methods,[28] and within the confines of the truth and the common good.

Theology has its legitimate place in the University alongside other disciplines. It has proper principles and methods which define it as a branch of knowledge. Theologians enjoy this same freedom so long as they are faithful to these principles and methods.

Bishops should encourage the creative work of theologians. They serve the Church through research done in a way that respects theological method. They seek to understand better, further develop, and more effectively communicate the meaning of Christian Revelation as transmitted in Scripture and Tradition and in the Church's Magisterium. They also investigate the ways in which theology can shed light on specific questions raised by contemporary culture. At the same time, since theology seeks an understanding of revealed truth whose authentic interpretation is entrusted to the Bishops of the Church,[29] it is intrinsic to the principles and methods of their research and teaching in their academic discipline that theologians respect the authority of the Bishops, and assent to Catholic doctrine according to the degree of authority with which it is taught.[30] Because of their interrelated roles, dialogue between Bishops and theologians is essential; this is especially true today,

---

26   Cf. Vatican Council II, Declaration on Religious Liberty *Dignitatis Humanae*, no. 2: AAS 58 (1966), 930-931.

27   John Paul II, Address to Leaders of Catholic Higher Education, Xavier University of Louisiana, U.S.A., 12 September 1987, no. 4: AAS 80 (1988), 764.

28   Vatican Council II, Pastoral Constitution on the Church in the Modern World *Gaudium et Spes*, no. 59: AAS 58 (1966), 1080.

29   Cf. Vatican Council II, Dogmatic Constitution on Divine Revelation *Dei Verbum*, nos. 8-10: AAS 58 (1966), 820-822.

30   Cf. Vatican Council II, Dogmatic Constitution on the Church *Lumen Gentium*, no. 25: AAS 57 (1965), 29-31.

when the results of research are so quickly and so widely communicated through the media.[31]

B. The Mission of Service of a Catholic University

30. The basic mission of a University is a continuous quest for truth through its research, and the preservation and communication of knowledge for the good of society. A Catholic University participates in this mission with its own specific characteristics and purposes.

1. SERVICE TO CHURCH AND SOCIETY

31. Through teaching and research, a Catholic University offers an indispensable contribution to the Church. In fact, it prepares men and women who, inspired by Christian principles and helped to live their Christian vocation in a mature and responsible manner, will be able to assume positions of responsibility in the Church. Moreover, by offering the results of its scientific research, a Catholic University will be able to help the Church respond to the problems and needs of this age.

32. A Catholic University, as any University, is immersed in human society; as an extension of its service to the Church, and always within its proper competence, it is called on to become an ever more effective instrument of cultural progress for individuals as well as for society. Included among its research activities, therefore, will be a study of *serious contemporary problems* in areas such as the dignity of human life, the promotion of justice for all, the quality of personal and family life, the protection of nature, the search for peace and political stability, a more just sharing in the world's resources, and a new economic and political order that will better serve the human community at a national and international level. University research will seek to discover the roots and causes of the serious problems of our time, paying special attention to their ethical and religious dimensions.

If need be, a Catholic University must have the courage to speak uncomfortable truths which do not please public opinion, but which are necessary to safeguard the authentic good of society.

33. A specific priority is the need to examine and evaluate the predominant values and norms of modern society and culture in a Christian perspective, and the responsibility to try to communicate to society those *ethical and religious principles which give full meaning to human life*. In this way a University can contribute further to the development of a true Christian anthropology, founded on the person of Christ, which will bring the dynamism of the creation and redemption to bear on reality and on the correct solution to the problems of life.

34. The Christian spirit of service to others for the *promotion of social justice* is of particular importance for each Catholic University, to be shared by its teachers and developed in its students. The Church is firmly committed to the integral growth of

---

31   Cf. "Instruction on the Ecclesial Vocation of the Theologian" of the Congregation for the Doctrine of the Faith of 24 May 1990.

all men and women.[32] The Gospel, interpreted in the social teachings of the Church, is an urgent call to promote "the development of those peoples who are striving to escape from hunger, misery, endemic diseases, and ignorance; of those who are looking for a wider share in the benefits of civilization and a more active improvement of their human qualities; of those who are aiming purposefully at their complete fulfillment."[33] Every Catholic University feels responsible to contribute concretely to the progress of the society within which it works: for example, it will be capable of searching for ways to make university education accessible to all those who are able to benefit from it, especially the poor or members of minority groups who customarily have been deprived of it. A Catholic University also has the responsibility, to the degree that it is able, to help to promote the development of the emerging nations.

35. In its attempts to resolve these complex issues that touch on so many different dimensions of human life and of society, a Catholic University will insist on cooperation among the different academic disciplines, each offering its distinct contribution in the search for solutions; moreover, since the economic and personal resources of a single Institution are limited, cooperation in *common research projects* among Catholic Universities, as well as with other private and governmental institutions, is imperative. In this regard, and also in what pertains to the other fields of the specific activity of a Catholic University, the role played by various national and international associations of Catholic Universities is to be emphasized. Among these associations the mission of *The International Federation of Catholic Universities*, founded by the Holy See,[34] is particularly to be remembered. The Holy See anticipates further fruitful collaboration with this Federation.

36. Through programs of *continuing education* offered to the wider community, by making its scholars available for consulting services, by taking advantage of modern means of communication, and in a variety of other ways, a Catholic University can assist in making the growing body of human knowledge and a developing understanding of the faith available to a wider public, thus expanding university services beyond its own academic community.

37. In its service to society, a Catholic University *will relate especially to the academic, cultural, and scientific world* of the region in which it is located. Original forms of dialogue and collaboration are to be encouraged between the Catholic Universities and the other Universities of a nation on behalf of development, of understanding between cultures, and of the defense of nature in accordance with an awareness of the international ecological situation.

Catholic Universities join other private and public institutions in serving the public interest through higher education and research; they are one among the

---

32 Cf. John Paul II, Encyclical Letter *Sollicitudo Rei Socialis*, nos. 27-34: AAS 80 (1988), 547-560.

33 Paul VI, Encyclical Letter *Populorum Progressio*, no. 1: AAS 59 (1967), 257.

34 "Therefore, in that there has been a pleasing multiplication of centers of higher learning, it has become apparent that it would be opportune for the faculty and the alumni to unite in common association which, working in reciprocal understanding and close collaboration, and based upon the authority of the Supreme Pontiff, as father and universal doctor, they might more efficaciously spread and extend the light of Christ." (Pius XII, Apostolic Letter *Catholicas Studiorum Universitates*, with which The International Federation of Catholic Universities was established: AAS 42 [1950], 386).

variety of different types of institutions that are necessary for the free expression of cultural diversity, and they are committed to the promotion of solidarity and its meaning in society and in the world. Therefore, they have the full right to expect that civil society and public authorities will recognize and defend their institutional autonomy and academic freedom; moreover, they have the right to the financial support that is necessary for their continued existence and development.

2. PASTORAL MINISTRY

38. Pastoral ministry is that activity of the University which offers the members of the university community an opportunity to integrate religious and moral principles with their academic study and non-academic activities, *thus integrating faith with life*. It is part of the mission of the Church within the University, and is also a constitutive element of a Catholic University itself, both in its structure and in its life. A university community concerned with promoting the Institution's Catholic character will be conscious of this pastoral dimension and sensitive to the ways in which it can have an influence on all university activities.

39. As a natural expression of the Catholic identity of the University, the university community *should give a practical demonstration of its faith in its daily activity*, with important moments of reflection and of prayer. Catholic members of this community will be offered opportunities to assimilate Catholic teaching and practice into their lives and will be encouraged to participate in the celebration of the sacraments, especially the Eucharist as the most perfect act of community worship. When the academic community includes members of other Churches, ecclesial communities, or religions, their initiatives for reflection and prayer in accordance with their own beliefs are to be respected.

40. Those involved in pastoral ministry will encourage teachers and students to become more aware of their responsibility towards those who are suffering physically or spiritually. Following the example of Christ, they will be particularly attentive to the poorest and to those who suffer economic, social, cultural or religious injustice. This responsibility begins within the academic community, but it also finds application beyond it.

41. Pastoral ministry is an indispensable means by which Catholic students can, in fulfillment of their baptism, *be prepared for active participation in the life of the Church*; it can assist in developing and nurturing the value of marriage and family life, fostering vocations to the priesthood and religious life, stimulating the Christian commitment of the laity and imbuing every activity with the spirit of the Gospel. Close cooperation between pastoral ministry in a Catholic University and the other activities within the local Church, under the guidance or with the approval of the diocesan Bishop, will contribute to their mutual growth.[35]

---

35 The *Code of Canon Law* indicates the general responsibility of the Bishop toward university students: "The diocesan bishop is to have serious pastoral concern for students by erecting a parish for them or by assigning priests for this purpose on a stable basis; he is also to provide for Catholic university centers at universities, even non-Catholic ones, to give assistance, especially spiritual to young people." (CIC, can. 813).

42. Various associations or movements of spiritual and apostolic life, especially those developed specifically for students, can be of great assistance in developing the pastoral aspects of university life.

3. CULTURAL DIALOGUE

43. By its very nature, a University develops culture through its research, helps to transmit the local culture to each succeeding generation through its teaching, and assists cultural activities through its educational services. It is open to all human experience and is ready to dialogue with and learn from any culture. A Catholic University shares in this, offering the rich experience of the Church's own culture. In addition, a Catholic University, aware that human culture is open to Revelation and transcendence, is also a primary and privileged place for a *fruitful dialogue between the Gospel and culture*.

44. Through this dialogue a Catholic University assists the Church, enabling it to come to a better knowledge of diverse cultures, discern their positive and negative aspects, to receive their authentically human contributions, and to develop means by which it can make the faith better understood by the men and women of a particular culture.[36] While it is true that the Gospel cannot be identified with any particular culture and transcends all cultures, it is also true that "the Kingdom which the Gospel proclaims is lived by men and women who are profoundly linked to a culture, and the building up of the Kingdom cannot avoid borrowing the elements of human culture or cultures."[37] "A faith that places itself on the margin of what is human, of what is therefore culture, would be a faith unfaithful to the fullness of what the Word of God manifests and reveals, a decapitated faith, worse still, a faith in the process of self-annihilation."[38]

45. A Catholic University must become *more attentive to the cultures of the world of today*, and to the *various cultural traditions existing within the Church* in a way that will promote a continuous and profitable dialogue between the Gospel and modern society. Among the criteria that characterize the values of a culture are above all, the *meaning of the human person*, his or her liberty, dignity, *sense of responsibility*, and openness to the transcendent. To a respect for persons is joined *the preeminent value of the family*, the primary unit of every human culture.

Catholic Universities will seek to discern and evaluate both the aspirations and the contradictions of modern culture, in order to make it more suited to the total

---

36 "Living in various circumstances during the course of time, the Church, too, has used in her preaching the discoveries of different cultures to spread and explain the message of Christ to all nations, to probe it and more deeply understand it, and to give it better expression in liturgical celebrations and in the life of the diversified community of the faithful." (Vatican Council II, Pastoral Constitution on the Church in the Modern World *Gaudium et Spes*, no. 58: AAS 58 [1966], 1079).

37 Paul VI, Apostolic Exhortation *Evangelii Nuntiandi*, no. 20: AAS 68 (1976), 18. Cf. Vatican Council II, Pastoral Constitution on the Church in the Modern World *Gaudium et Spes*, no. 58: AAS 58 (1966), 1079.

38 John Paul II, Address to Intellectuals, to Students and to University Personnel at Medellín, Colombia, 5 July 1986, no. 3: AAS 79 (1987), 99. Cf. also Vatican Council II, Pastoral Constitution on the Church in the Modern World *Gaudium et Spes*, no. 58: AAS 58 (1966), 1079.

development of individuals and peoples. In particular, it is recommended that by means of appropriate studies, the impact of modern technology and especially of the mass media on persons, the family, and the institutions and whole of modem culture be studied deeply. Traditional cultures are to be defended in their identity, help-ing them to receive modern values without sacrificing their own heritage, which is a wealth for the whole of the human family. Universities, situated within the ambience of these cultures, will seek to harmonize local cultures with the positive contributions of modern cultures.

46. An area that particularly interests a Catholic University is the *dialogue between Christian thought and the modern sciences*. This task requires persons par-ticularly well versed in the individual disciplines and who are at the same time adequately prepared theologically, and who are capable of confronting epistemo-logical questions at the level of the relationship between faith and reason. Such dialogue concerns the natural sciences as much as the human sciences which posit new and complex philosophical and ethical problems. The Christian researcher should demonstrate the way in which human intelligence is enriched by the higher truth that comes from the Gospel: "The intelligence is never diminished, rather, it is stimulated and reinforced by that interior fount of deep understanding that is the Word of God, and by the hierarchy of values that results from it. . . . In its unique manner, the Catholic University helps to manifest the superiority of the spirit, that can never, without the risk of losing its very self, be placed at the service of some-thing other than the search for truth."[39]

47. Besides cultural dialogue, a Catholic University, in accordance with its spe-cific ends, and keeping in mind the various religious-cultural contexts, following the directives promulgated by competent ecclesiastical authority, can offer a contri-bution to ecumenical dialogue. It does so to further the search for unity among all Christians. In interreligious dialogue it will assist in discerning the spiritual values that are present in the different religions.

4. EVANGELIZATION

48. The primary mission of the Church is to preach the Gospel in such a way that a relationship between faith and life is established in each individual and in the socio-cultural context in which individuals live and act and communicate with one another. Evangelization means "bringing the Good News into all the strata of humanity, and through its influence transforming humanity from within and making it new. . . . It is a question not only of preaching the Gospel in ever wider geographic areas or to ever greater numbers of people, but also of affecting and, as it were, upset-ting, through the power of the Gospel, humanity's criteria of judgment, determining values, points of interest, lines of thought, sources of inspiration, and models of life, which are in contrast with the Word of God and the plan of salvation."[40]

---

39   Paul VI, to the Delegates of The International Federation of Catholic Universities, 27 November 1972: AAS 64 (1972), 770.

40   Paul VI, Apostolic Exhortation *Evangelii Nuntiandi*, nos. 18ff.: AAS 68 (1976), 17-18.

49. By its very nature, each Catholic University makes an important contribution to the Church's work of evangelization. It is a living *institutional* witness to Christ and his message, so vitally important in cultures marked by secularism, or where Christ and his message are still virtually unknown. Moreover, all the basic academic activities of a Catholic University are connected with and in harmony with the evangelizing mission of the Church: research carried out in the light of the Christian message which puts new human discoveries at the service of individuals and society; education offered in a faith-context that forms men and women capable of rational and critical judgment and conscious of the transcendent dignity of the human person; professional training that incorporates ethical values and a sense of service to individuals and to society; the dialogue with culture that makes the faith better understood, and the theological research that translates the faith into contemporary language. "Precisely because it is more and more conscious of its salvific mission in this world, the Church wants to have these centers closely connected with it; it wants to have them present and operative in spreading the authentic message of Christ."[41]

PART II
GENERAL NORMS

ARTICLE 1. THE NATURE OF THESE NORMS

§ 1. These General Norms are based on, and are a further development of, the *Code of Canon Law* and the complementary Church legislation, without prejudice to the right of the Holy See to intervene should this become necessary. They are valid for all Catholic Universities and other Catholic Institutes of Higher Studies throughout the world.

§ 2. The General Norms are to be applied concretely at the local and regional levels by Episcopal Conferences and other Assemblies of Catholic Hierarchy[43] in conformity with the *Code of Canon Law* and complementary Church legislation, taking into account the Statutes of each University or Institute and, as far as possible and appropriate, civil law. After review by the Holy See,[44] these local or regional "Ordinances" will be valid for all Catholic Universities and other Catholic Institutes of Higher Studies in the region, except for Ecclesiastical Universities and Faculties. These latter Institutions, including Ecclesiastical Faculties which are part

---

41 Paul VI, Address to Presidents and Rectors of the Universities of the Society of Jesus, 6 August 1975, no. 2: AAS 67 (1975), 533. Speaking to the participants of the International Congress on Catholic Universities, 25 April 1989, I added (no. 5): "Within a Catholic University the evangelical mission of the Church and the mission of research and teaching become *interrelated* and *coordinated*": Cf. AAS 81 (1989), 1220.

42 Cf. in particular the Chapter of the Code: "Catholic Universities and other Institutes of Higher Studies" (CIC, cann. 807-814).

43 Episcopal Conferences were established in the Latin Rite. Other Rites have other Assemblies of Catholic Hierarchy.

44 Cf. CIC, Can. 455, § 2.

of a Catholic University, are governed by the norms of the Apostolic Constitution *Sapientia Christiana.*[45]

§ 3. A University established or approved by the Holy See, by an Episcopal Conference or another Assembly of Catholic Hierarchy, or by a diocesan Bishop is to incorporate these General Norms and their local and regional applications into its governing documents, and conform its existing Statutes both to the General Norms and to their applications, and submit them for approval to the competent ecclesiastical Authority. It is contemplated that other Catholic Universities, that is, those not established or approved in any of the above ways, with the agreement of the local ecclesiastical Authority, will make their own the General Norms and their local and regional applications, internalizing them into their governing documents, and, as far as possible, will conform their existing Statutes both to these General Norms and to their applications.

ARTICLE 2. THE NATURE OF A CATHOLIC UNIVERSITY

§ 1. A Catholic University, like every university, is a community of scholars representing various branches of human knowledge. It is dedicated to research, to teaching, and to various kinds of service in accordance with its cultural mission.

§ 2. A Catholic University, as Catholic, informs and carries out its research, teaching, and all other activities with Catholic ideals, principles and attitudes. It is linked with the Church either by a formal, constitutive and statutory bond or by reason of an institutional commitment made by those responsible for it.

§ 3. Every Catholic University is to make known its Catholic identity, either in a mission statement or in some other appropriate public document, unless authorized otherwise by the competent ecclesiastical Authority. The University, particularly through its structure and its regulations, is to provide means which will guarantee the expression and the preservation of this identity in a manner consistent with § 2.

§ 4. Catholic teaching and discipline are to influence all university activities, while the freedom of conscience of each person is to be fully respected.[46] Any official action or commitment of the University is to be in accord with its Catholic identity.

§ 5. A Catholic University possesses the autonomy necessary to develop its distinctive identity and pursue its proper mission. Freedom in research and teaching is recognized and respected according to the principles and methods of each individual discipline, so long as the rights of the individual and of the community are preserved within the confines of the truth and the common good.[47]

---

45 Cf. *Sapientia Christiana*: AAS 71 (1979), 469-521. Ecclesiastical Universities and Faculties are those that have the right to confer academic degrees by the authority of the Holy See.

46 Cf. Vatican Council II, Declaration on Religious Liberty *Dignitatis Humanae*, no. 2: AAS 58 (1966), 930-931.

47 Cf. Vatican Council II, Pastoral Constitution on the Church in the Modern World *Gaudium et Spes*, nos. 57 and 59: AAS 58 (1966), 1077-1080; *Gravissimum Educationis*, no. 10: AAS 58 (1966), 737.

ARTICLE 3. THE ESTABLISHMENT OF A CATHOLIC UNIVERSITY

§ 1. A Catholic University may be established or approved by the Holy See, by an Episcopal Conference or another Assembly of Catholic Hierarchy, or by a diocesan Bishop.

§ 2. With the consent of the diocesan Bishop, a Catholic University may also be established by a Religious Institute or other public juridical person.

§ 3. A Catholic University may also be established by other ecclesiastical or lay persons; such a University may refer to itself as a Catholic University only with the consent of the competent ecclesiastical Authority, in accordance with the conditions upon which both parties shall agree.[48]

§ 4. In the cases of §§ 1 and 2, the Statutes must be approved by the competent ecclesiastical Authority.

ARTICLE 4. THE UNIVERSITY COMMUNITY

§ 1. The responsibility for maintaining and strengthening the Catholic identity of the University rests primarily with the University itself. While this responsibility is entrusted principally to university authorities (including, when the positions exist, the Chancellor and/or a Board of Trustees or equivalent body), it is shared in varying degrees by all members of the university community, and therefore calls for the recruitment of adequate university personnel, especially teachers and administrators, who are both willing and able to promote that identity. The identity of a Catholic University is essentially linked to the quality of its teachers and to respect for Catholic doctrine. It is the responsibility of the competent Authority to watch over these two fundamental needs in accordance with what is indicated in Canon Law.[49]

§ 2. All teachers and all administrators, at the time of their appointment, are to be informed about the Catholic identity of the Institution and its implications, and about their responsibility to promote, or at least to respect, that identity.

§ 3. In ways appropriate to the different academic disciplines, all Catholic teachers are to be faithful to, and all other teachers are to respect, Catholic doctrine and morals in their research and teaching. In particular, Catholic theologians, aware that they fulfill a mandate received from the Church, are to be faithful to the

---

48   Both the establishment of such a university and the conditions by which it may refer to itself as a Catholic University are to be in accordance with the prescriptions issued by the Holy See, Episcopal Conference or other Assembly of Catholic Hierarchy.

49   Canon 810 of CIC specifies the responsibility of the competent Authorities in this area: § 1 "It is the responsibility of the authority who is competent in accord with the statutes to provide for the appointment of teachers to Catholic universities who, besides their scientific and pedagogical suitability, are also outstanding in their integrity of doctrine and probity of life; when those requisite qualities are lacking they are to be removed from their positions in accord with the procedure set forth in the statutes. § 2 The conference of bishops and the diocesan bishops concerned have the duty and right of being vigilant that in these universities the principles of Catholic doctrine are faithfully observed." Cf. also Article 5, 2 ahead in these "Norms."

Magisterium of the Church as the authentic interpreter of Sacred Scripture and Sacred Tradition.[50]

§ 4. Those university teachers and administrators who belong to other Churches, ecclesial communities, or religions, as well as those who profess no religious belief, and also all students, are to recognize and respect the distinctive Catholic identity of the University. In order not to endanger the Catholic identity of the University or Institute of Higher Studies, the number of non-Catholic teachers should not be allowed to constitute a majority within the Institution, which is and must remain Catholic.

§ 5. The education of students is to combine academic and professional development with formation in moral and religious principles and the social teachings of the Church; the program of studies for each of the various professions is to include an appropriate ethical formation in that profession. Courses in Catholic doctrine are to be made available to all students.[51]

ARTICLE 5. THE CATHOLIC UNIVERSITY WITHIN THE CHURCH

§ 1. Every Catholic University is to maintain communion with the universal Church and the Holy See; it is to be in close communion with the local Church and in particular with the diocesan Bishops of the region or nation in which it is located. In ways consistent with its nature as a University, a Catholic University will contribute to the Church's work of evangelization.

§ 2. Each Bishop has a responsibility to promote the welfare of the Catholic Universities in his diocese and has the right and duty to watch over the preservation and strengthening of their Catholic character. If problems should arise concerning this Catholic character, the local Bishop is to take the initiatives necessary to resolve the matter, working with the competent university authorities in accordance with established procedures[52] and, if necessary, with the help of the Holy See.

§ 3. Periodically, each Catholic University, to which Article 3, 1, and 2 refers, is to communicate relevant information about the University and its activities to the competent ecclesiastical Authority. Other Catholic Universities are to communicate this information to the Bishop of the diocese in which the principal seat of the Institution is located.

ARTICLE 6. PASTORAL MINISTRY

§ 1. A Catholic University is to promote the pastoral care of all members of the university community, and to be especially attentive to the spiritual development of

---

50   Vatican Council II, Dogmatic Constitution on the Church *Lumen Gentium*, no. 25: AAS 57 (1965), 29; *Dei Verbum*, nos. 8-10: AAS 58 (1966), 820-822; Cf. CIC, can. 812: "It is necessary that those who teach theological disciplines in any institute of higher studies have a mandate from the competent ecclesiastical authority."

51   Cf. CIC, can 811 § 2.

52   For Universities to which Article 3 §§ 1 and 2 refer, these procedures are to be established in the university statutes approved by the competent ecclesiastical Authority; for other Catholic Universities, they are to be determined by Episcopal Conferences or other Assemblies of Catholic Hierarchy.

those who are Catholics. Priority is to be given to those means which will facilitate the integration of human and professional education with religious values in the light of Catholic doctrine, in order to unite intellectual learning with the religious dimension of life.

§ 2. A sufficient number of qualified people—priests religious, and lay persons—are to be appointed to provide pastoral ministry for the university community, carried on in harmony and cooperation with the pastoral activities of the local Church under the guidance or with the approval of the diocesan Bishop. All members of the university community are to be invited to assist the work of pastoral ministry, and to collaborate in its activities.

ARTICLE 7. COOPERATION

§ 1. In order better to confront the complex problems facing modern society, and in order to strengthen the Catholic identity of the Institutions, regional, national, and international cooperation is to be promoted in research, teaching, and other university activities among all Catholic Universities, including Ecclesiastical Universities and Faculties.[53] Such cooperation is also to be promoted between Catholic Universities and other Universities, and with other research and educational Institutions, both private and governmental.

§ 2. Catholic Universities will, when possible and in accord with Catholic principles and doctrine, cooperate with government programs and the programs of other national and international Organizations on behalf of justice, development, and progress.

TRANSITIONAL NORMS

Art. 8. The present Constitution will come into effect on the first day of the academic year 1991.

Art. 9. The application of the Constitution is committed to the Congregation for Catholic Education, which has the duty to promulgate the necessary directives that will serve towards that end.

Art. 10. It will be the competence of the Congregation for Catholic Education, when with the passage of time circumstances require it, to propose changes to be made in the present Constitution in order that it may be adapted continuously to the needs of Catholic Universities.

Art. 11. Any particular laws or customs presently in effect that are contrary to this Constitution are abolished. Also, any privileges granted up to this day by the Holy See whether to physical or moral persons that are contrary to this present Constitution are abolished.

---

53   Cf. CIC, can. 820. Cf. also *Sapientia Christiana*, Norms of Application, Article 49: AAS 71 (1979), 512.

CONCLUSION

The mission that the Church, with great hope, entrusts to Catholic Universities holds a cultural and religious meaning of vital importance because it concerns the very future of humanity. The renewal requested of Catholic Universities will make them better able to respond to the task of bringing the message of Christ to man, to society, to the various cultures: "Every human reality, both individual and social has been liberated by Christ: persons, as well as the activities of men and women, of which culture is the highest and incarnate expression. The salvific action of the Church on cultures is achieved, first of all, by means of persons, families, and educators . . . Jesus Christ, our Savior, offers his light and his hope to all those who promote the sciences, the arts, letters, and the numerous fields developed by modern culture. Therefore, all the sons and daughters of the Church should become aware of their mission and discover how the strength of the Gospel can penetrate and regenerate the mentalities and dominant values that inspire individual cultures, as well as the opinions and mental attitudes that are derived from it."[54]

It is with fervent hope that I address this Document to all the men and women engaged in various ways in the significant mission of Catholic higher education.

Beloved Brothers and Sisters, my encouragement and my trust go with you in your weighty daily task that becomes ever more important, more urgent and necessary on behalf of Evangelization for the future of culture and of all cultures. The Church and the world have great need of your witness and of your capable, free, and responsible contribution.

Given in Rome, at Saint Peter's, on 15 August, the Solemnity of the Assumption of the Blessed Virgin Mary into Heaven, in the year 1990, the twelfth of the Pontificate.

---

54   John Paul II, to the Pontifical Council for Culture, 13 January 1989, no. 2: AAS 81 (1989), 857-858.

Address to Catholic Educators

Pope Benedict XVI
April 17, 2008
Given at the Catholic University of America

Your Eminences,
Dear Brother Bishops,
Distinguished Professors, Teachers and Educators,

"How beautiful are the footsteps of those who bring good news" (*Rom* 10:15-17). With these words of Isaiah quoted by Saint Paul, I warmly greet each of you—bearers of wisdom—and through you the staff, students and families of the many and varied institutions of learning that you represent. It is my great pleasure to meet you and to share with you some thoughts regarding the nature and identity of Catholic education today. I especially wish to thank Father David O'Connell, President and Rector of the Catholic University of America. Your kind words of welcome are much appreciated. Please extend my heartfelt gratitude to the entire community—faculty, staff and students—of this University.

Education is integral to the mission of the Church to proclaim the Good News. First and foremost every Catholic educational institution is a place to encounter the living God who in Jesus Christ reveals his transforming love and truth (cf. *Spe Salvi*, no. 4). This relationship elicits a desire to grow in the knowledge and understanding of Christ and his teaching. In this way those who meet him are drawn by the very power of the Gospel to lead a new life characterized by all that is beautiful, good, and true; a life of Christian witness nurtured and strengthened within the community of our Lord's disciples, the Church.

The dynamic between personal encounter, knowledge and Christian witness is integral to the *diakonia* of truth which the Church exercises in the midst of humanity. God's revelation offers every generation the opportunity to discover the ultimate truth about its own life and the goal of history. This task is never easy; it involves the entire Christian community and motivates each generation of Christian educators to ensure that the power of God's truth permeates every dimension of the institutions they serve. In this way, Christ's Good News is set to work, guiding both teacher and student towards the objective truth which, in transcending the particular and the subjective, points to the universal and absolute that enables us to proclaim with confidence the hope which does not disappoint (cf. Rm 5:5). Set against personal struggles, moral confusion and fragmentation of knowledge, the noble goals of scholarship and education, founded on the unity of truth and in service of the person and the community, become an especially powerful instrument of hope.

Dear friends, the history of this nation includes many examples of the Church's commitment in this regard. The Catholic community here has in fact made education one of its highest priorities. This undertaking has not come without great sacrifice. Towering figures, like Saint Elizabeth Ann Seton and other founders and foundresses, with great tenacity and foresight, laid the foundations of what is today a remarkable network of parochial schools contributing to the spiritual well-being of the Church and the nation. Some, like Saint Katharine Drexel, devoted their lives to educating those whom others had neglected—in her case, African Americans and Native Americans. Countless dedicated Religious Sisters, Brothers, and Priests together with selfless parents have, through Catholic schools, helped generations of immigrants to rise from poverty and take their place in mainstream society.

This sacrifice continues today. It is an outstanding apostolate of hope, seeking to address the material, intellectual and spiritual needs of over three million children and students. It also provides a highly commendable opportunity for the entire Catholic community to contribute generously to the financial needs of our institutions. Their long-term sustainability must be assured. Indeed, everything possible must be done, in cooperation with the wider community, to ensure that they are accessible to people of all social and economic strata. No child should be denied his or her right to an education in faith, which in turn nurtures the soul of a nation.

Some today question the Church's involvement in education, wondering whether her resources might be better placed elsewhere. Certainly in a nation such as this, the State provides ample opportunities for education and attracts committed and generous men and women to this honorable profession. It is timely, then, to reflect on what is particular to our Catholic institutions. How do they contribute to the good of society through the Church's primary mission of evangelization?

All the Church's activities stem from her awareness that she is the bearer of a message which has its origin in God himself: in his goodness and wisdom, God chose to reveal himself and to make known the hidden purpose of his will (cf. Eph 1:9; *Dei Verbum*, no. 2). God's desire to make himself known, and the innate desire of all human beings to know the truth, provide the context for human inquiry into the meaning of life. This unique encounter is sustained within our Christian community: the one who seeks the truth becomes the one who lives by faith (cf. *Fides et Ratio*, no. 31). It can be described as a move from "I" to "we," leading the individual to be numbered among God's people.

This same dynamic of communal identity—to whom do I belong?—vivifies the ethos of our Catholic institutions. A university or school's Catholic identity is not simply a question of the number of Catholic students. It is a question of conviction—do we really believe that only in the mystery of the Word made flesh does the mystery of man truly become clear (cf. *Gaudium et Spes*, no. 22)? Are we ready to commit our entire self—intellect and will, mind and heart—to God? Do we accept the truth Christ reveals? Is the faith tangible in our universities and schools? Is it given fervent expression liturgically, sacramentally, through prayer, acts of charity, a concern for justice, and respect for God's creation? Only in this way do we really bear witness to the meaning of who we are and what we uphold.

From this perspective one can recognize that the contemporary "crisis of truth" is rooted in a "crisis of faith." Only through faith can we freely give our assent to God's testimony and acknowledge him as the transcendent guarantor of the truth he reveals. Again, we see why fostering personal intimacy with Jesus Christ and communal witness to his loving truth is indispensable in Catholic institutions of learning. Yet we all know, and observe with concern, the difficulty or reluctance many people have today in entrusting themselves to God. It is a complex phenomenon and one which I ponder continually. While we have sought diligently to engage the intellect of our young, perhaps we have neglected the will. Subsequently we observe, with distress, the notion of freedom being distorted. Freedom is not an opting out. It is an opting in—a participation in Being itself. Hence authentic freedom can never be attained by turning away from God. Such a choice would ultimately disregard the very truth we need in order to understand ourselves. A particular responsibility therefore for each of you, and your colleagues, is to evoke among the young the desire for the act of faith, encouraging them to commit themselves to the ecclesial life that follows from this belief. It is here that freedom reaches the certainty of truth. In choosing to live by that truth, we embrace the fullness of the life of faith which is given to us in the Church.

Clearly, then, Catholic identity is not dependent upon statistics. Neither can it be equated simply with orthodoxy of course content. It demands and inspires much more: namely that each and every aspect of your learning communities reverberates within the ecclesial life of faith. Only in faith can truth become incarnate and reason truly human, capable of directing the will along the path of freedom (cf. *Spe Salvi*, no. 23). In this way our institutions make a vital contribution to the mission of the Church and truly serve society. They become places in which God's active presence in human affairs is recognized and in which every young person discovers the joy of entering into Christ's "being for others" (cf. ibid., no. 28).

The Church's primary mission of evangelization, in which educational institutions play a crucial role, is consonant with a nation's fundamental aspiration to develop a society truly worthy of the human person's dignity. At times, however, the value of the Church's contribution to the public forum is questioned. It is important therefore to recall that the truths of faith and of reason never contradict one another (cf. First Vatican Ecumenical Council, Dogmatic Constitution on the Catholic Faith *Dei Filius*, IV: DS 3017; St. Augustine, *Contra Academicos*, III, 20, 43). The Church's mission, in fact, involves her in humanity's struggle to arrive at truth. In articulating revealed truth she serves all members of society by purifying reason, ensuring that it remains open to the consideration of ultimate truths. Drawing upon divine wisdom, she sheds light on the foundation of human morality and ethics, and reminds all groups in society that it is not praxis that creates truth but truth that should serve as the basis of praxis. Far from undermining the tolerance of legitimate diversity, such a contribution illuminates the very truth which makes consensus attainable, and helps to keep public debate rational, honest and accountable. Similarly the Church never tires of upholding the essential moral categories of right and wrong, without which hope could only wither, giving way to cold pragmatic calculations of utility which render the person little more than a pawn on some ideological chess-board.

With regard to the educational forum, the *diakonia* of truth takes on a heightened significance in societies where secularist ideology drives a wedge between truth and faith. This division has led to a tendency to equate truth with knowledge and to adopt a positivistic mentality which, in rejecting metaphysics, denies the foundations of faith and rejects the need for a moral vision. Truth means more than knowledge: knowing the truth leads us to discover the good. Truth speaks to the individual in his or her entirety, inviting us to respond with our whole being. This optimistic vision is found in our Christian faith because such faith has been granted the vision of the *Logos*, God's creative Reason, which in the Incarnation, is revealed as Goodness itself. Far from being just a communication of factual data—"informative"—the loving truth of the Gospel is creative and life-changing—"performative" (cf. *Spe Salvi*, no. 2). With confidence, Christian educators can liberate the young from the limits of positivism and awaken receptivity to the truth, to God and his goodness. In this way you will also help to form their conscience which, enriched by faith, opens a sure path to inner peace and to respect for others.

It comes as no surprise, then, that not just our own ecclesial communities but society in general has high expectations of Catholic educators. This places upon you a responsibility and offers an opportunity. More and more people—parents in particular—recognize the need for excellence in the human formation of their children. As *Mater et Magistra*, the Church shares their concern. When nothing beyond the individual is recognized as definitive, the ultimate criterion of judgment becomes the self and the satisfaction of the individual's immediate wishes. The objectivity and perspective, which can only come through a recognition of the essential transcendent dimension of the human person, can be lost. Within such a relativistic horizon the goals of education are inevitably curtailed. Slowly, a lowering of standards occurs. We observe today a timidity in the face of the category of the good and an aimless pursuit of novelty parading as the realization of freedom. We witness an assumption that every experience is of equal worth and a reluctance to admit imperfection and mistakes. And particularly disturbing, is the reduction of the precious and delicate area of education in sexuality to management of 'risk,' bereft of any reference to the beauty of conjugal love.

How might Christian educators respond? These harmful developments point to the particular urgency of what we might call "intellectual charity." This aspect of charity calls the educator to recognize that the profound responsibility to lead the young to truth is nothing less than an act of love. Indeed, the dignity of education lies in fostering the true perfection and happiness of those to be educated. In practice "intellectual charity" upholds the essential unity of knowledge against the fragmentation which ensues when reason is detached from the pursuit of truth. It guides the young towards the deep satisfaction of exercising freedom in relation to truth, and it strives to articulate the relationship between faith and all aspects of family and civic life. Once their passion for the fullness and unity of truth has been awakened, young people will surely relish the discovery that the question of what they can know opens up the vast adventure of what they ought to do. Here they will experience "in what" and "in whom" it is possible to hope, and be inspired to contribute to society in a way that engenders hope in others.

Dear friends, I wish to conclude by focusing our attention specifically on the paramount importance of your own professionalism and witness within our Catholic universities and schools. First, let me thank you for your dedication and generosity. I know from my own days as a professor, and I have heard from your Bishops and officials of the Congregation for Catholic Education, that the reputation of Catholic institutes of learning in this country is largely due to yourselves and your predecessors. Your selfless contributions—from outstanding research to the dedi-cation of those working in inner-city schools—serve both your country and the Church. For this I express my profound gratitude.

In regard to faculty members at Catholic colleges universities, I wish to reaf-firm the great value of academic freedom. In virtue of this freedom you are called to search for the truth wherever careful analysis of evidence leads you. Yet it is also the case that any appeal to the principle of academic freedom in order to justify positions that contradict the faith and the teaching of the Church would obstruct or even betray the university's identity and mission; a mission at the heart of the Church's *munus docendi* and not somehow autonomous or independent of it.

Teachers and administrators, whether in universities or schools, have the duty and privilege to ensure that students receive instruction in Catholic doctrine and practice. This requires that public witness to the way of Christ, as found in the Gospel and upheld by the Church's Magisterium, shapes all aspects of an insti-tution's life, both inside and outside the classroom. Divergence from this vision weakens Catholic identity and, far from advancing freedom, inevitably leads to con-fusion, whether moral, intellectual or spiritual.

I wish also to express a particular word of encouragement to both lay and Religious teachers of catechesis who strive to ensure that young people become daily more appreciative of the gift of faith. Religious education is a challenging apostolate, yet there are many signs of a desire among young people to learn about the faith and practice it with vigor. If this awakening is to grow, teachers require a clear and precise understanding of the specific nature and role of Catholic educa-tion. They must also be ready to lead the commitment made by the entire school community to assist our young people, and their families, to experience the har-mony between faith, life and culture.

Here I wish to make a special appeal to Religious Brothers, Sisters and Priests: do not abandon the school apostolate; indeed, renew your commitment to schools especially those in poorer areas. In places where there are many hollow promises which lure young people away from the path of truth and genuine freedom, the consecrated person's witness to the evangelical counsels is an irreplaceable gift. I encourage the Religious present to bring renewed enthusiasm to the promotion of vocations. Know that your witness to the ideal of consecration and mission among the young is a source of great inspiration in faith for them and their families.

To all of you I say: bear witness to hope. Nourish your witness with prayer. Account for the hope that characterizes your lives (cf. 1 Pt 3:15) by living the truth which you propose to your students. Help them to know and love the One you have encountered, whose truth and goodness you have experienced with joy. With Saint Augustine, let us say: "we who speak and you who listen acknowledge ourselves as fellow disciples of a single teacher" (*Sermons*, 23:2). With these sentiments of com-munion, I gladly impart to you, your colleagues and students, and to your families, my Apostolic Blessing.

Address to Participants in the Plenary Session of the Congregation for Catholic Education

Pope Francis
February 13, 2014

Dear Cardinals,
Venerable Brothers in the Episcopate and in the Priesthood,
Dear Brothers and Sisters,

I extend a special welcome to the Cardinals and Bishops who were recently appointed members of this Congregation, and I thank the Cardinal Prefect for the words with which he introduced this meeting.

The topics on your agenda are challenging, indeed, such as updating the Apostolic Constitution *Sapientia Christiana*, strengthening the identity of Catholic universities and preparing for anniversaries that are coming in 2015, such as the 50th anniversary of the Conciliar Declaration *Gravissimum Educationis* and the 25th anniversary of the Apostolic Constitution *Ex Corde Ecclesiae*. Catholic education is one of the most important challenges for the Church, engaged as she is today in implementing the new evangelization in a historical and cultural context which is in constant flux. In this perspective, I would like to draw your attention to three aspects.

The first aspect concerns the *importance of dialogue in education*. Of late, you have developed the theme of an education for intercultural dialogue in Catholic schools with the publication of a specific document. In fact, Catholic schools and universities are attended by many non-Christian students as well as non-believers. Catholic educational institutions offer everyone an education aimed at the integral development of the person that responds to right of all people to have access to knowledge and understanding. But they are equally called to offer to all the Christian message—respecting fully the freedom of all and the proper methods of each specific scholastic environment—namely that Jesus Christ is the meaning of life, of the cosmos and of history.

Jesus began to preach the Good News in the "Galilee of the Gentiles," a crossroads for people of different races, cultures and religions. In some ways this context is similar to today's world. The profound changes that have led to the ever spreading multicultural societies requires those who work in schools and universities to become involved in the educational programs of exchange and dialogue, with a bold and innovative fidelity able to bring together the Catholic identity to meet the different "souls" existing in a multicultural society. I think with appreciation of the contribution which religious institutions and other ecclesial institutes offer through the foundation and management of Catholic schools in contexts strongly marked by cultural and religious pluralism.

The second aspect is the *quality preparation of formators*. We cannot improvise. We must take this seriously. In the meeting I had with the Superiors General, I underlined that today education is directed at a *changing* generation and, therefore, every educator—and the entire Church who is the mother educator—is called "*to change*," or know how to communicate with the young people before them.

I would like to limit myself to recalling the features of an educator and his or her specific duty. To educate is an act of love, it is to give life. And love is demanding, it calls for the best resources, for a reawakening of the passion to begin this path patiently with young people. The educator in Catholic schools must be, first and foremost, competent and qualified but, at the same time, someone who is rich in humanity and capable of being with young people in a style of pedagogy that helps promote their human and spiritual growth. Youth are in need of quality teaching along with values that are not only articulated but witnessed to. Consistency is an indispensable factor in the education of young people! Consistency! We cannot grow and we cannot educate without consistency: consistency and witness!

For this, an educator is himself in need of permanent formation. It is necessary to invest so that teachers and supervisors may maintain a high level of professionalism and also maintain their faith and the strength of their spiritual impetus. And in this permanent formation too I would suggest a need for retreats and spiritual exercises for educators. It is a beautiful thing to offer courses on the subject, but it is also necessary to offer spiritual exercises and retreats focused on prayer! For consistency requires effort but most of all it is a gift and a grace. We must ask for it!

The last aspect concerns *educational institutions*, that is, schools and Catholic and ecclesial universities. The 50th anniversary of the Conciliar Declaration, the 25th anniversary of *Ex Corde Ecclesiae* and the updating of *Sapientia Christiana* lead us to reflect seriously on the many formational institutions around the world and on their duty to be an expression of a living presence of the Gospel in the field of education, of science and of culture. Catholic academic institutions cannot isolate themselves from the world, they must know how to enter bravely into the aeropagus of current culture and open dialogue, conscious of the gift that they can offer to everyone.

Dear ones, education is a great open building site in which the Church has always been present through her institutions and projects. Today we must encourage this commitment on all levels and renew the commitment of all engaged in the new evangelization. On this horizon, I thank you all for your work and I invoke through the intercession of the Virgin Mary the perpetual help of the Holy Spirit for you and your work. I ask you to please pray for me and for my ministry. And from my heart, I bless you. Thank you!

III. Curial Documents

Instruction *Donum Veritatis*

On the Ecclesial Vocation of the Theologian

Congregation for the Doctrine of the Faith

May 24, 1990

INTRODUCTION

1. The truth which sets us free is a gift of Jesus Christ (cf. Jn 8:32). Man's nature calls him to seek the truth while ignorance keeps him in a condition of servitude. Indeed, man could not be truly free were no light shed upon the central questions of his existence including, in particular, where he comes from and where he is going. When God gives Himself to man as a friend, man becomes free, in accordance with the Lord's word: "No longer do I call you servants, for the servant does not know what his master is doing; but I have called you friends, for all that I have heard from my Father I have made known to you" (Jn 15:15). Man's deliverance from the alienation of sin and death comes about when Christ, the Truth, becomes the "way" for him (cf. Jn 14:6).

In the Christian faith, knowledge and life, truth and existence are intrinsically connected. Assuredly, the truth given in God's revelation exceeds the capacity of human knowledge, but it is not opposed to human reason. Revelation in fact penetrates human reason, elevates it, and calls it to give an account of itself (cf. 1 Pt 3:15). For this reason, from the very beginning of the Church, the "standard of teaching" (cf. Rom 6:17) has been linked with baptism to entrance into the mystery of Christ. The service of doctrine, implying as it does the believer's search for an understanding of the faith, i.e., theology, is therefore something indispensable for the Church.

Theology has importance for the Church in every age so that it can respond to the plan of God "who desires all men to be saved and to come to the knowledge of the truth" (1 Tm 2:4). In times of great spiritual and cultural change, theology is all the more important. Yet it also is exposed to risks since it must strive to "abide" in the truth (cf. Jn 8:31), while at the same time taking into account the new problems which confront the human spirit. In our century, in particular, during the periods of preparation for and implementation of the Second Vatican Council, theology contributed much to a deeper "understanding of the realities and the words handed on."[1] But it also experienced and continues to experience moments of crisis and tension.

The Congregation for the Doctrine of the Faith deems it opportune then to address to the Bishops of the Catholic Church, and through them her theologians,

---

1 Dogmatic Constitution *Dei Verbum*, no. 8.

the present Instruction which seeks to shed light on the mission of theology in the Church. After having considered truth as God's gift to His people (I), the instruction will describe the role of theologians (II), ponder the particular mission of the Church's Pastors (III), and finally, propose some points on the proper relationship between theologians and pastors (IV). In this way, it aims to serve the growth in understanding of the truth (cf. Col 1:10) which ushers us into that freedom which Christ died and rose to win for us (cf. Gal 5:1).

THE TRUTH: GOD'S GIFT TO HIS PEOPLE

2. Out of His infinite love, God desired to draw near to man, as he seeks his own proper identity, and walk with him (cf. Lk 24:15) . He also wanted to free him from the snares of the "father of lies" (cf. Jn 8:44) and to open the way to intimacy with Himself so that man could find there, superabundantly, full truth and authentic freedom. This plan of love, conceived by "the Father of lights" (Jas 1:17; cf. 1 Pt 2:9; 1 Jn 1:5) and realized by the Son victorious over death (cf. Jn 8:36), is continually made present by the Spirit who leads "to all truth" (Jn 16:13).

3. The truth possesses in itself a unifying force. It frees men from isolation and the oppositions in which they have been trapped by ignorance of the truth. And as it opens the way to God, it, at the same time, unites them to each other. Christ destroyed the wall of separation which had kept them strangers to God's promise and to the fellowship of the covenant (cf. Eph 2:12–14). Into the hearts of the faithful He sends His Spirit through whom we become nothing less than "one" in Him (cf. Rom 5:5; Gal 3:28). Thus thanks to the new birth and the anointing of the Holy Spirit (cf. Jn 3:5; 1 Jn 2:20, 27), we become the one, new People of God whose mission it is, with our different vocations and charisms, to preserve and hand on the gift of truth. Indeed, the whole Church, as the "salt of the earth" and "the light of the world" (cf. Mt 5:13 f.), must bear witness to the truth of Christ which sets us free.

4. The People of God respond to this calling "above all by means of the life of faith and charity, and by offering to God a sacrifice of praise." More specifically, as far as the "life of faith" is concerned, the Second Vatican Council makes it clear that "the whole body of the faithful who have an anointing that comes from the holy one (cf. 1 Jn 2:20. 27) cannot err in matters of belief." And "this characteristic is shown in the supernatural sense of the faith of the whole people, when 'from the bishops to the last of the faithful' they manifest a universal consent in matters of faith and morals."[2]

5. In order to exercise the prophetic function in the world, the People of God must continually reawaken or "rekindle" its own life of faith (cf. 2 Tm 1:6). It does this particularly by contemplating ever more deeply, under the guidance of the Holy Spirit, the contents of the faith itself and by dutifully presenting the reasonableness of the faith to those who ask for an account of it (cf. 1 Pt 3:15). For the sake of this mission, the Spirit of truth distributes among the faithful of every rank special graces "for the common good" (1 Cor 12:7–11).

---

2   Dogmatic Constitution *Lumen Gentium*, no. 12.

II. THE VOCATION OF THE THEOLOGIAN

6. Among the vocations awakened in this way by the Spirit in the Church is that of the theologian. His role is to pursue in a particular way an ever deeper understanding of the Word of God found in the inspired Scriptures and handed on by the living Tradition of the Church. He does this in communion with the Magisterium which has been charged with the responsibility of preserving the deposit of faith.

By its nature, faith appeals to reason because it reveals to man the truth of his destiny and the way to attain it. Revealed truth, to be sure, surpasses our telling. All our concepts fall short of its ultimately unfathomable grandeur (cf. Eph 3:19). Nonetheless, revealed truth beckons reason—God's gift fashioned for the assimilation of truth—to enter into its light and thereby come to understand in a certain measure what it has believed. Theological science responds to the invitation of truth as it seeks to understand the faith. It thereby aids the People of God in fulfilling the Apostle's command (cf. 1 Pt 3:15) to give an accounting for their hope to those who ask it.

7. The theologian's work thus responds to a dynamism found in the faith itself. Truth, by its nature, seeks to be communicated since man was created for the perception of truth and from the depths of his being desires knowledge of it so that he can discover himself in the truth and find there his salvation (cf. 1 Tm 2:4). For this reason, the Lord sent forth His apostles to make "disciples" of all nations and teach them (cf. Mt 28:19 f.). Theology, which seeks the "reasons of faith" and offers these reasons as a response to those seeking them, thus constitutes an integral part of obedience to the command of Christ, for men cannot become disciples if the truth found in the word of faith is not presented to them (cf. Rom 10:14 f.).

Theology therefore offers its contribution so that the faith might be communicated. Appealing to the understanding of those who do not yet know Christ, it helps them to seek and find faith. Obedient to the impulse of truth which seeks to be communicated, theology also arises from love and love's dynamism. In the act of faith, man knows God's goodness and begins to love Him. Love, however, is ever desirous of a better knowledge of the beloved.[3] From this double origin of theology, inscribed upon the interior life of the People of God and its missionary vocation, derives the method with which it ought to be pursued in order to satisfy the requirements of its nature.

8. Since the object of theology is the Truth which is the living God and His plan for salvation revealed in Jesus Christ, the theologian is called to deepen his own life of faith and continuously unite his scientific research with prayer.[4] In this way, he will become more open to the "supernatural sense of faith" upon which he depends, and it will appear to him as a sure rule for guiding his reflections and helping him assess the correctness of his conclusions.

---

3   Cf. St. Bonaventure, *Prooem. in I Sent.*, q. 2, ad 6: "*Quando fides non assentit propter rationem, sed propter amorem eius cui assentit, desiderat habere rationes.*"

4   Cf. John Paul II, "*Discorso in occasione della consegna del premio internazionale Paulo VI a Hans Urs von Balthasar,*" June 23, 1984: *Insegnamenti di Giovanni Paolo II*, VII, 1 (1984) 1911–1917.

9. Through the course of centuries, theology has progressively developed into a true and proper science. The theologian must therefore be attentive to the epistemological requirements of his discipline, to the demands of rigorous critical standards, and thus to a rational verification of each stage of his research. The obligation to be critical, however, should not be identified with the critical spirit which is born of feeling or prejudice. The theologian must discern in himself the origin of and motivation for his critical attitude and allow his gaze to be purified by faith. The commitment to theology requires a spiritual effort to grow in virtue and holiness.

10. Even though it transcends human reason, revealed truth is in profound harmony with it. It presumes that reason by its nature is ordered to the truth in such a way that, illumined by faith, it can penetrate to the meaning of Revelation. Despite the assertions of many philosophical currents, but in conformity with a correct way of thinking which finds confirmation in Scripture, human reason's ability to attain truth must be recognized as well as its metaphysical capacity to come to a knowledge of God from creation.[5]

Theology's proper task is to understand the meaning of revelation and this, therefore, requires the utilization of philosophical concepts which provide "a solid and correct understanding of man, the world, and God"[6] and can be employed in a reflection upon revealed doctrine. The historical disciplines are likewise necessary for the theologian's investigations. This is due chiefly to the historical character of revelation itself which has been communicated to us in "salvation history." Finally, a consultation of the "human sciences" is also necessary to understand better the revealed truth about man and the moral norms for his conduct, setting these in relation to the sound findings of such sciences.

It is the theologian's task in this perspective to draw from the surrounding culture those elements which will allow him better to illumine one or other aspect of the mysteries of faith. This is certainly an arduous task that has its risks, but it is legitimate in itself and should be encouraged.

Here it is important to emphasize that when theology employs the elements and conceptual tools of philosophy or other disciplines, discernment is needed. The ultimate normative principle for such discernment is revealed doctrine which itself must furnish the criteria for the evaluation of these elements and conceptual tools and not *vice versa.*

11. Never forgetting that he is also a member of the People of God, the theologian must foster respect for them and be committed to offering them a teaching which in no way does harm to the doctrine of the faith.

The freedom proper to theological research is exercised within the Church's faith. Thus while the theologian might often feel the urge to be daring in his work, this will not bear fruit or "edify" unless it is accompanied by that patience which permits maturation to occur. New proposals advanced for understanding the faith "are but an offering made to the whole Church. Many corrections and broadening of perspectives within the context of fraternal dialogue may be needed before the moment comes when the whole Church can accept them." Consequently, "this very

---

5   Cf. Vatican Council I, Dogmatic Constitution *De Fide Catholica, De Revelatione,* c. 1: DS 3026.

6   Decree *Optatam Totius,* no. 15.

disinterested service to the community of the faithful," which theology is, "entails in essence an objective discussion, a fraternal dialogue, an openness and willingness to modify one's own opinions."[7]

12. Freedom of research, which the academic community rightly holds most precious, means an openness to accepting the truth that emerges at the end of an investigation in which no element has intruded that is foreign to the methodology corresponding to the object under study.

In theology this freedom of inquiry is the hallmark of a rational discipline whose object is given by Revelation, handed on and interpreted in the Church under the authority of the Magisterium, and received by faith. These givens have the force of principles. To eliminate them would mean to cease doing theology. In order to set forth precisely the ways in which the theologian relates to the Church's teaching authority, it is appropriate now to reflect upon the role of the Magisterium in the Church.

III. THE MAGISTERIUM OF THE CHURCH'S PASTORS

13. "God graciously arranged that the things he had once revealed for the salvation of all peoples should remain in their entirety, throughout the ages, and be transmitted to all generations."[8] He bestowed upon His Church, through the gift of the Holy Spirit, a participation in His own infallibility.[9] Thanks to the "supernatural sense of Faith," the People of God enjoys this privilege under the guidance of the Church's living Magisterium, which is the sole authentic interpreter of the Word of God, written or handed down, by virtue of the authority which it exercises in the name of Christ.[10]

14. As successors of the apostles, the bishops of the Church "receive from the Lord, to whom all power is given in heaven and on earth, the mission of teaching all peoples and of preaching the Gospel to every creature, so that all men may attain to salvation . . . ."[11] They have been entrusted then with the task of preserving, explaining, and spreading the Word of God of which they are servants.[12]

It is the mission of the Magisterium to affirm the definitive character of the Covenant established by God through Christ with His People in a way which is consistent with the "eschatological" nature of the event of Jesus Christ. It must protect God's People from the danger of deviations and confusion, guaranteeing

---

7   John Paul II, "*Discorso ai teologi ad Altötting*," November 18, 1980: AAS 73 (1981) 104; cf. also Paul VI, "*Discorso ai membri della Commissione Teologica Internazionale*," October 11, 1972: AAS 64 (1972) 682–683; John Paul II, "*Discorso ai membri della Commissione Teologica Internazionale*," October 26, 1979: AAS 71 (1979) 1428–1433.

8   Dogmatic Constitution *Dei Verbum*, no. 7.

9   Cf. Congregation for the Doctrine of the Faith, Decl. *Mysterium Ecclesiae*, no. 2: AAS 65 (1973) 398 f.

10   Cf. Dogmatic Constitution *Dei Verbum*, no. 10.

11   Dogmatic Constitution *Lumen Gentium*, no. 24.

12   Cf. Dogmatic Constitution *Dei Verbum*, no. 10.

them the objective possibility of professing the authentic faith free from error, at all times and in diverse situations. It follows that the sense and the weight of the Magisterium's authority are only intelligible in relation to the truth of Christian doctrine and the preaching of the true Word. The function of the Magisterium is not, then, something extrinsic to Christian truth, nor is it set above the faith. It arises directly from the economy of the faith itself, inasmuch as the Magisterium is, in its service to the Word of God, an institution positively willed by Christ as a constitutive element of His Church. The service to Christian truth which the Magisterium renders is thus for the benefit of the whole People of God called to enter the liberty of the truth revealed by God in Christ.

15. Jesus Christ promised the assistance of the Holy Spirit to the Church's Pastors so that they could fulfill their assigned task of teaching the Gospel and authentically interpreting Revelation. In particular, He bestowed on them the charism of infallibility in matters of faith and morals. This charism is manifested when the Pastors propose a doctrine as contained in Revelation and can be exercised in various ways. Thus it is exercised particularly when the bishops in union with their visible head proclaim a doctrine by a collegial act, as is the case in an ecumenical council, or when the Roman Pontiff, fulfilling his mission as supreme Pastor and Teacher of all Christians, proclaims a doctrine *ex cathedra.*[13]

16. By its nature, the task of religiously guarding and loyally expounding the deposit of divine Revelation (in all its integrity and purity), implies that the Magisterium can make a pronouncement "in a definitive way"[14] on propositions which, even if not contained among the truths of faith, are nonetheless intimately connected with them, in such a way, that the definitive character of such affirmations derives in the final analysis from revelation itself.[15]

What concerns morality can also be the object of the authentic Magisterium because the Gospel, being the Word of Life, inspires and guides the whole sphere of human behavior. The Magisterium, therefore, has the task of discerning, by means of judgments normative for the consciences of believers, those acts which in themselves conform to the demands of faith and foster their expression in life and those which, on the contrary, because intrinsically evil, are incompatible with such demands. By reason of the connection between the orders of creation and redemption and by reason of the necessity, in view of salvation, of knowing and observing the whole moral law, the competence of the Magisterium also extends to that which concerns the natural law.[16]

---

13   Cf. Dogmatic Constitution *Lumen Gentium,* no. 25; Congregation for the Doctrine of the Faith, Declaration *Mysterium Ecclesiae,* no. 3: AAS 65 (1973) 400 f.

14   Cf. *Professio Fidei et Iusiurandum Fidelitatis: AAS* 81 (1989) 104 f.: "*Omnia et singula quae circa doctrinam de fide vel moribus ab eadem definitive proponuntur.*"

15   Cf. Dogmatic Constitution *Lumen Gentium,* no. 25; Congregation for the Doctrine of the Faith, Declaration *Mysterium Ecclesiae,* nos. 3–5: AAS 65 (1973) 400–404; *Professio Fidei et Iusiurandum Fidelitatis:* AAS 81 (1989) 104 f.

16   Cf. Paul VI, Encyclical *Humanae Vitae,* no. 4: AAS 60 (1968), 483.

Revelation also contains moral teachings which *per se* could be known by natural reason. Access to them, however, is made difficult by man's sinful condition. It is a doctrine of faith that these moral norms can be infallibly taught by the Magisterium.[17]

17. Divine assistance is also given to the successors of the apostles teaching in communion with the successor of Peter, and in a particular way, to the Roman Pontiff as Pastor of the whole Church, when exercising their ordinary Magisterium, even should this not issue in an infallible definition or in a "definitive" pronouncement but in the proposal of some teaching which leads to a better understanding of Revelation in matters of faith and morals and to moral directives derived from such teaching.

One must therefore take into account the proper character of every exercise of the Magisterium, considering the extent to which its authority is engaged. It is also to be borne in mind that all acts of the Magisterium derive from the same source, that is, from Christ who desires that His People walk in the entire truth. For this same reason, magisterial decisions in matters of discipline, even if they are not guaranteed by the charism of infallibility, are not without divine assistance and call for the adherence of the faithful.

18. The Roman Pontiff fulfills his universal mission with the help of the various bodies of the Roman Curia and in particular with that of the Congregation for the Doctrine of the Faith in matters of doctrine and morals. Consequently, the documents issued by this Congregation expressly approved by the Pope participate in the ordinary Magisterium of the successor of Peter.[18]

19. Within the particular Churches, it is the bishop's responsibility to guard and interpret the Word of God and to make authoritative judgments as to what is or is not in conformity with it. The teaching of each bishop, taken individually, is exercised in communion with the Roman Pontiff, Pastor of the universal Church, and with the other bishops dispersed throughout the world or gathered in an ecumenical council. Such communion is a condition for its authenticity.

Member of the Episcopal College by virtue of his sacramental ordination and hierarchical communion, the bishop represents his Church just as all the bishops, in union with the Pope, represent the Church universal in the bonds of peace, love, unity, and truth. As they come together in unity, the local Churches, with their own proper patrimonies, manifest the Church's catholicity. The episcopal conferences for their part contribute to the concrete realization of the collegial spirit (*affectus*).[19]

20. The pastoral task of the Magisterium is one of vigilance. It seeks to ensure that the People of God remain in the truth which sets free. It is therefore a complex and diversified reality. The theologian, to be faithful to his role of service to the

---

17   Cf. Vatican Council I, Dogmatic Constitution *Dei Filius*, Ch. 2; DS 3005.

18   Cf. *Code of Canon Law*, cc. 360–361; Paul VI, Apostolic Constitution *Regimini Ecclesiae Universae*, August 15, 1967, nos. 29–40: AAS 59 (1967) 879–899; John Paul II, Apostolic Constitution *Pastor Bonus*, June 28, 1988: AAS 80 (1988) 873–874.

19   Dogmatic Constitution *Lumen Gentium*, nos. 22–23. As it is known, following upon the Second Extraordinary Synod of Bishops, the Holy Father gave the Congregation for Bishops the task of exploring the "Theological-Juridical Status of Episcopal Conferences."

truth, must take into account the proper mission of the Magisterium and collaborate with it. How should this collaboration be understood? How is it put into practice and what are the obstacles it may face? These questions should now be examined more closely.

IV. THE MAGISTERIUM AND THEOLOGY

A. Collaborative Relations

21. The living Magisterium of the Church and theology, while having different gifts and functions, ultimately have the same goal: preserving the People of God in the truth which sets free and thereby making them "a light to the nations." This service to the ecclesial community brings the theologian and the Magisterium into a reciprocal relationship. The latter authentically teaches the doctrine of the Apostles. And, benefiting from the work of theologians, it refutes objections to and distortions of the faith and promotes, with the authority received from Jesus Christ, new and deeper comprehension, clarification, and application of revealed doctrine. Theology, for its part, gains, by way of reflection, an ever deeper understanding of the Word of God found in the Scripture and handed on faithfully by the Church's living Tradition under the guidance of the Magisterium. Theology strives to clarify the teaching of Revelation with regard to reason and gives it finally an organic and systematic form.[20]

22. Collaboration between the theologian and the Magisterium occurs in a special way when the theologian receives the canonical mission or the mandate to teach. In a certain sense, such collaboration becomes a participation in the work of the Magisterium, linked, as it then is, by a juridic bond. The theologian's code of conduct, which obviously has its origin in the service of the Word of God, is here reinforced by the commitment the theologian assumes in accepting his office, making the profession of faith, and taking the oath of fidelity.[21]

From this moment on, the theologian is officially charged with the task of presenting and illustrating the doctrine of the faith in its integrity and with full accuracy.

23. When the Magisterium of the Church makes an infallible pronouncement and solemnly declares that a teaching is found in Revelation, the assent called for is that of theological faith. This kind of adherence is to be given even to the teaching of the ordinary and universal Magisterium when it proposes for belief a teaching of faith as divinely revealed.

When the Magisterium proposes "in a definitive way" truths concerning faith and morals, which, even if not divinely revealed, are nevertheless strictly and intimately connected with Revelation, these must be firmly accepted and held.[22]

---

20   Cf. Paul VI, "*Discorso ai partecipanti al Congresso internazionale di Teologia del Concilio Vaticano II*," October 1, 1966: *Insegnamenti di Paolo VI*: AAS 58 (1966) 892f.

21   Cf. *Code of Canon Law*, c. 833; *Professio Fidei et Iusiurandum Fidelitatis*: AAS 81 (1989) 104f.

22   The text of the new Profession of Faith (cf. no. 15) makes explicit the kind of assent called for by these teachings in these terms: "*Firmiter etiam amplector et retineo . . .*"

When the Magisterium, not intending to act "definitively," teaches a doctrine to aid a better understanding of Revelation and make explicit its contents, or to recall how some teaching is in conformity with the truths of faith, or finally to guard against ideas that are incompatible with these truths, the response called for is that of the religious submission of will and intellect.[23] This kind of response cannot be simply exterior or disciplinary but must be understood within the logic of faith and under the impulse of obedience to the faith.

24. Finally, in order to serve the People of God as well as possible, in particular, by warning them of dangerous opinions which could lead to error, the Magisterium can intervene in questions under discussion which involve, in addition to solid principles, certain contingent and conjectural elements. It often only becomes possible with the passage of time to distinguish between what is necessary and what is contingent.

The willingness to submit loyally to the teaching of the Magisterium on matters *per se* not irreformable must be the rule. It can happen, however, that a theologian may, according to the case, raise questions regarding the timeliness, the form, or even the contents of magisterial interventions. Here the theologian will need, first of all, to assess accurately the authoritativeness of the interventions which becomes clear from the nature of the documents, the insistence with which a teaching is repeated, and the very way in which it is expressed.[24]

When it comes to the question of interventions in the prudential order, it could happen that some Magisterial documents might not be free from all deficiencies. Bishops and their advisors have not always taken into immediate consideration every aspect or the entire complexity of a question. But it would be contrary to the truth, if, proceeding from some particular cases, one were to conclude that the Church's Magisterium can be habitually mistaken in its prudential judgments, or that it does not enjoy divine assistance in the integral exercise of its mission. In fact, the theologian, who cannot pursue his discipline well without a certain competence in history, is aware of the filtering which occurs with the passage of time. This is not to be understood in the sense of a relativization of the tenets of the faith. The theologian knows that some judgments of the Magisterium could be justified at the time in which they were made, because while the pronouncements contained true assertions and others which were not sure, both types were inextricably connected. Only time has permitted discernment and, after deeper study, the attainment of true doctrinal progress.

25. Even when collaboration takes place under the best conditions, the possibility cannot be excluded that tensions may arise between the theologian and the Magisterium. The meaning attributed to such tensions and the spirit with which they are faced are not matters of indifference. If tensions do not spring from hostile and contrary feelings, they can become a dynamic factor, a stimulus to both the Magisterium and theologians to fulfill their respective roles while practicing dialogue.

26. In the dialogue, a two-fold rule should prevail. When there is a question of the communion of faith, the principle of the "unity of truth" (*unitas veritatis*)

---

23   Cf. Dogmatic Constitution *Lumen Gentium*, no. 25; *Code of Canon Law*, c. 752.

24   Dogmatic Constitution *Lumen Gentium*, no. 25 §1.

applies. When it is a question of differences which do not jeopardize this communion, the "unity of charity" (*unitas caritatis*) should be safeguarded.

27. Even if the doctrine of the faith is not in question, the theologian will not present his own opinions or divergent hypotheses as though they were non-arguable conclusions. Respect for the truth as well as for the People of God requires this discretion (cf. Rom 14:1–15; 1 Cor 8; 10: 23–33). For the same reasons, the theologian will refrain from giving untimely public expression to them.

28. The preceding considerations have a particular application to the case of the theologian who might have serious difficulties, for reasons which appear to him well-founded, in accepting a non-irreformable magisterial teaching.

Such a disagreement could not be justified if it were based solely upon the fact that the validity of the given teaching is not evident or upon the opinion that the opposite position would be the more probable. Nor, furthermore, would the judgment of the subjective conscience of the theologian justify it because conscience does not constitute an autonomous and exclusive authority for deciding the truth of a doctrine.

29. In any case there should never be a diminishment of that fundamental openness loyally to accept the teaching of the Magisterium as is fitting for every believer by reason of the obedience of faith. The theologian will strive then to understand this teaching in its contents, arguments, and purposes. This will mean an intense and patient reflection on his part and a readiness, if need be, to revise his own opinions and examine the objections which his colleagues might offer him.

30. If, despite a loyal effort on the theologian's part, the difficulties persist, the theologian has the duty to make known to the Magisterial authorities the problems raised by the teaching in itself, in the arguments proposed to justify it, or even in the manner in which it is presented. He should do this in an evangelical spirit and with a profound desire to resolve the difficulties. His objections could then contribute to real progress and provide a stimulus to the Magisterium to propose the teaching of the Church in greater depth and with a clearer presentation of the arguments.

In cases like these, the theologian should avoid turning to the "mass media," but have recourse to the responsible authority, for it is not by seeking to exert the pressure of public opinion that one contributes to the clarification of doctrinal issues and renders service to the truth.

31. It can also happen that at the conclusion of a serious study, undertaken with the desire to heed the Magisterium's teaching without hesitation, the theologian's difficulty remains because the arguments to the contrary seem more persuasive to him. Faced with a proposition to which he feels he cannot give his intellectual assent, the theologian nevertheless has the duty to remain open to a deeper examination of the question.

For a loyal spirit, animated by love for the Church, such a situation can certainly prove a difficult trial. It can be a call to suffer for the truth, in silence and prayer, but with the certainty, that if the truth really is at stake, it will ultimately prevail.

B. The Problem of Dissent

32. The Magisterium has drawn attention several times to the serious harm done to the community of the Church by attitudes of general opposition to Church teaching which even come to expression in organized groups. In his Apostolic Exhortation *Paterna cum Benevolentia*, Paul VI offered a diagnosis of this problem which is still apropos.[25] In particular, he addresses here that public opposition to the Magisterium of the Church also called "dissent," which must be distinguished from the situation of personal difficulties treated above. The phenomenon of dissent can have diverse forms. Its remote and proximate causes are multiple.

The ideology of philosophical liberalism, which permeates the thinking of our age, must be counted among the factors which may exercise their remote or indirect influence. Here arises the tendency to regard a judgment as having all the more validity to the extent that it proceeds from the individual relying upon his own powers. In such a way freedom of thought comes to oppose the authority of tradition, which is considered a cause of servitude. A teaching handed on and generally received is *a priori* suspect and its truth contested. Ultimately, freedom of judgment understood in this way is more important than the truth itself. We are dealing then here with something quite different from the legitimate demand for freedom in the sense of absence of constraint as a necessary condition for the loyal inquiry into truth. In virtue of this exigency, the Church has always held that "nobody is to be forced to embrace the faith against his will."[26]

The weight of public opinion when manipulated and its pressure to conform also have their influence. Often models of society promoted by the "mass media" tend to assume a normative value. The view is particularly promoted that the Church should only express her judgment on those issues which public opinion considers important and then only by way of agreeing with it. The Magisterium, for example, could intervene in economic or social questions but ought to leave matters of conjugal and family morality to individual judgment.

Finally, the plurality of cultures and languages, in itself a benefit, can indirectly bring on misunderstandings which occasion disagreements.

In this context, the theologian needs to make a critical, well-considered discernment, as well as have a true mastery of the issues, if he wants to fulfill his ecclesial mission and not lose, by conforming himself to this present world (cf. Rom 12:2; Eph 4:23), the independence of judgment which should be that of the disciples of Christ.

33. Dissent has different aspects. In its most radical form, it aims at changing the Church following a model of protest which takes its inspiration from political society. More frequently, it is asserted that the theologian is not bound to adhere to any Magisterial teaching unless it is infallible. Thus a kind of theological positivism is adopted, according to which, doctrines proposed without exercise of the

---

25   Cf. Paul VI, Apostolic Exhortation *Paterna cum Benevolentia*, December 8, 1974: AAS 67 (1975) 5–23. Cf. also Congregation for the Doctrine of the Faith, Declaration *Mysterium Ecclesiae*: AAS 65 (1973) 396–408.

26   Declaration *Dignitatis Humanae*, no. 10.

charism of infallibility are said to have no obligatory character about them, leaving the individual completely at liberty to adhere to them or not. The theologian would accordingly be totally free to raise doubts or reject the non-infallible teaching of the Magisterium particularly in the case of specific moral norms. With such critical opposition, he would even be making a contribution to the development of doctrine.

34. Dissent is generally defended by various arguments, two of which are more basic in character. The first lies in the order of hermeneutics. The documents of the Magisterium, it is said, reflect nothing more than a debatable theology. The second takes theological pluralism sometimes to the point of a relativism which calls the integrity of the faith into question. Here the interventions of the Magisterium would have their origin in one theology among many theologies, while no particular theology, however, could presume to claim universal normative status. In opposition to and in competition with the authentic Magisterium, there thus arises a kind of "parallel magisterium" of theologians.[27]

Certainly, it is one of the theologian's tasks to give a correct interpretation to the texts of the Magisterium and to this end he employs various hermeneutical rules. Among these is the principle which affirms that magisterial teaching, by virtue of divine assistance, has a validity beyond its argumentation, which may derive at times from a particular theology. As far as theological pluralism is concerned, this is only legitimate to the extent that the unity of the faith in its objective meaning is not jeopardized.[28] Essential bonds link the distinct levels of unity of faith, unity-plurality of expressions of the faith, and plurality of theologies. The ultimate reason for plurality is found in the unfathomable mystery of Christ who transcends every objective systematization. This cannot mean that it is possible to accept conclusions contrary to that mystery and it certainly does not put into question the truth of those assertions by which the Magisterium has declared itself.[29] As to the "parallel magisterium," it can cause great spiritual harm by opposing itself to the Magisterium of the Pastors. Indeed, when dissent succeeds in extending its influence to the point of shaping a common opinion, it tends to become the rule of conduct. This cannot but seriously trouble the People of God and lead to contempt for true authority.[30]

---

27 The notion of a "parallel magisterium" of theologians in opposition to and in competition with the Magisterium of the Pastors is sometimes supported by reference to some texts in which St. Thomas Aquinas makes a distinction between the *"magisterium cathedrae pastoralis"* and *"magisterium cathedrae magisterialis"* (*Contro Impugnantes*, c. 2; Quodlib. III, q. 4, a.l (9); *In IV.Sent.* 19, 2, 2, q. 3 sol. 2 ad 4). Actually, these texts do not give any support to this position for St. Thomas was absolutely certain that the right to judge in matters of doctrine was the sole responsibility of the *officium praelationis*.

28 Paul VI, Apostolic Exhortation *Paterna cum Benevolentia*, no. 4: AAS 67 (1975) 14–15.

29 Cf. Paul VI, "*Discorso ai membri della Commissione Teologica Internazionale,*" October 11, 1973: AAS 65 (1973) 555–559.

30 Cf. John Paul II, Encyclical *Redemptor Hominis*, no. 19: AAS 71 (1979) 308; "*Discorso ai fedeli di Managua,*" March 4, 1983, no. 7: AAS 75 (1983) 723; "*Discorso ai religiosi a Guatemala,*" March 8, 1983, no. 3: AAS 75 (1983) 746; "*Discorso ai vescovi a Lima,*" February 2, 1985, no. 5: AAS 77 (1985) 874; "*Discorso alla Conferenza dei vescovi belgi a Malines,*" May 18, 1985, no. 5: *Insegnamenti di Giovanni Paolo II*, VIII, 1 (1985) 1481; "*Discorso ad alcuni vescovi americani in visita ad limina,*" October 15, 1988, no. 6: L'Osservatore Romano, October 16, 1988, 4.

35. Dissent sometimes also appeals to a kind of sociological argumentation which holds that the opinion of a large number of Christians would be a direct and adequate expression of the "supernatural sense of the faith."

Actually, the opinions of the faithful cannot be purely and simply identified with the *sensus fidei*.[31] The sense of the faith is a property of theological faith; and, as God's gift which enables one to adhere personally to the Truth, it cannot err. This personal faith is also the faith of the Church since God has given guardianship of the Word to the Church. Consequently, what the believer believes is what the Church believes. The *sensus fidei* implies then by its nature a profound agreement of spirit and heart with the Church, *sentire cum Ecclesia*.

Although theological faith as such then cannot err, the believer can still have erroneous opinions since all his thoughts do not spring from faith.[32] Not all the ideas which circulate among the People of God are compatible with the faith. This is all the more so given that people can be swayed by a public opinion influenced by modern communications media. Not without reason did the Second Vatican Council emphasize the indissoluble bond between the *sensus fidei* and the guidance of God's People by the Magisterium of the Pastors. These two realities cannot be separated.[33] Magisterial interventions serve to guarantee the Church's unity in the truth of the Lord. They aid her to "abide in the truth" in face of the arbitrary character of changeable opinions and are an expression of obedience to the Word of God.[34] Even when it might seem that they limit the freedom of theologians, these actions, by their fidelity to the faith which has been handed on, establish a deeper freedom which can only come from unity in truth.

36. The freedom of the act of faith cannot justify a right to dissent. In fact this freedom does not indicate at all freedom with regard to the truth but signifies the free self-determination of the person in conformity with his moral obligation to accept the truth. The act of faith is a voluntary act because man, saved by Christ the Redeemer and called by Him to be an adopted son (cf. Rom 8:15; Gal 4:5; Eph 1:5; Jn 1:12), cannot adhere to God unless, "drawn by the Father" (Jn 6:44), he offer God the rational homage of his faith (cf. Rom 12:1). As the Declaration *Dignitatis Humanae* recalls,[35] no human authority may overstep the limits of its competence and claim the right to interfere with this choice by exerting pressure or constraint. Respect for religious liberty is the foundation of respect for all the rights of man.

One cannot then appeal to these rights of man in order to oppose the interventions of the Magisterium. Such behavior fails to recognize the nature and mission of the Church which has received from the Lord the task to proclaim the truth of salvation to all men. She fulfills this task by walking in Christ's footsteps, knowing

---

31 Cf. John Paul II, Apostolic Exhortation *Familiaris Consortio*, no. 5: AAS 74 (1982) 85–86.

32 Cf. the formula of the Council of Trent, sess. VI, cap. 9: fides "*cui non potest subesse falsum*": DS 1534; cf. St. Thomas Aquinas, *Summa Theologiae*, II-II, q. 1, a. 3, ad 3: "*Possibile est enim hominem fidelem ex coniectura humana falsum aliquid aestimare. Sed quod ex fide falsum aestimet, hoc est impossibile.*"

33 Cf. Dogmatic Constitution *Lumen Gentium*, no. 12.

34 Cf. Dogmatic Constitution *Dei Verbum*, no. 10.

35 Declaration *Dignitatis Humanae*, nos. 9–10.

that "truth can impose itself on the mind only by virtue of its own truth, which wins over the mind with both gentleness and power."[36]

37. By virtue of the divine mandate given to it in the Church, the Magisterium has the mission to set forth the Gospel's teaching, guard its integrity, and thereby protect the Faith of the People of God. In order to fulfill this duty, it can at times be led to take serious measures as, for example, when it withdraws from a theologian, who departs from the doctrine of the faith, the canonical mission or the teaching mandate it had given him, or declares that some writings do not conform to this doctrine. When it acts in such ways, the Magisterium seeks to be faithful to its mission of defending the right of the People of God to receive the message of the Church in its purity and integrity and not be disturbed by a particular dangerous opinion.

The judgment expressed by the Magisterium in such circumstances is the result of a thorough investigation conducted according to established procedures which afford the interested party the opportunity to clear up possible misunderstandings of his thought. This judgment, however, does not concern the person of the theologian but the intellectual positions which he has publicly espoused. The fact that these procedures can be improved does not mean that they are contrary to justice and right. To speak in this instance of a violation of human rights is out of place for it indicates a failure to recognize the proper hierarchy of these rights as well as the nature of the ecclesial community and her common good. Moreover, the theologian who is not disposed to think with the Church (*sentire cum Ecclesia*) contradicts the commitment he freely and knowingly accepted to teach in the name of the Church.[37]

38. Finally, argumentation appealing to the obligation to follow one's own conscience cannot legitimate dissent. This is true, first of all, because conscience illumines the practical judgment about a decision to make, while here we are concerned with the truth of a doctrinal pronouncement. This is furthermore the case because while the theologian, like every believer, must follow his conscience, he is also obliged to form it. Conscience is not an independent and infallible faculty. It is an act of moral judgment regarding a responsible choice. A right conscience is one duly illumined by faith and by the objective moral law and it presupposes, as well, the uprightness of the will in the pursuit of the true good.

The right conscience of the Catholic theologian presumes not only faith in the Word of God whose riches he must explore, but also love for the Church from whom he receives his mission, and respect for her divinely assisted Magisterium. Setting up a supreme magisterium of conscience in opposition to the Magisterium of the Church means adopting a principle of free examination incompatible with the economy of Revelation and its transmission in the Church and thus also with a correct understanding of theology and the role of the theologian. The propositions of faith are not the product of mere individual research and free criticism of the Word of God but constitute an ecclesial heritage. If there occurs a separation from

---

36   Ibid. no. 1.

37   Cf. John Paul II, Apostolic Constitution *Sapientia Christiana*, April 15, 1979, no. 27, 1: AAS 71 (1979) 483; *Code of Canon Law*, c. 812.

the Bishops who watch over and keep the apostolic tradition alive, it is the bond with Christ which is irreparably compromised.[38]

39. The Church, which has her origin in the unity of the Father, Son, and Holy Spirit,[39] is a mystery of communion. In accordance with the will of her founder, she is organized around a hierarchy established for the service of the Gospel and the People of God who live by it. After the pattern of the members of the first community, all the baptized with their own proper charisms are to strive with sincere hearts for a harmonious unity in doctrine, life, and worship (cf. Acts 2:42). This is a rule which flows from the very being of the Church. For this reason, standards of conduct, appropriate to civil society or the workings of a democracy, cannot be purely and simply applied to the Church. Even less can relationships within the Church be inspired by the mentality of the world around it (cf. Rom 12:2). Polling public opinion to determine the proper thing to think or do, opposing the Magisterium by exerting the pressure of public opinion, making the excuse of a "consensus" among theologians, maintaining that the theologian is the prophetical spokesman of a "base" or autonomous community which would be the source of all truth, all this indicates a grave loss of the sense of truth and of the sense of the Church.

40. The Church "is like a sacrament, a sign and instrument, that is, of communion with God and of unity among all men."[40] Consequently, to pursue concord and communion is to enhance the force of her witness and credibility. To succumb to the temptation of dissent, on the other hand, is to allow the "leaven of infidelity to the Holy Spirit" to start to work.[41]

To be sure, theology and the Magisterium are of diverse natures and missions and cannot be confused. Nonetheless they fulfill two vital roles in the Church which must interpenetrate and enrich each other for the service of the People of God.

It is the duty of the Pastors by virtue of the authority they have received from Christ Himself to guard this unity and to see that the tensions arising from life do not degenerate into divisions. Their authority, which transcends particular positions and oppositions, must unite all in the integrity of the Gospel which is the "word of reconciliation" (cf. 2 Cor 5:18–20).

As for theologians, by virtue of their own proper charisms, they have the responsibility of participating in the building up of Christ's Body in unity and truth. Their contribution is needed more than ever, for evangelization on a world scale requires the efforts of the whole People of God.[42] If it happens that they encounter difficulties due to the character of their research, they should seek their solution in trustful dialogue with the Pastors, in the spirit of truth and charity which is that of the communion of the Church.

---

38 Cf. Paul VI, Apostolic Exhortation *Paterna cum Benevolentia*, no. 4: AAS 67 (1975)15.

39 Cf. Dogmatic Constitution *Lumen Gentium*, no. 4.

40 Dogmatic Constitution *Lumen Gentium*, no. 1.

41 Cf. Paul VI, Apostolic Exhortation *Paterna cum Benevolentia*, nos. 2–3: AAS 67 (1975) 10–11.

42 Cf. John Paul II, Post-Synodal Apostolic Exhortation *Christifideles Laici*, nos. 32–35: AAS 81 (1989) 451–459.

41. Both Bishops and theologians will keep in mind that Christ is the definitive Word of the Father (cf. Heb 1:2) in whom, as St. John of the Cross observes: "God has told us everything all together and at one time."[43] As such, He is the Truth who sets us free (cf. Jn 8:36; 14:6). The acts of assent and submission to the Word entrusted to the Church under the guidance of the Magisterium are directed ultimately to Him and lead us into the realm of true freedom.

CONCLUSION

42. The Virgin Mary is Mother and perfect Icon of the Church. From the very beginnings of the New Testament, she has been called blessed because of her immediate and unhesitating assent of faith to the Word of God (cf. Lk 1:38, 45) which she kept and pondered in her heart (cf. Lk 2:19, 51). Thus did she become a model and source of help for all of the People of God entrusted to her maternal care. She shows us the way to accept and serve the Word. At the same time, she points out the final goal, on which our sights should ever be set, the salvation won for the world by her Son Jesus Christ which we are to proclaim to all men.

At the close of this Instruction, the Congregation for the Doctrine of the Faith earnestly invites Bishops to maintain and develop relations of trust with theologians in the fellowship of charity and in the realization that they share one spirit in their acceptance and service of the Word. In this context, they will more easily overcome some of the obstacles which are part of the human condition on earth. In this way, all can become ever better servants of the Word and of the People of God, so that the People of God, persevering in the doctrine of truth and freedom heard from the beginning, may abide also in the Son and the Father and obtain eternal life, the fulfillment of the Promise (cf. 1 Jn 2:24–25).

This Instruction was adopted at a Plenary Meeting of the Congregation for the Doctrine of the Faith and was approved at an audience granted to the undersigned Cardinal Prefect by the Supreme Pontiff, Pope John Paul II, who ordered its publication.

Given at Rome, at the Congregation for the Doctrine of the Faith, on May 24, 1990, the Solemnity of the Ascension of the Lord.

Joseph Card. Ratzinger
Prefect

Alberto Bovone
Titular Archbishop of Caesarea in Numidia
Secretary

---

43   St. John of the Cross, *Ascent of Mount Carmel*, II, 22, 3.

The Presence of the Church in the University and in University Culture

Congregation for Catholic Education • Pontifical Council for the Laity • Pontifical Council for Culture
May 22, 1994

FOREWORD:
NATURE, AIM AND INTENDED READERS
OF THE DOCUMENT

The University and, more widely, university culture, constitute a reality of decisive importance. In this field, vital questions are at stake and profound cultural changes present new challenges. The Church owes it to herself to advert to them in her mission of proclaiming the Gospel.[1]

In the course of their *ad limina* visits, many Bishops have expressed their desire to find help in meeting new and serious problems that are rapidly emerging and for which those responsible are at times unprepared. The usual pastoral methods often prove ineffective and even the most zealous are discouraged. Various dioceses and Bishops' conferences have undertaken pastoral reflection and action that already provide elements of response. Religious communities and apostolic movements are also approaching with fresh generosity the new challenges of university pastoral action.

For a sharing of these initiatives and a global assessment of the situation, the Congregation for Catholic Education, the Pontifical Council for the Laity and the Pontifical Council for Culture undertook a new consultation of the Bishops' Conferences, of religious Institutes and of various ecclesial bodies and movements. A first synthesis of the replies was presented on 28 October 1987 to the Synod of Bishops on the vocation and mission of the laity in the church and in the world.[2] This documentation has been enriched in many meetings, and also by the reactions of the institutions concerned to the published text and by the publication of studies and research on the action of Christians in the university world.

---

1   This pastoral concern is evidenced in the Church's Magisterium, for example, in the addresses to university people of Pope John Paul II. (Cf. Giovanni Paolo II: *Discorsi alle Università*, Camerino, 1991). Of particular significance was the Pope's address of 8 March 1982 for a "work session on university apostolate" with the clergy of Rome. (Cf. *L'Osservatore Romano*, English Edition, 3 May 1982, 6-7).

2   This synthesis, presented by Cardinal Paul Poupard on behalf of the three dicasteries, was published on 25 March 1988 and reproduced in several languages. (Cf. *Origins* vol. 18, N. 7, 30 June 1988, 109-112; *La Documentation Catholique*, n. 1964, 19 June 1988, 623-628; *Ecclesia* N. 2381, 23 July 1988, 1105-1110; *La Civiltà Cattolica* an. 139, 21 May 1988, N. 3310, 364-374).

It has been possible in this way to ascertain a number of facts, to formulate questions in precise terms and to indicate certain guidelines on the basis of the apostolic experience of people involved in the university world.

The present document, drawing attention to the more significant questions and initiatives, is intended as an instrument for study and action at the service of the particular Churches. It is addressed in the first place to the Episcopal Conference and, in a special way, to Bishops who are directly concerned due to the presence in their dioceses of Universities or Institutes of Higher Studies. But the facts and the orientations presented here are intended, at the same time, for all those who take part in university pastoral action under the guidance of the Bishops: priests, lay people, religious Institutes, ecclesial movements. The suggestions made for the new evangelization are meant to inspire deeper reflection on the part of all those concerned and a renewal of pastoral action.

AN URGENT NEED

The University was, in its earliest stages, one of the most significant expressions of the Church's pastoral concern. Its birth was linked to the development of the schools set up in the Middle Ages by the Bishops of the great episcopal sees. If the vicissitudes of history have led the *Universitas magistrorum et scholarium* to become more and more autonomous, the Church nevertheless continues to nourish the same concern that gave rise to this institution.[3] The Church's presence in the University is not, in fact, a task that would remain, as it were, external to the mission of proclaiming the faith. "The synthesis between culture and faith is a necessity not only for culture, but also for faith . . . A faith that does not become culture is a faith that is not fully received, not entirely thought through and faithfully lived."[4] The faith that the Church proclaims is a *fides quaerens intellectum* that must penetrate the human intellect and heart, that must be thought out in order to be lived. The Church's presence cannot, therefore, be limited to a cultural and scientific contribution: it must offer a real opportunity for encountering Christ.

Concretely, the Church's presence and mission in university culture take varied and complementary forms. In the first place, there is the task of giving support to the Catholics engaged in the life of the University as professors, students, researchers or non-academic staff. The Church is concerned with proclaiming the gospel to all those, within the University, to whom it is still unknown and who are ready to receive it in freedom. Her action also takes the form of sincere dialogue and loyal cooperation with all members of the university community who are concerned for the cultural development of the human person and of all the people involved.

This approach requires pastoral workers to see the University as a specific environment with its own problems. The success of their commitment depends, indeed, to a great extent on the relations they establish with this milieu, and which at times are still only embryonic. University pastoral action often remains, in fact,

---

3   Cf. John Paul II, Apostolic Constitution *Ex Corde Ecclesiae*, 15 August 1990, no. 1.

4   John Paul II, *Autograph Letter instituting the Pontifical Council for Culture*, 20 May 1982, in AAS 74 (1983), 683-688.

on the fringe of ordinary pastoral action. The whole Christian community must therefore become aware of its pastoral and missionary responsibility in relation to the university milieu.

I. SITUATION OF THE UNIVERSITY

In the space of half a century, the University as institution has undergone a notable transformation. One cannot generalize, however, about the features of this transformation in all countries. Such changes do not apply equally to all the academic centers of a single region. Each University is marked by its historical, cultural, social, economic and political context. This great variety calls for careful adaptation in the forms that the Church's presence will take.

1. **In many countries, especially in certain developed countries,** after the confrontation of the years '68–'70 and the institutional crisis that threw the University into a certain confusion, several trends, both positive and negative, emerged. Clashes and crises, and in particular, the collapse of ideologies and utopias that were once dominant, have left deep marks. The University, that was formerly reserved for the privileged, has become wide open for a vast public, both in its initial teaching and through continuing education. This is a significant feature of the democratization of social and cultural life. In many cases, students have come in such numbers that the infrastructures, the services and even traditional teaching methods can prove inadequate. In certain cultural contexts, moreover, various factors have brought about crucial changes in the position of the teaching staff. Between isolation and collegiality, diverse professional commitments and family life, they see a decline in their academic and social status, their authority and their security. The concrete situation of the students is also a cause for anxiety. Structures are often lacking for welcoming and supporting them and for community life. Many of them, transplanted far from their family to a strange town, suffer from loneliness. In addition, contact with the professors is often limited, and the students find themselves without guidance in face of problems of adjustment which they are unable to solve. At times, they have to enter an environment marked by the influence of attitudes of a socio-political kind and by the claim to unlimited freedom in all fields of research and scientific experimentation. Finally, in some cases, the young university students are confronted with the prevalence of a relativistic liberalism, a scientific positivism and a certain pessimism caused by the insecurity of professional prospects in the current economic crisis.

2. **Elsewhere, the University has lost part of its prestige.** The proliferation of Universities and their specialization have created a situation of great disparity. Some enjoy unquestioned prestige, while others are barely able to offer a mediocre standard of teaching. The University no longer has a monopoly of research in fields where specialized Institutes and Research Centers, both private and public, achieve excellence. These Institutes and Centers are part, in any case, of a specific cultural context, of the "university culture," that generates a characteristic *forma mentis* or mindset: the importance attached to the force of reasoned argument, the

development of a critical spirit, a high level of compartmentalized information and little capacity for synthesis, even within specific sectors.

3. **Living in this changing culture with a desire for truth and an attitude of service in conformity with the Christian ideal,** has, at times, become difficult. In the past, becoming a student, and even more so a professor, was everywhere an unquestionable social promotion. Today, the context of university studies is often marked by new difficulties, of a material or moral order, that rapidly become human and spiritual problems with unforeseeable consequences.

4. **In many countries, the University meets with great difficulties in the effort for renewal** that is constantly required by the evolution of society, the development of new sectors of knowledge, the demands of economies in crisis. Society aspires to a University that will meet its specific needs, starting from employment for all. In this way, the industrial world is having a notable impact on the University, with its specific demands for rapid and reliable technical services. This "professionalization" with its undeniable benefits, does not always go together with a "university" formation in a sense of values, in professional ethics and in an approach to other disciplines, as a complement to the necessary specialization.

5. **In contrast to the *"professionalization"* of some Institutes,** many Faculties, especially of Arts, Philosophy, Political Science and Law, often limit themselves to providing a generic formation in their own discipline, without reference to possible professional outlets for their students. In many countries, of medium development, government authorities use the Universities as "parking areas" to reduce the tensions caused by unemployment among the youth.

6. **Another inescapable fact emerges:** whereas the University, by vocation, has a primary role to play in the development of culture, it is exposed, in many countries, to two opposing risks: either passively to submit to the dominant cultural influences, or to become marginal in relation to them. It is difficult to face these situations, because the University often ceases to be a "community of students and teachers in search of truth," becoming a mere "instrument" in the hands of the State and of the dominant economic forces. The only aim is then to assure the technical and professional training of specialists, without giving of education of the person the central place it has by right. Moreover—and this is not without grave consequence—many students attend the University without finding there a human formation that would help them towards the necessary discernment about the meaning the bases and development of values and ideals; they live in a state of uncertainty, with the added burden for their future.

7. **In countries which were or still are subjected to a materialistic and atheistic ideology,** especially in the fields of the human sciences, of philosophy and history. As a result, even in some countries that have passed through radical changes on the political level, there is not yet sufficient freedom of thought to discern, where necessary, the dominant trends, and to perceive the relativistic liberalism that is often concealed within them. A certain skepticism begins to arise concerning the very idea of truth.

8. **Everywhere one notices great diversification in the fields of knowledge.** The different disciplines have succeeded in defining their specific field of investigation and truth claims, and in recognizing the legitimate complexity and the

diversity of their methods. There is a danger, becoming more and more evident, that research workers, teachers and students will close themselves within their specific field of knowledge, seeing only a fragment of reality.

9. **In some disciplines, there is emerging a new positivism, with no ethical reference:** science for the sake of science. "Utilitarian" formation takes precedent over integral humanism, tending to neglect the needs and expectations of persons, to censure or stifle the most basic questions of personal and social existence. The development of scientific techniques in the fields of biology, communications and automation, raises new and crucial ethical questions. The more human beings become capable of mastering nature, the more they depend on technology, the more they need to protect their own freedom. This raises new questions about the approaches and the epistemological criteria of the different disciplines.

10. **The skepticism and indifference** engendered by the prevailing secularism exist together with a new and ill-defined searching of a religious kind. In the climate of uncertainty that characterizes the intellectual horizon of teachers and students, the University at times provides a context for the development of aggressive nationalistic behavior. But, in some situations, the climate of confrontation gives way to conformism.

11. **The development of university education** *"at a distance"* or *"tele-education"* (correspondence, audio-visual techniques, etc.) makes information more widely accessible; but the personal contact between teacher and student is in danger of disappearing, together with the human formation bound up with this indispensable relationship. Some mixed forms are a judicious combination of "tele-education" and occasional contacts between teacher and student; this could be a good way of developing university formation.

12. **Inter-university and international cooperation** shows real progress. The more developed academic centers can help the less advanced; this is at times, but not always, to the advantage of the latter. The major Universities can, indeed, exercise a certain technical and even ideological "domination" beyond their national frontiers, to the detriment of the less favored countries.

13. **The place women are taking in the University,** and the general widening of access to university studies already constitute a well-established tradition in some countries. Elsewhere, they come as a new development, offering an exceptional opportunity for renewal, and an enrichment of university life.

14. **The central role of Universities** in development programs brings with it a tension between the pursuit of the new culture engendered by modernity and the safeguard and promotion of traditional cultures. In responding to its vocation, however, the University lacks a "guiding idea," an anchor for its multiple activities. This is at the root of the present crisis of identity and purpose in an institution that, of its nature, is directed towards the search for truth. The chaos of thought and the poverty of basic criteria sterilize the process that should produce educational proposals capable of meeting the new problems. In spite of its imperfections, by vocation, the University, with the other Institutions of higher education, remains a privileged place for the development of knowledge and formation, and plays a fundamental role in preparing leaders for the society of the 21st century.

15. **A renewed pastoral effort.** The presence of Catholics in the University is, in itself, a question and a hope for the Church. In many countries, this "presence" is, indeed, at one and the same time, numerically impressive and relatively modest in its effect. Too many teachers and students consider their faith a strictly private affair, or do not perceive the impact their university life has on their Christian existence. Their presence in the University seems like a parenthesis in their life of faith. Some, among them even priests or religious, in the name of university autonomy, go so far as to refrain from any explicit witness to their faith. Others use this autonomy to spread doctrines contrary to the Church's teaching. This situation is aggravated by the lack of theologians with competence in the scientific and technical fields, and of professors specialized in the sciences who have a good theological formation. Obviously, this calls for a renewed awareness, leading to a new pastoral effort. Moreover, while appreciating the praiseworthy initiatives undertaken in various places, one cannot fail to see that the Christian presence often seems limited to isolated groups, sporadic initiatives, the occasional witness of well-known personalities and the action of one or another movement.

II. PRESENCE OF THE CHURCH IN THE UNIVERSITY AND UNIVERSITY CULTURE

1. Presence in the structures of the University

Sent by Christ to all human beings of every culture, the Church tries to share with them the good news of salvation. Having received through Christ the revealed Truth about God and humankind, she has the mission to provide, through her message of truth, an opening for authentic freedom. Founded on the mandate received from Christ, she seeks to cast light on cultural values and expressions, to correct and purify them, where necessary, in the light of faith, in order to bring them to their fullness of meaning.[5]

Within the University, the Church's pastoral action, in its rich complexity, has in the first place a subjective aspect: the evangelization of people. From this point of view, the Church enters into dialogue with real people: men and women, professors, students, staff, and, through them, with the cultural trends that characterize this milieu. But one cannot forget the objective aspect: the dialogue between faith and the different disciplines of knowledge. In the context of the University, the appearance of new cultural trends is, indeed, closely linked to the great questions concerning humanity: the value of the human person, the meaning of human existence and action, and especially conscience and freedom. At this level, Catholic intellectuals should give priority to promoting a renewed and vital synthesis between faith and culture.

The Church must not forget that her action is carried out in the particular situation of each university Center and that her presence in the University is a service rendered to the people concerned in their two-fold dimension: personal and social.

---

5   Cf. John Paul II, Encyclical *Veritatis Splendor*, no. 30-31.

The type of presence is therefore different in each country, which bears the marks of its historical, cultural, religious and legislative tradition. In particular, where the legislation permits, the Church cannot forsake her institutional action within the University. She seeks to support and foster the teaching of theology wherever possible. At the institutional level, the university Chaplaincy has a special importance on the campus. By offering a wide range of both doctrinal and spiritual formation, it constitutes, in fact, an important source for the proclamation of the Gospel. Through the stimulus and awareness given through the Chaplaincy, university pastoral action can hope to achieve its aim, that is, to create within the university environment a Christian community and a missionary faith commitment.

Religious Orders and Congregations bring a specific presence to the Universities. By the wealth and diversity of their charism—especially their educational charism—they contribute to the Christian formation of teachers and students. In their pastoral options, these religious communities, that are much in demand for primary and secondary education, should take into consideration what is at stake in their presence within higher education; they should be careful not to draw back in any way, under pretext of entrusting to others the mission corresponding to their vocation.

To be accepted and influential, the Church's institutional presence in university culture must be of good quality. Often there is a lack of personnel, or at times of the necessary financial resources. This situation calls for creativity and an adequate pastoral effort.

2. The Catholic University

Among the different institutional forms of the Church's presence in the university world, emphasis must be placed on the Catholic University, itself an institution of the Church.

The existence of a large number of Catholic Universities—differing greatly according to regions and countries, from a large number to a total absence—is in itself a richness and an essential factor of the Church's presence within university culture. However, this investment does not always produce the fruit for which one might legitimately hope.

Important indications for the specific role of the Catholic University were given in the Apostolic Constitution *Ex Corde Ecclesiae*, published on 15 August 1990. The Constitution points out that the institutional identity of the Catholic University depends on its realizing together its characteristics as "*University*" and as "*Catholic*." It only achieves its full identity when, at one and the same time, it gives proof of being rigorously serious as a member of the international community of knowledge and expresses its Catholic identity through an explicit link with the Church, at both local and universal levels; an identity which marks concretely the life, the services and the programs of the university community. In this way, by its very existence, the Catholic University achieves its aim of guaranteeing, in an institutional form, a Christian presence in the university world. From this stems its specific mission, characterized by several inseparable features.

In order to carry out its function in relation to the Church and to society, the Catholic University must study the grave problems of the day and propose solutions that express the religious and ethical values proper to a Christian vision of the human person.

Next comes university pastoral action in the strict sense. In this respect, the challenges the Catholic University has to meet are not substantially different from those confronting other academic centers. However, we should stress that an academic institution which defines itself as "*Catholic*" is committed to university pastoral action at the same depth as the goals it sets for itself: the integral formation of the people, men and women, who, in the academic context, are called to active participation in the life of society and of the Church.

A further aspect of the mission of the Catholic University is, finally, a commitment to dialogue between faith and culture, and the development of a culture rooted in faith. Even in this regard, if there must be concern for the development of a culture in harmony with faith wherever baptized persons are involved in the life of the University, this is still more urgent in the context of the Catholic University, called to become, in a special way, a significant interlocutor of the academic, cultural and scientific world.

Clearly, the Church's concern for the University—in the direct service of people and the evangelization of culture—necessarily has a point of reference in the Catholic University. The growing demand for a qualified presence of baptized people in university culture becomes, in this way, a call to the whole Church to become more and more aware of the specific vocation of the Catholic University and to facilitate its development as an effective instrument of the Church's evangelizing mission.

3. Fruitful initiatives already implemented

In response to the demands of university culture, many local Churches have taken appropriate action in various ways:

1. Appointment by the Bishops' Conference of university Chaplains with an ad hoc formation, a specific status and adequate support.
2. Creation, for university pastoral action, of diversified diocesan teams that show the specific responsibility of the laity and the diocesan character of these apostolic units.
3. First steps in a pastoral approach to University Rectors/Presidents and Faculty Professors, whose milieu is often dominated by technical and professional concerns.
4. Action taken for the setting up of "*Departments of Religious Sciences*," capable of opening up new horizons for teachers and students, and compatible with the mission of the Church. In these Departments, Catholics should play a prominent role, especially when Faculties of Theology are lacking in the university structures.
5. Institution of regular courses on morals and professional ethics in specialized Institutes and Centers of higher education.
6. Support for dynamic ecclesial movements. University pastoral action achieves better results when it is based on groups or movements and

associations—at times, few in numbers but of high quality—that have the support of the dioceses and Bishops' Conferences.

7. Stimulus for a university pastoral action that is not limited to a general and undifferentiated "*pastoral action for youth*," but which takes as its starting-point the fact that many young people are deeply influenced by the "*university environment*." It is there, to a great extent, that they have their encounter with Christ and bear their witness as Christians. The aim is therefore to educate and accompany the young people, enabling them to live in faith the concrete reality of their milieu and their own activities and commitments.

8. Facilitating dialogue between theologians, philosophers and scientists, for a profound renewal of attitudes and to create new and fruitful relations between Christian Faith, theology, philosophy and the sciences in their concrete search for truth. Experience shows that university people, priests and especially lay people, are in the forefront in maintaining and promoting cultural debate on the great questions regarding humanity, science, society and the new challenges for the human spirit. It is for Catholic teachers and their associations, in particular, to promote interdisciplinary initiatives, and cultural encounters, inside and outside the University, combining critical method and confidence in reason, in order to bring face to face, in the language of the different cultures, metaphysical and scientific positions and the affirmations of faith.

III. PASTORAL SUGGESTIONS AND GUIDELINES

1. Pastoral suggestions from local Churches

1. A **consultation** conducted by the "*ad hoc*" episcopal Commissions would make it possible to have a better idea of the different initiatives for university pastoral action and for the presence of Christians in the University, and to prepare guidelines to support fruitful apostolic undertakings and to promote those seen to be necessary.

2. The **setting up of a National Commission** for questions related to the University and to Culture would help the local Churches to share their experiences and their capabilities. It would be for the Commission to sponsor a program of activities, reflection and meetings on "*Evangelization and Cultures*," intended for the seminaries and the formation centers for religious and laity; one section would be devoted explicitly to university culture.

3. **At diocesan level,** in university towns, it would be good to encourage the setting up of a specialized commission, composed of priests and Catholic university people, teachers and students. The aim would be to provide useful indications for university pastoral action and for the activity of Christians in the fields of education and research. The commission would be a help to the Bishop in the exercise of his

specific mission of promoting and confirming the various initiatives in the diocese and facilitating contact with national or international initiatives. By virtue of his pastoral task at the service of his Church, the diocesan Bishop bears the first responsibility for the presence and pastoral action of the Church in the State Universities, as well as in the Catholic Universities and other private institutions.

4. **At parish level,** it would be desirable for the Christian communities—priests, religious and lay faithful—to pay greater attention to students and teachers, and also to the apostolate of the university Chaplaincies. The parish is of its nature a community, within which fruitful relationships can be established for a more effective service of the Gospel. It plays a considerable role through its capacity to welcome people, especially when it facilitates the setting up and functioning of "*Student Hostels*" and "*University Residences.*" The success of the evangelization of the University and of university culture depends to a great extent on the commitment of the whole local Church.

5. The **university parish** is, in some places, an institution more necessary than ever. It supposes the presence of one or more priests, with a good preparation for this specific apostolate. The parish is unique as a milieu for communication with all the variety of the academic world. It makes possible relations with people from the fields of culture, art and science; at the same time, it allows the Church to penetrate into this complex milieu. As a place of meeting and of Christian reflection and formation, it opens to young people the doors of a Church hitherto unknown or misunderstood, and opens the Church up to the students, their questions and their apostolic dynamism. As a privileged place for the liturgical celebration of the sacraments, it is, above all, the place of the Eucharist, heart of every Christian community, source and summit of every apostolate.

6. Wherever possible, university pastoral action should create or intensify relations between Catholic Universities or Faculties and all other university milieus, in varied forms of collaboration.

7. The present situation is an urgent call to organize the formation of qualified pastoral workers within parishes and Catholic movements and associations. It urgently demands the implementation of a long-term strategy, for cultural and theological formation requires appropriate preparation. Concretely, many dioceses are not in a position to set up and carry out a formation of this kind at university level. This demand can be met by sharing the resources of dioceses, specialized religious Institutes and lay groups.

8. In every situation, the *presence* of the Church must be seen as a "*plantatio*" (planting) of the Christian community in the university milieu, through witness, proclamation of the gospel and the service of charity. This presence will mean growth for the "*Christifideles*" (Faithful) and a help in approaching those who are far from Jesus Christ. In this perspective, it seems important to develop and promote:

> — a catechetical pedagogy characterized by a "*sense of community,*" offering a variety of proposals, the possibility of differentiated itineraries and responses to the real needs of concrete persons;
> — a pedagogy of personal guidance: welcome, availability and friendship, interpersonal relationships, discernment of the

> circumstances in which students are living and concrete means for their improvement.
> — a pedagogy for the deepening of faith and spiritual life, rooted in the Word of god, shared in depth through sacramental and liturgical life.

9. Finally, the presence of the Church in the University calls for a common witness of Christians. This ecumenical witness, inseparable from the missionary dimension, is an important contribution to Christian unity. Without prejudice to the pastoral care of the Catholic faithful, ecumenical collaboration will take the forms and respect the limits established by the Church. It supposes an adequate formation and will be particularly fruitful in the study of social questions and, in general, of all questions related to humankind, to the meaning of human existence and activity.[6]

2. Developing the apostolate of the laity, especially of teachers

"*The Christian vocation is, of its nature, a vocation to the apostolate.*"[7] This statement of the Second Vatican Council, when applied to university pastoral action, is a resounding challenge to responsibility for Catholic teachers, intellectuals and students. The apostolic commitment of the faithful is a sign of vitality and spiritual progress for the whole Church. Developing in university people this consciousness of the duty of apostolate is consistent with the pastoral orientations of Vatican II. At the heart of the university community, faith becomes in this way a radiating source of new life, and of genuinely Christian culture. The lay faithful enjoy a legitimate autonomy in the exercise of their specific apostolic vocation. Pastors are invited, not only to recognize this specificity, but to give it warm support. This apostolate starts and develops from professional relationships, common cultural interests and the sharing of daily life in the different sectors of university activity. The individual apostolate of Catholic lay people is "*the starting-point and condition of the whole lay apostolate, even in its organized expression, and admits of no substitute.*"[8] Nevertheless, it remains necessary and urgent for the Catholics present in the University to give a witness of communion and unity. In this respect, the ecclesial movements are particularly valuable.

Catholic teachers play a fundamental role for the Church's presence in university culture. In certain cases, their quality and generosity can even make up for imperfections in the structures. The apostolic commitment of the Catholic teacher who gives priority to respect and service for individuals—colleagues and students— offers the witness of the "*new Man, always ready to render an account to anyone who asks for the hope that is in him, and to do it with courtesy and respect*" (cf. 1 Pt 3:15-16). The University is certainly a limited sector of society, but qualitatively, its influence is in greater proportion to its quantitative dimension. By contrast, however,

---

6   Cf. Pontifical Council for Promoting Christian Unity, *Directory for the Application of Principles and Norms on Ecumenism*, Vatican City, 1993, nos. 211-216.

7   Second Vatican Council, Decree on the Apostolate of the Laity, *Apostolicam Actuositatem*, no. 2.

8   Ibid, no. 16.

even the figure of the Catholic intellectual seems to have almost disappeared from certain university contexts, where the students feel painfully the lack of genuine mentors whose constant presence and availability would provide a *"companionship"* of high quality.

This witness of the Catholic teacher certainly does not consist in filling disciplines that are being taught with religious subject matter. Rather, it means opening up the horizon to the ultimate and fundamental questions, with the stimulating generosity of an active presence for the often inarticulate demands of young minds in search of points of reference and certainties, of guidance and purpose. Their life tomorrow in society depends on this. Even more do the Church and the University expect from priests teaching in the University a high standard of competence and a sincere ecclesial communion.

Unity grows in diversity, resisting the temptation to unify and formalize activities. The variety of apostolic initiatives and resources, far from opposing ecclesial unity, requires and enriches it. Pastors will take into account the legitimate characteristics of the university spirit: diversity and spontaneity, respect for personal freedom and responsibility, resistance to any attempt at imposing uniformity.

Catholic movements or groups should be encouraged to multiply and to grow; but it is important also to recognize and to vitalize associations of the Catholic laity that boast a long and fruitful tradition of university apostolate. The apostolate, exercised by lay people, is fruitful to the extent that it is ecclesial. The criteria for evaluation of the different commitments include doctrinal consistency with Catholic identity, together with an exemplary moral and professional standard, ensuring the radiating authenticity of the lay apostolate, of which spiritual life is the guarantee.

CONCLUSION

Among the immense fields of apostolate and action for which the Church is responsible, university culture is one of the most promising, but also one of the most difficult. This particular milieu has so great an influence on the social and cultural life of nations, and on it depends to a great extent the future of the Church and that of society. Within it the Church maintains an apostolic presence and action at both the institutional and the personal levels, with the specific cooperation of priests and lay people, administrative staff, teachers and students.

Consultation and meetings with many Bishops and university people have shown the importance of cooperation between the different ecclesial bodies concerned. The Congregation for Catholic Education, the Pontifical Council for the Laity and the Pontifical Council for Culture express again their readiness to facilitate exchanges, and to promote meetings at the level of Bishops' Conferences, Catholic International Organizations and of Commissions for Teaching, Education and Culture acting in this particular field.

Service of the individuals involved in the University, and through them, service of society, the presence of the Church in the university milieu enters into the process of inculturation of the faith, as a requirement of evangelization. On the threshold of a new millennium, of which university culture will be a major component, the duty of proclaiming the Gospel becomes more urgent. It calls for faith communities able to transmit the Good News of Christ to all those who are formed, who teach and who exercise their activity in the context of university culture. The urgency of this apostolic commitment is great, for the University is one of the most fruitful centers for the creation of culture.

"Fully aware of a pastoral urgency that calls for an absolutely special concern for culture (. . .) the Church calls upon the lay faithful to be present, as signs of courage and intellectual creativity, in the privileged places of culture, that is, the world of education—school and University—in places of scientific and technological research, the areas of artistic creativity and work in the humanities. Such a presence is destined not only for the recognition and possible purification of the elements that critically burden existing culture, but also for the elevation of these cultures through the riches which have their source in the Gospel and the Christian faith."[9]

Vatican City, Pentecost, 22 May 1994

Pio Card. Laghi
Prefect of the Congregation for Catholic Education

Eduardo Card. Pironio
President of the Pontifical Council for the Laity

Paul Card. Poupard
President of the Pontifical Council for Culture

---

9   John Paul II, Post-Synodal Apostolic Exhortation *Christifideles Laici*, on the Vocation and Mission of the Laity in the Church and in the world, December 30, 1988, no. 44.

Second World Congress for the Pastoral Care of Foreign Students

Final Document

Pontifical Council for the Pastoral Care of the Migrants and Itinerant People The Event

April 2007

The Congress was held at the "Casa Maria Immacolata," in Rome, and was organized by the Pontifical Council for the Pastoral Care of Migrants and Itinerant People, on the topic: "The Foreign Students and the Instruction *Erga migrantes caritas Christi.*" Its President and Secretary chaired the sessions of the meeting. Two officials of the Dicastery were present as well. Bishops, priests, religious men and women, and lay people, attended as representatives of eighteen countries (Argentina, Australia, Austria, Belgium, Canada, France, Germany, Great Britain, Ireland, Italy, Netherlands, Portugal, South Africa, Spain, Sweden—for the Nordic Countries—, Switzerland, Tanzania, USA) and of CCEE and CELAM. There were two fraternal Delegates (from the Anglican Communion and the World Council of Churches), delegates of various religious congregations (Legionaries of Christ, Salesians), and of Opus Dei and representatives of lay associations and ecclesial movements (IYCS, MIEC, SECIS, UCSEI, KAAD, AII, Focolare, Community of Saint'Egidio) and two observers.

With a warm welcome, the President of the Pontifical Council, H. Em. Stephen Fumio Cardinal Hamao, opened the Congress by highlighting the importance of foreign students [here we use the expression "foreign students," which is quite traditional, although some countries prefer the term "international students"], who call for the attention and pastoral care of the Universal Church and the particular Churches. Archbishop Agostino Marchetto, Secretary of the Dicastery, presented the theme and the agenda of the meeting and likewise offered some criteria for a specific pastoral care of foreign students. He also indicated a vast and important field of apostolate, which requires such a specific pastoral vision. Then the two fraternal Delegates, Rev. Dr. Richard Burridge, representing the Archbishop of Canterbury, and Dr. Gary Vachicouras, Delegate of W.C.C., greeted the assembly. After this, all the participants presented themselves.

On the second day, after the celebration of the Holy Mass to implore the Holy Spirit for assistance, the situation of foreign students in the world was presented by the Rev. Canon Charles de Hemptinne, President of SECIS (Service of European Churches for International Students), based on the answers to a questionnaire sent previously. This was followed by a Round Table at which the representatives of the different countries, institutions and associations presented their points of view and shared their experiences. On his part, H. E. Archbishop Robert Sarah,

Secretary of the Congregation for the Evangelization of Peoples, introduced the topic *"The Ecumenical, Inter-religious and Intercultural Dimension of the Pastoral Care for Foreign Students"* (Erga Migrantes Caritas Christi (EMCC), nos. 49-69), followed by study groups.

On the third day, H.E. Msgr. Cesare Nosiglia, Archbishop-Delegate of the CCEE for the Pastoral Care in Universities, who was supposed to speak on the *"Guidelines for Pastoral Care in the Universities of Europe, with special attention given to Pastoral Agents and their Formation"* (EMCC, nos. 70-88), delegated Msgr. Leuzzi to read his text because he could not attend the meeting. Later on Archbishop Michael Miller, Secretary of the Congregation for Catholic Education, delivered a speech entitled *"Towards a Missionary Pastoral Care of Proclamation, Evangelization and Dialogue"* (EMCC, nos. 89-104), followed by a second series of workshops.

The summit of the Congress was the participation in the Holy Mass for Roman University students, presided over by H.E. Card. Camillo Ruini, followed by an audience with the Holy Father for all participants.

The words of the Pope were received with great joy. He said:

"I am also pleased on this occasion to welcome those taking part in the World Congress of Pastoral Care for Foreign Students, organized by the Pontifical Council for the Pastoral Care of Migrants and Itinerant People. I address an affectionate welcome to everyone. [...]

I would now like to turn my attention to the foreign students. Their presence is a growing phenomenon and is an important field of pastoral action for the Church. Indeed, young people who leave their own country in order to study encounter many problems and especially the risk of an identity crisis and a loss of spiritual and moral values.

Moreover, for many young people the possibility of studying abroad is a unique opportunity to become better able to contribute to the development of their own countries and participate actively in the Church's mission. It is important to continue on the journey undertaken to meet the needs of these brothers and sisters of ours."

On the last day, the assembly listened to the reports of the workshops and the propositions of the Congress for the Final Document. Reaffirming their firm intention to pursue the work of these days, in a spirit of collaboration and some kind of coordination, the participants examined strategies for the future, taking into account methodologies and objectives, which are summarized in the following conclusions and recommendations.

With words of thanks, Card. Stephen Fumio Hamao closed the Congress.

CONCLUSIONS

Theological

- Jesus Christ is our icon of the "man on the move" (Lk 9:58; EMCC 15).
- Christ said "I was a stranger and you made me welcome" (Mt 25:35).

- We are all immigrants in the Church: that is, we enter the Church through baptism.
- The Church is the pilgrim people of God, on the way to "our heavenly home".'
- Hospitality is part of our essential ecclesial identity; human encounter is vital.
- As "Christ welcomes us" (Rom 15:7), so do we welcome the stranger in our pastoral care towards foreign students.

On the Reality

The phenomenon of student migration is complex.

It is a global reality, it is a gift also.

Students are "special" migrants between continents, within continents and within countries.

Various types of foreign students exist, for example:

- "free movers": they are students who are self-financed and are culturally connected;
- the "invited students" who receive scholarships;
- refugee or "economic migrant" students (who are sometimes illegal or transient);

Also we can find various types of professors who are mobile.

It is important to know why students move and how they are recruited.

In any case, with the globalization of learning, university education has become a commodity, bought and sold. The Church nevertheless believes that education is a public good, not just a commodity, and that students are human persons who need to be respected as such.

Foreign student recruitment has become also a global business.

- The wealthy generally have open access to higher education, while poor students face many challenges.
- Many countries are privatizing university education and for students its cost can be a heavy burden.
- University fees are often much higher for foreign students than for local citizens.
- But some countries, agencies and universities offer scholarships.

Pastoral care for foreign students has an ecumenical, an inter-religious and an intercultural dimension and is a partnership involving the university, the host country and that of origin, the local Churches and chaplaincies, as well as student organizations and the foreign students themselves.

Pastoral welcome and solidarity is also a "bridge" between peoples, but with the following consequences:

- Foreign students experience culture shock and secularization, which sometimes lead to the loss of faith. Students who are unprepared are also an easy target for conversion to other denominations or religions (here the question of proselytism and sects is to be considered). However many of them are an example of faith in secularized areas.
- Some foreign students face a "double estrangement": first from their host country and then from their home country upon their return.
- Many foreign students initially plan to return home after their studies, but do not do so for a variety of reasons (search for a better standard of living, politically not safe to return, relationships)
- Foreign students seek more than just spiritual help: they also need concrete things.
- There is often little formal training for chaplains and pastoral agents concerning the specific needs of the pastoral care for foreign students.

Pastoral Response

The pastoral care (ministry) for foreign students takes on many different shapes and forms in different countries, but there are many good, positive examples of welcome and solidarity (offering advocacy, scholarships, housing, emergency funding, helping to obtain visas, etc.).

Responding to the specific needs of human mobility (foreign students) is an important part of the Church's mission. In fact:

- Chaplaincies create a place of meeting and sharing; a place of openness, free from prejudice.
- Some chaplaincies have a unique and specialized pastoral care for foreign students.
- Others incorporate foreign students into local chaplaincy programs or connect them with the local parish.
- Many chaplains focus on hospitality and create "a safe place" ministry.
- Liturgy is an important dimension of the Catholic pastoral care for foreign students.
- Therefore many chaplaincies offer Liturgies celebrated in their languages. When Liturgy is held in the language of the host country, readings and hymns are to be fittingly adapted to include foreign students.
- Spiritual, social and cultural events are of special importance to them.
- Chaplains work with the "International Student Office" in the universities.

- "International Student Offices" provide opportunities for cultural integration, as well as help and advice about visas, economic matters and studies.
- In some countries, chaplaincies provide hostels for foreign students.
- Not every university chaplaincy has a priest.
- In any case, Catholic leaders are important for the students.
- Some of them desire to have contacts with the university chaplaincy in the host country before they arrive.
- Sometimes Church pastors are so focused on other church issues that it is difficult for them to emphasize or dedicate themselves to a specific pastoral care for foreign students.

RECOMMENDATIONS

For Chaplains and University Pastoral Agents

As chaplains and university pastoral agents we have to:

1. Seek time when foreign students can "speak about faith with pride" and humility and all will "listen with respect." Dialogue is vital also in these cases.
2. Recognize that every encounter is at heart a reciprocal friendship; chaplaincy is a path to developing a healthy community of friends in Christ and/or in humanity.
3. Participate with joy in the festivals and cultural celebrations of foreign students and, with deep sorrow, in their pains and fatigue.
4. Remain in contact with alumni so that current foreign students will learn how their predecessors contribute positively to their home country.
5. Connect foreign students with good host families.
6. Create a welcoming committee to foster communication between foreign students and the Catholic community upon arrival.
7. Listen with patience, sympathy and attentive ears to student reality, recognizing the importance of direct hospitality, if possible.
8. Encourage collaboration between the university chaplain and pastoral agents, the whole diocesan community and student organizations.
9. Help foreign students find accommodations, assisting eventually and when possible in their search for employment and finding financial sponsors (cf. *Gaudium et Spes*, no. 60, and the Universal Declaration on Human Rights, art. 26).
10. Develop leadership qualities of foreign students for them to help one another and to have their own cultural gifts valued by their host community. They must also be capable of receiving from the latter (Church and society).

11. Encourage foreign students to appreciate their vocation of service in their home country, when they return, and to contribute to the transformation of their countries human and spiritual condition.
12. Create attractive web pages for chaplaincies, given that many foreign students select their university through web searches.
13. Not to forget the specific pastoral care for foreign students in the strict sense of the word (Liturgy, Word of God, Sacraments, spiritual formation), because of social issues.
14. Work ecumenically, with a perspective of interdenominational education, open to inter-religious dialogue, without forgetting each one's own identity.

For Dioceses or Episcopal Conferences

We encourage them to:

1. Make adequate provisions for chaplains and campus ministers at all higher education institutions, taking care also of their preparation.
2. Provide special services for foreign students who are identified as "refugees" and IDPs, also by offering scholarships.
3. Provide, as far as possible, social assistance to foreign students in need, regarding their legal and social rights, and the necessary paper work.
4. Establish appropriate contact with civil authorities, human rights organizations, health and psychological organizations, etc., to improve the condition of foreign students.
5. Also invite foreign students to help create a pastoral plan for themselves. Catholic student groups and student leaders in the chaplaincy play an important role in the pastoral care of foreign students and in advocating on their behalf, both in the university and in broader society.
6. Help foreign students face the challenges of secularization.
7. Have a national, continental and universal vision of this specific pastoral care. A national Bishop Promoter in this field could be appointed.

Pontifical Council

We would like to ask the Pontifical Council to:

1. Help create the conviction that a worldwide directory of university chaplaincies is important, so that from the grassroots level a form of cooperation would emerge towards a concrete realization of this project. It could be simpler to start at the national level.

2. Clarify the connections from chaplain to bishop, to national bishops' conference and then to the offices of the Holy See.
3. Encourage university chaplains to engage in appropriate ecumenical and inter-religious dialogue.
4. Continue to gather chaplains from all over the world to share experiences and deepen their understanding of the specific pastoral care for foreign students.
5. Promote the pastoral care of foreign students in the local Churches.
6. Encourage all Church authorities to adapt to the globalization of education.
7. On the diocesan, national, and international levels, to encourage effective pastoral planning for the needs of foreign students.
8. Continue to gather together members of the various Dicasteries of the Roman Curia to respond together to the pastoral concerns of foreign students.
9. Establish opportunities to study the worldwide realities of foreign students and their economic, personal and spiritual needs.

Interreligious Dialogue and Catholic Higher Education from a Migration Perspective

Pontifical Council for the Pastoral Care of Migrants and Itinerant People

August 2007

Migrations are one of the most complex challenges facing our world today. The inevitable changes brought about in society by the arrival of immigrants of a different ethnic origin are therefore a matter of public debate. In fact the migration question is high up on the international list of such matters. International migrants worldwide are estimated to number some 190,600,000, of whom 49% are women. The biggest concentration of migrants, some 60% of the total, is to be found in the industrialised countries. It is estimated that between 10% and 15% of these are illegal, while almost half are economically active, working and earning. Among migrants, there are also those who are forced to migrate (refugees) and IDPs.

Then there is the matter of international students, about 2 million in the world (half a million in the United States).

Our work consists in discerning facts and aspects of migration that will help us understand better the phenomenon so as to interpret this "sign of the times"[1] in a Christian light and offer our pastoral service to the world of human mobility. Migrations have always been at the center of the Church's care.[2] Initiatives of many kinds show that the Church has carefully followed developments in this changeable sector and has been actively engaged, especially pastorally but also in the purely social and humanitarian field, to ensure that foreigners should be fully accepted and integrated into society. The Church's ultimate aim is an authentic communion with

---

1   Cf. Benedict XVI, Message for the World Day of Migrants and Refugees 2006: *L'Osservatore Romano* 254 (Oct. 29, 2005), 4; A. Marchetto, "Migrations: a sign of the times": published by the Pontifical Council for the Pastoral Care of Migrants and Itinerant People, *The Church's Care for Migrants* (*Quaderni Universitari*, Part I), Libreria Editrice Vaticana, Vatican City 2005, 28-40.

2   To take the last century only: With prophetic intuition Pius XII wrote his Apostolic Constitution *Exsul Familia* (AAS XLIV [1952] 649-704), considered the Magna Charta of the Church's thought on migrations. Later Paul VI, continuing and practising the teaching of the Second Vatican Ecumenical Council, wrote the Motu Proprio *Pastoralis Migratorum Cura* (AAS LXI [1969] 601-603), promulgating the Instruction of the Congregation for Bishops *De Pastorali Migratorum Cura* (AAS LXI [1969] 614-643). Then, in 1978, the Pontifical Commission for the Pastoral Care of Migration and Tourism addressed a circular letter to the Episcopal Conferences *The Church and Human Mobility* (AAS LXX [1978] 357-378). Cf. Instruction *Erga Migrantes Caritas Christi* (EMCC), nos. 19-33, see note 3; Pontifical Council for the Pastoral Care of Migrants and Itinerant People (editor), *The Church's care for migrants* (*Quaderni Universitari* Part I), Libreria Editrice Vaticana, Vatican City 2005, A. Marchetto, "The Church of the Council and pastoral care of welcome": *People on the Move* XXXVIII (102, 2006), 131-145.

respect for legitimate diversities and with no intent of proselytism in the negative sense attached to the term today. In any event, for immigrants, too, rights go hand in hand with duties.

The recent activity of the Holy See shows careful attention to the continuous changes in the phenomenon of mobility and to the different requirements of people today. The aim is "to respond especially to the new spiritual and pastoral needs of migrants" in "an ecumenical and interreligious vision of the phenomenon because migrants now include Christians not in full communion with the catholic Church and growing numbers of persons of other religions, in particular Moslems" (*Erga Migrantes Caritas Christi* (EMCC) no. 3).[3]

A field in which the Church is constantly committed at various levels especially pastorally is that of basic human rights, which are valid for migrants too. Specific initiatives and Messages of the Holy Father, various activities to stir the conscience of international organizations and the governments of migrants' home countries, their temporary residence or their host countries all form part of the Church's strategy. In this the sacredness of the human person,[4] especially when weak and marginalised, remains central. This has led to "important developments in the realms of theology and pastoral work, namely: the centrality of the person and the defence of the rights of migrants, men or women, and of their children; the ecclesial and missionary dimension of migrations; the revaluation of the lay apostolate and the value of different cultures in the work of evangelisation; the safeguarding and appreciation of minorities even within the Church itself; the importance of dialogue both within the sphere of the Church and with others outside it; the specific contribution of emigration to world peace" (EMCC no. 27). For this reason the Church is extremely anxious to welcome all migrants and accompany them pastorally, especially when the influx of legal migrants is accompanied by illegal migrants who are a source of worry and are quite often criminalised. Moreover the presence of unscrupulous evil-doers, speculating on human tragedy and encouraging human slave trading, increases xenophobia and sometimes gives rise to racialism (cf. EMCC nos. 29 and 41).

The Instruction *Erga migrantes caritas Christi* makes suitable proposals for projects consonant with the lives of migrants. With regard to their reception it distinguishes between "*help* in general (immediate short-term reception), real *reception* (longer-term projects) and *integration* (a long-term objective to be followed up constantly)" (no. 42). In the last named case, an important question is looked at and the difficult concept of how to integrate migrants in the society of the host country is examined in a new light: the idea of assimilation is rejected in favour of meeting and legitimate cultural exchange. In fact the Instruction insists on the creation of intercultural societies with their component elements capable of interacting and

---

3   In 2004 the Pontifical Council for the Pastoral Care of Migrants and Itinerant People published the Instruction *Erga Migrantes Caritas Christi*: AAS XCVI (2004) 762-822 and *People on the Move* XXXVI (95, 2004) and the website: *www.vatican.va/roman_curia/pontifical_councils/migrants/*. See also the comments on the Instruction in *People on the Move* XXXVII (98, 2005), 23-125, especially on the topics of ecumenism and the interreligious dialogue, 45-63.

4   See for example the Pontifical Message for the World Day of Peace 2007 on "The human person, the heart of peace": *L'Osservatore Romano* 146 (44.429; Dec. 13, 2006), 4-5.

enriching each other, which goes beyond a multicultural concept limited to a mere juxtaposition of different cultures.[5]

Dialogue, especially intercultural and interreligious dialogue, is the Church's mission today because "in recent years the presence of immigrants of other religions in traditionally Christian countries has become more and more marked" (EMCC no. 59). The great diversity of their cultural and religious origins poses new challenges and new outlooks, giving dialogue a central place in the pastoral care of migrants. The Church is called to develop "a dialogue that must be practised in the conviction that the Church is the ordinary way of salvation and that it alone possesses the full ness of the means of salvation" (ibid.). At the same time "everything possible must be done to help migrants of other religions so that they do not lose the transcendent dimension of life" (ibid.).

In the matter of human mobility the Church offers its help to all, irrespective of race or religion, respecting in all the inalienable dignity of the human person created in the image of God and redeemed by the Blood of Christ. To dialogue with others "requires that the catholic communities welcoming them should be all the more aware of their own identity, verify their faith in Christ, know well what their faith teaches, rediscover their missionary calling and therefore commit themselves to bear witness to Jesus the Lord and His gospel. This is . . . the prerequisite for conducting a sincere dialogue that is open, respects all, but is neither ingenuous nor ill equipped" (EMCC no. 60).[6]

Certain values are common to both the Christian faith and other beliefs. But it must be borne in mind that "beside these convergences there are also divergences, some of which have to do with the legitimate acquisitions of modern times" (EMCC no. 66). For immigrants therefore the first step they must take is to respect the laws and values of their host society, including its religious values, otherwise it becomes meaningless to talk of integration. The Church for its part is called to live its identity to the full; it must not fail to bear witness, including the "respectful proclamation" of its faith (cf. EMCC no. 9). Finally, another thing to be remembered is the important principle of reciprocity,[7] "understood not as a mere give-and-take attitude but as a relationship based on mutual respect and on justice in juridical and religious dealings. Reciprocity is also an attitude of the heart and the spirit that enables us to live together everywhere with equal rights and duties. A healthy reciprocity urges us to become an "advocate" for the rights

---

5   The topics of this important chapter in the pastoral care of human mobility are dealt with in *Migranti e pastorale d'accoglienza*, edited by the Pontifical Council for the Pastoral Care of Migrants and Itinerant People (*Quaderni Universitari*, Part II), Libreria Editrice Vaticana, Vatican City 2006.

6   Cf. The minutes of the XVII Plenary Session of our Pontifical Council held from 15 to 17 May 2006 on the subject of "Migration and movement from and to countries of Islamic majority": *People on the Move* XXXVIII (101 Suppl., 2006). For the interreligious dialogue see in particular 187-224. Number 11 of the conclusions and recommendations is of special interest: "It was moreover seen how important it is to distinguish what these societies can or cannot tolerate in Islamic culture, what must be respected or shared in relation to the faithful of other religions (see EMCC nos. 65 and 66), so as to be able to give indications to politicians too for drawing up civil legislation that will respect the competence of all": ibid. 43.

7   Benedict XVI, too, has made reference to this. See *People on the Move* XXXVIII (101 Suppl., 2006), 5.

of minorities when our own religious community forms the majority. This reminds us of the numerous Christian migrants in countries where the majority of the population is not Christian and in which the right of freedom of religion is severely restricted or suppressed" (EMCC no. 64).

It remains true, however, that solidarity, cooperation, interdependence among nations and the just distribution of the goods of the earth all indicate the vital need to work with determination especially in those countries where migrations originate so as to remove the inequalities that lead individuals or populations to abandon their own natural and cultural environment (cf. EMCC nos. 4; 8-9; 39-43). For its part the Church never ceases to encourage all, but in particular Christian communities, to be open and welcoming to others including migrants. The Church affirms that "in spite of the repeated failure of human projects, even noble projects, Christians, stirred by the phenomenon of mobility, are aware of their calling to be always and repeatedly a sign of fraternity and communion in the world, showing respect for differences and solidarity in their meeting with others" (EMCC no. 102).

Finally it must be recognized that migration is a process in constant evolution, that it will continue to be present as society develops and will transform our world into an intercultural world in which dialogue, including dialogue in the ecumenical and interreligious fields, will enable us to learn to live with our legitimate diversities.

With the help of the background I have sketched it will not be difficult for you to single out the points of contact with "Catholic Higher Education," bearing in mind especially international students,[8] but not only these.

Here there is ample room for study and research especially by catholic universities and, I would say, by colleges and also seminaries. I would also draw attention to letters addressed by our Pontifical Council in conjunction with other offices of the Roman Curia to the Bishops of the Oriental Catholic Churches and to Diocesan Ordinaries on the pastoral care of human mobility, to the superiors and general superiors of the institutes of consecrated life, the societies of apostolic life and the secular institutes, to Diocesan Bishops and the rectors of seminaries, to the heads and members of Church movements and lay associations.[9]

---

8   See the final statement of the Second World Congress for the Pastoral Care of International Students organized by the Pontifical Council for the Pastoral Care of Migrants and Itinerant People in December 2005: *www.vatican.va/roman_curia/pontifical_councils/migrants/s_index_intstudents/rc_pc_migrants_sectionint students_it.htm*. The First Congress with the theme: The Role of the Church in the World of Foreign Students. *Proceedings of the First World Congress on the Pastoral Care of Foreign Students* (Rome, September 17-19, 1996) published by *Leberit Printing Press*, Rome 1996.

9   See *People on the Move* XXXVII (No. 99, 2005) 89-221.

In conclusion I would say that today "Catholic Higher Education," while respecting the specific role of all others, cannot and must not fail to play its part in the sector of human mobility and in the specific pastoral care pertaining to that field.

Address given at the luncheon session organized by the Lay Center at Foyer Unitas Rome, June 20, 2007.

> Archbishop Agostino Marchetto
> *Secretary*
> *Pontifical Council for the Pastoral Care*
> *of Migrants and Itinerant People*

IV. United States Conference of Catholic Bishops' Documents

Catholic Higher Education and the Pastoral Mission of the Church

Statement of the U.S. Bishops on Catholic Higher Education

1980

I. THE MINISTRY OF CATHOLIC HIGHER EDUCATION

As we enter the 20th decade of Catholic higher education in the United States, we wish to express in a formal fashion our profound gratitude and esteem for those in this ministry. They serve the entire American people in every field of learning. They also serve the church in three indispensable ways. Catholic colleges and universities strive to bring faith and reason into an intellectually disciplined and constructive encounter. In addition, they are called to be communities of faith and worship that provide the young men and women of our country and church with opportunities to mature in mind, body, heart and soul. Without that maturity, they cannot function effectively as the future leaders of American business, government, culture and religion. Finally, our schools are serving increasingly the educational needs of adults as they seek to advance their learning at various stages of their lives.

During his recent visit in the United States, our Holy Father, Pope John Paul II, emphasized the importance of these functions of Catholic colleges and universities. Speaking to representatives of these institutions at the Catholic University of America, he stated that Catholic colleges and universities "must train young men and women of outstanding knowledge who, having made a personal synthesis between faith and culture, will be both capable and willing to assume tasks in the service of the community and of society in general, and to bear witness to their faith before the world."[1]

Catholic colleges and universities of the United States have been a significant part of the Catholic community and of American higher education since Georgetown University was founded in 1789 by the first bishop of Baltimore, John Carroll. Their growth since then has been extraordinary. They constitute the largest group of Catholic institutions of higher education in the world, a striking testimonial to the generosity and commitment of the clergy, religious and laity in our country. They have produced great numbers of American leaders both in public life and in the church.

From the schools at Antioch and Alexandria, the monastic and cathedral schools, to the medieval universities of Paris and Bologna, the church has fostered schools dedicated to the integration of the Christian faith and culture. This same

---

1   Origins, Oct. 25, 1979, para. 3.

concern led to the creation of such institutions in the New World as the University of Santo Domingo in 1533 and the many others which followed it.

The Second Vatican Council clarified the reason for the church's commitment to higher education when it said that people who devote themselves to the various disciplines of philosophy, history, science and the arts can help elevate the human family to a better understanding of truth, goodness and beauty, and to the formation of judgments which embody universal values.[2]

The world is good because it reflects its Creator. Human culture is good to the extent that it reflects the plan and purpose of the Creator, but it bears the wounds of sin. The church wishes to make the Gospel of Jesus Christ present to the world and to every sector of humanity at every stage of history. The Catholic college or university seeks to do this by educating men and women to play responsible roles in the contemporary world in the framework of that most important historical fact: the sending of the Son by the Father to reconcile, to vivify, to spread the good news, to call all the world to a restoration in Christ Jesus.[3]

The Catholic Church is, of course, not the only religious body in the United States to recognize the enormous importance of colleges and universities that seek to broaden human knowledge and understanding as part of their commitment to a particular religious faith. We note the ongoing contribution of Jewish and Protestant colleges and universities. At the recent national congress of church-related colleges and universities, delegates of 23 churches and their affiliated colleges came to a deeper understanding of their need for each other. They discovered that they have many of the same problems and challenges, and can assist one another in facing them.

During the decade of the '80s, all church-related colleges and universities will meet new challenges and new pressures. The burdens of inflation and of excessive governmental regulation will probably increase.[4] Moreover, the number of men and women of traditional college age will decline at a rate of almost half a million a year,[5] placing great economic stresses on all colleges and universities. Finally, there will be the continuing need for a clear definition by each institution of its religious identity and mission. All who are dedicated to the vitality of church-related higher education must work to surmount these challenges.

The future of church-related education is essential to the preservation of pluralism in higher education. The historic vitality of American Catholic colleges and universities has been indispensable to that pluralism.

---

2   Cf. "The Church in the Modern World," no. 57.

3   Cf. *Sapientia Christiana*, 4-5.

4   Indeed, during the past decade some colleges and universities, founded by Catholics, lay or clerical or religious, which have long presumed and styled themselves to be Catholic, have found themselves required to refrain from such designation as a condition for government aid to the institution. We regret the presence of such pressures and look to their removal in a timely fashion.

5   U.S. Bureau of the Census, Current Population Reports, series P-25, no. 704, 1977, 38-60 and no. 721, 1978, 9-11, as cited in Exhibit 3. Policy Analysis Service Reports, vol. 4, no. 2 (December 1978), American Council on Education.

A distinctive contribution to that pluralism has been the significant role played by women. To have so many women as presidents, major administrators and faculty of Catholic colleges has been unique in the annals of American higher education.

II. A PASTORAL MESSAGE TO CATHOLIC COLLEGES AND UNIVERSITIES

Our statement is intended as a pastoral message addressed first of all to those engaged in the ministry of Catholic higher education and then to the church at large. It speaks about the pastoral dimension of the life of the Catholic college and university.

This dimension is only one aspect of Catholic higher education. The church attaches great importance to higher learning, both for its own sake and for the life of the church. This was acknowledged in "The Catholic University in the Modern World," issued by the Second Congress of Delegates of the Catholic Universities of the World, convened in November 1972 by the Sacred Congregation for Catholic Education.[6] The document "Relations of American Catholic Colleges and Universities with the Church," issued in 1976 by the Association of Catholic Colleges and Universities[7] describes how Catholic colleges and universities function in the American context. This pastoral message need not restate all that in detail but it does reaffirm the intellectual importance of Catholic colleges and universities in the modern world.

Identity and Mission

One of our expectations is that Catholic colleges and universities continue to manifest, with unmistakable clarity, their Catholic identity and mission. The Holy Father has said that their character must be safeguarded,[8] and that the term "Catholic" should never be "a mere label, either added or dropped according to the pressures of varying factors."[9]

The Catholic identity of these institutions should be evident to faculty, students and the general public. Policies, practices, programs and general spirit should communicate to everyone that the institution is a community of scholars dedicated to the ideals and values of Catholic higher education.

Trustees and administrators have an extremely important role to discharge in maintaining fidelity to the nature of the institution and the kind of education the students' experience. We look in a special way, however, to faculties for the leadership to accomplish this.

---

6   "The Catholic University in the Modern World," College Newsletter, National Catholic Educational Association, March 1973. Cf. also the letter to presidents of Catholic universities of Cardinal G.M. Garrone, April 25, 1973, then prefect of the Sacred Congregation for Catholic Education.

7   Occasional Papers on Catholic Higher Education, April 1976.

8   John Paul II to members of the Council of the International Federation of Catholic Universities and Rectors of the Catholic Universities of Europe, Rome, Feb. 24, 1979, no. 3.

9   At the Catholic University of America, para. 3.

The many faculty members who come from other religious traditions can make a special contribution to the breadth of your students' experience. However, those faculty members who completely share the Catholic vision and heritage of faith carry the greatest responsibility to maintain the Catholic character of these institutions. The recruitment and retention of committed and competent Catholic faculty are essential.

Many Catholic colleges and universities are making serious efforts to renew their Catholic identity and mission within the guidelines provided by the Second Vatican Council, and thus remain true to their heritage while they adapt to modern circumstances. Academic freedom and institutional independence in pursuit of the mission of the institution are essential components of educational quality and integrity; commitment to the Gospel and the teachings and heritage of the Catholic Church provide the inspiration and enrichment that make a college fully Catholic.

Liberal Arts

The Catholic identity of a college or university is effectively manifested only in a context of academic excellence. Policies, standards, curricula, governance and administration should accord, therefore, with the norms of quality accepted in the wider academic community.

A necessary, though not sufficient, element in the identity of undergraduate programs in Catholic institutions is the provision of a liberal education of high quality. But that education must go beyond secular humanism, which also emphasizes the liberal arts. Catholic institutions of higher learning can uniquely fuse the traditional study of arts and sciences with the light of faith in the synthesis we call Christian and Catholic humanism. That synthesis provides an integral view of human existence—one that gives true meaning, purpose and value to the study of all the disciplines. Indeed the Christian and Catholic view of human nature is a sound guide through the moral dilemmas that are so frequent in contemporary society and technology.

We are concerned that the erosion in the teaching of the liberal arts in American higher education today might compromise their important part in teaching the ideals of Christian humanism. That is why we urge Catholic colleges and universities to preserve and strengthen the teaching of the liberal arts in undergraduate and pre-professional education. Particularly in professional and graduate programs the faculty and students should address human and religious issues that are intrinsic to a humane education. An institution's Catholic identity is largely expressed in a curriculum that shows how the values of the Judeo-Christian view of life illuminate all fields of study and practice.

Theology

Theological education is a major concern of the bishops since we are responsible before God and before his people for "a heritage of faith that the church has the duty of preserving in its untouchable purity, and of presenting . . . to the people of our time in a way that is as understandable and persuasive as possible."[10]

For its part, "one of the principal tasks of a Catholic university, and one which it alone is able to accomplish adequately, will be to make theology relevant to all human knowledge and reciprocally all human knowledge relevant to theology."[11]

The early American Catholic colleges were founded in part to protect the faith of students. The mission of Catholic institutions has broadened considerably since that time. They are full partners in the higher-education community of the nation, offering wide diversity of academic programs and degrees. With all this diversity, however, theological education has maintained a role that is central to their mission. We are grateful for this continued emphasis and take note of the improvement of education in theology and religious studies in Catholic colleges since the Second Vatican Council. Recent progress in exegesis and patristic research has enriched biblical, liturgical and historic theology and has contributed to progress in systematic, pastoral and moral theology. We also appreciate the efforts to pursue the ecumenical and interreligious directives of the council by providing students with the opportunity to learn of other religious traditions.

Theology is not the same as faith or spirituality or holiness. These, too, are important values of Catholic education, but here we want to emphasize that the distinguishing mark of every Catholic college or university is that, in an appropriate fashion, it offers its students an introduction to the Catholic theological heritage. This is a moral obligation owed to students.

In fulfilling this obligation a theological faculty should take "prudent account of the maturity and previous preparation of the students,"[12] and should be cautious about private speculation of a kind that might undermine the students' foundations of faith in God's revealed truth. It is advisable, however, that students be encouraged to cope with their personal problems of faith and to consider the religious dimensions of the major issues in our contemporary culture and society. Theology should enable students to think and act within a vision of life that includes religious values. A truly liberating and elevating education is incomplete without the study of theology or religion.

For this reason, scholars in theology and other religious studies "make an indispensable contribution to the integrity of the university, which in order to embrace the fullness of human experience, must take its religious dimension into account."[13]

Although the majority of Catholic institutions are undergraduate colleges, some are universities with graduate and professional programs of theology. Graduate teachers and students, enriched by sacred scripture, the traditions of the church and its magisterium, can utilize the professional tools of their discipline to explore Catholic teaching in depth and to discern its applicability to the problems of our times. Because many of the graduates of these programs in theology will be engaged

---

10 "On Evangelization" (Paul VI, 1975), no. 3.

11 "The Catholic University in the Modern World," para. 4.

12 "The Catholic University in the Modern World," para. 4, cf. "On Evangelization," no. 78.

13 "The Catholic University in the Modern World," no. 26.

in the ministry of teaching religion, the faculty will have special reason to show respect for the authentic teaching of the church.

Christian Formation of Teachers

The Christian formation of teachers has always been basic to the educational mission of the church. Until a few years ago, Catholic schools were staffed almost exclusively by men and women, priests and religious, who had not only received training in a formal Christian formation program, but who also had available ongoing opportunities for growth and development in their spiritual and professional lives.

Today lay persons have become the overwhelming majority in virtually every Catholic school. They come to Catholic schools with a variety of teacher-preparation backgrounds, motivations and perspectives. Usually, this formation is achieved at secular universities where the prospective teacher is exposed to either a theological pluralism or receives no special training at all in this field. This is in stark contrast to those who previously were formed in a specifically Catholic environment and emerged certain and secure in their understanding of Catholic tradition and practice.

Therefore, teacher-preparation programs adequate for public schools are inadequate for teachers in Catholic schools. They omit the necessary spiritual and ministerial formation which must be an integral part of the professional preparation of the Catholic school teacher. This need is urgent and can best be met by the Catholic colleges and universities who alone possess the unique resources and desire to be of service to the Catholic community.

Catholic institutions of higher education which have teacher-preparation programs are urged to provide Christian formation programs for educators, who are evangelizers by call and covenant and mission. Only those teachers who have been formed theologically and spiritually can respond to the call of professional ministry in Christian education according to the vision of Jesus Christ and his church.

Theologians and Bishops

We bishops, for our part, look to biblical scholars and theologians for assistance in understanding and explicating the gospel message within the framework of the church's theological traditions, and for helping the church's judgment to mature on current questions.[14] In the words of the Second Vatican Council, "furthermore, while adhering to the methods and requirements proper to theology, theologians are invited to seek continually for more suitable ways of communicating doctrine to the men and women of their times. For the deposit of faith or revealed truths are one thing; the manner in which they are formulated without violence to their meaning and significance is another."[15]

The Holy Father, when speaking at the Catholic University of America, said:

"I want to say a special word of gratitude, encouragement and guidance for theologians. The church needs her theologians, particularly in this time and age as

---

14   Cf. "On Divine Revelation," no. 12.

15   "The Church in the Modern World," no. 62.

profoundly marked by deep changes in all areas of life and society. The bishops of the church, to whom the Lord has entrusted the keeping of the unity of the faith and the preaching of the message—individual bishops for their dioceses; and bishops collegially with the successor of Peter for the universal church—we all need your work, your dedication and the fruits of your reflection. We desire to listen to you and we are eager to receive the valued assistance of your responsible scholarship."[16]

Tension sometimes occurs as we seek to satisfy the respective claims of faith and reason, and to distinguish the doctrinal and pastoral responsibilities of bishops from the particular tasks of theologians. The pope alluded to this tension when he said "the theologian's contribution will be enriching to the church only if it takes into account the proper function of the bishops and the rights of the faithful. It devolves upon the bishops of the church to safeguard the Christian authenticity and unity of faith and moral teaching."[17]

Bishops and the theological community share a mutual but not identical responsibility to the church. Like theology, the ecclesiastical magisterium is subject to the word of God, which it serves.[18] As Pope John Paul II has reminded us: "In putting themselves at the service of the truth, the magisterium and the theologians are joined together by common ties, namely by the word of God, by the sensus fidei, which has been alive in the church in the past and is alive today, by the documents of tradition in which the faith of the people in general is set forth, and finally by pastoral and missionary considerations."[19]

Conscious of our different roles in the church, and also of our mutual responsibilities, we seek a fruitful cooperation with theologians. Together we must work to build up the body of Christ and to bring the truth and power of the Gospel to our society and culture with due respect for the legitimate autonomy of culture and of the sciences. [20]

We encourage the universities to develop ways which will bring bishops and theologians together with other members of the church and the academy to examine theological issues with wisdom and learning, with faith and with mutual charity and esteem. We shall all need to recall and to work for that "delicate balance . . . between the autonomy of a Catholic university and the responsibilities of the hierarchy."[21] There need be no conflict between the two.

Philosophy

Another major concern of ours is the study of philosophy. We do not see philosophy as merely one more subject area in the field of liberal arts, nor as an academic luxury

---

16 Para. 6.

17 Ibid.

18 "On Divine Revelation," no. 10.

19 Address to International Theological Commission, Origins, Nov. 29, 1979, para. 7.

20 Cf. "The Church in the Modern World," no. 59.

21 "The Catholic University in the Modern World," no. 52.

for those of speculative bent, but rather as an essential component of any education worthy of the name.

It is philosophy which familiarizes the student with the laws and patterns of human thought. It brings the student to face, in a disciplined academic fashion, the great questions about God, the world and humanity. It brings with itself an ever-increasing sense of the proportion and relationship that exist between the various aspects of reality and learning. Without solid philosophical grounding, both teachers and students in all fields of study cannot avoid the risk of superficiality and fragmentation.

Ethics

Catholic colleges and universities have the obligation to study and teach the moral and ethical dimensions of every discipline. They must guarantee that the moral considerations of the Catholic tradition are related to all programs of study and that the ethical implications of new findings are probed in what Pope John Paul II called a "proportionate development."[22] This is especially urgent in professional and technical studies because in a technologically oriented society it is often the professional who in fact makes many decisions involving human values.

Justice

Education for justice is a significant element in the general call to gospel holiness. We issued a call to justice on the occasion of our nation's bicentennial in 1976 and we repeat now that "we must expand and improve our programs of education for justice."[23]

Those who enjoy the benefits of Catholic higher education have the obligation to provide our society with leadership in matters of justice and human rights.

Knowledge of economics and politics will not in itself bring about justice, unless it is activated by human and religious ideals. However, religious ideals without the necessary secular expertise will not provide the kind of leadership needed to influence our complex society.

Many Catholic colleges and universities integrate social justice teaching with field education and experience. Students and faculty are encouraged to become personally aware of problems of injustice and their responsibility to be involved in the social process. These are responses we should expect from institutions which take the Gospel seriously.

For the college or university to be an authentic teacher of social justice, it must conduct its own affairs in a just way.[24] "Modern man listens more willingly to witnesses than to teachers, and if he does listen to teachers, it is because they are witnesses."[25] It is important that Catholic institutions of higher education continually

---

22   "The Redeemer of Man," no. 15.

23   "To Do the Work of Justice," 5.

24   Cf. "Fair Practices in Higher Education," Carnegie Council on Policy Studies in Higher Education, 1979.

25   Paul VI, address to members of the Council of the Laity, Oct. 2, 1974.

review their policies and personnel practices in order to ensure that social justice is a reality on campus. Fidelity to the social teachings of the church in this basic witness means there is no contradiction between practice and theory.

Minority Concerns

Another aspect of justice is the treatment of minority concerns. For much of its history, the Catholic Church in the United States bore the title of the "church of the immigrants," and these same immigrants frequently found opportunities for higher education in the Catholic colleges and universities. As new minority groups seek educational opportunities, Catholic institutions should strive to respond to their legitimate needs, providing student aid and an education which respects their culture while offering the benefits of the Christian heritage. We have in mind blacks, native Americans, Orientals and other minorities, but especially Hispanic-Americans, whose own Catholic culture is so rich and whose numbers are so great. We encourage our colleges and universities to institute pre-college programs for disadvantaged persons. We ask that attention be given to the need for the presence of minority persons on boards of trustees and faculties of these institutions.

The International Viewpoint

Because the unity of all people under God our Father is a fundamental principle of Catholic theology, an international point of view should be evident on the Catholic campus. Modern means of transportation and communication make possible a closer union of the peoples of the world by diminishing the distances that separate us. The way is thus being prepared for the familial closeness, the mutuality of service and the union of hearts which lie at the core of the Gospel and to which the human family is called. The present climate of competition, hostility and violence must be replaced by a constructive sharing of the earth's goods in a secure and peaceful environment. This suggests that international studies have an important place in the curriculum. It is also important and beneficial for students from other nations to be present on Catholic campuses. Their presence provides an opportunity for close associations which made possible an increased appreciation of others' culture and point of view.

Campus Ministry

This pastoral document envisions a Catholic university or college as an enterprise wholly committed to evangelical ministry. To relegate this ministry to the institution's periphery in an isolated department or office of "campus ministry" is to fault the university's or college's essential Catholic identity.

Trustees, administrators, faculties, parents and, above all, students need to see their whole college or university experience as a unique opportunity for the discovery of God's abiding presence and influence in the lives of people and in the signs of the times. At most and at best an office of campus ministry can be a catalyst to spark and to energize the total institution's involvement in a gospel-oriented evangelism. This office is badly degraded if it is regarded only as something like a bookstore or student union, some sort of a convenience for those students who want a little religion on the side of their higher education.

A university or college which has an ongoing, dynamic program to clarify its Catholic identity will expect the office of campus ministry to have a voice on a policy-making level and to insist in season and out of season on the preservation and enrichment of the institution's religious traditions.

Because campus ministry normally includes elements of parish ministry, e.g., counseling, preparation for the sacraments, preaching, liturgical worship and cooperation with diocesan activities, we are obliged to grant appropriate jurisdiction and authority to duly approved campus ministers at institutions of higher education in our dioceses. We see this duty not as one needlessly to restrict the highly commendable pastoral practices in campus ministry, but rather as one to give our official support and as far as possible our assistance to a ministry for which we have a share of responsibility. For this reason, we believe it to be of the utmost importance that those who are selected for this important ministry, whether they be clergy, religious or lay, be prepared for this kind of apostolate theologically and philosophically. They should present the authentic teaching of the church in a pastoral manner in the context of the academic communities in which they serve.

We would like university and college students to feel that they are not mere visitors in our diocese but are temporary residents for whose spiritual welfare we pray and work. There is merit, in a growing trend for bishops personally to visit university and college campuses for the celebration of liturgies and, on occasion, for close-up dialogue with students. Pope John Paul II has set a good example for our face-to-face conversations with students.

Though much progress lately has been made in improving the quality and extent of campus ministry on Catholic campuses there still is vast room for upgrading this important element of Catholic higher education. To a large extent, we fear, campus ministry still suffers badly from inadequate budgets and from too limited a staff. A very encouraging development, however, is team ministry in which laity, religious and priests combine their talents and experience for efficacious ministry.

In this ministry the gospel adage is controlling: "I know mine, and mine know me." To do the work of the Lord Jesus himself on a Catholic university or college campus is to have close personal contact with students who are ready to share their intimate hopes and anxieties with a person who truly can say, "I know you, and you know me." Obviously this ministry should not and cannot be limited to persons formally designated as campus ministers even though they rightfully are expected to take the lead.

We bishops, as best we can, wish to pledge our active cooperation with this kind of ministry on the campuses in our dioceses.

A Community of Faith

Pope John Paul II has repeatedly called for the Catholic campus to be a community of faith. In Mexico and in Poland, in Rome and in Washington, he has again and again returned to the same theme.[26] No more fitting ideal can be sought than to build a community which encourages intellectual growth and which calls to and supports a personal religious commitment.[27]

Growth in Christ is never an easy task. Indeed, in our times it is exceedingly difficult to live a fully Christian life. We honor those persons—especially young people—who reject the patterns of behavior which surround men and, as "children of light"[28] attempt to respond with fidelity to the grace of their baptism. It is that very grace which calls us to support one another as a company of believers.

All Catholic activity must of necessity be pointed to an objective that is ultimately religious: how to know God better and serve him more faithfully. The goals of a Catholic college are specified by its very nature as a place of learning. But learning itself does not constitute the perfect and fulfilled life. It needs to be integrated with our search for the Lord and in our living with our neighbor a life of faith in him and fidelity to his way. Our concern, then, is that students and faculty find on our campuses the community of faith which can encourage and support them in reaching for that goal. Unless a Catholic institution of higher learning fosters such a faith community it contradicts its own mission.

Residential students can more easily experience a campus-based community. For commuter students the formation of community is more difficult. We encourage dedicated persons to develop new ways to draw more students and faculty into communities of friends who help one another live strongly religious lives.

Adult Learners

Our concern for the welfare of the younger college students does not exclude the growing number of older students. These men and women seek education for new careers, to complete an interrupted education, or for the pleasure of learning. They constitute a growing proportion of the student body on our campuses. Their needs for an integrated Catholic education are similar to those of the younger students, but they must be addressed in different ways.

We appreciate the many programs developed by Catholic institutions to provide theological renewal and training for ministry to Catholic adults in the years since the Second Vatican Council. These programs illustrate a distinct form of service to the church community, which we hope will grow as we learn how to use the many resources of our institutions more effectively.

The Campus and Ecumenism

The Second Vatican Council called for strong ecumenical initiatives. The Catholic colleges have been responding not only with courses designed to acquaint Catholic

---

26 "To be what it ought to be, a Catholic college or university must set up, among its faculty and students, a real community which bears witness to a living and operative Christianity, a community where sincere commitment to scientific research and study goes together with a deep commitment to authentic Christian living." At the Catholic University of America, no. 3.

27 "The Catholic University in the Modern World," no. 10.

28 Eph 5:8.

students with other religious traditions, but with faculty members drawn from those traditions who have added a rich new dimension to departments of theology and religious studies. The Catholic college or university can be a fertile environment for further ecumenical activity and we encourage cooperative work with the local (and national) church to that end. Catholic faculty trained in biblical and theological sciences can offer leadership in the explorations and study in which we join with others outside the Catholic community.

Research

The church has always encouraged the advancement of human knowledge, because the more we know of truth the closer we come to God in whom truth ultimately resides. Catholic scholars, as Pope John Paul II urged, should examine all the fundamental questions in human culture with the highest degree of intellectual rigor. These scholars also have a special obligation to undertake research closely related to human and spiritual needs.[29] It is for this reason that the bishops of America in their bicentennial "Call to Action" urged scholars to undertake research in areas of pastoral concern, especially in issues of justice and peace.[30] In these efforts the church would be materially assisted if cooperative efforts could be organized to mobilize the combined research capabilities of the Catholic universities of this country. We shall work with the universities to find the resources necessary for research of high quality and utility.

III. THE SUPPORT FOR CATHOLIC HIGHER EDUCATION

We have addressed in particular those who work and study in Catholic colleges and universities; now we want to urge upon all in the church a firm support for this important ministry.

Religious Congregations

The entire church owes much to those generations of sisters, brothers and priests who provided higher education to their students, financed by their own labors and often by their own funds.

Today the numbers of clergy and religious are smaller at many Catholic colleges and universities. This is due, in part, to the decline in religious vocations and, in part, to entry into other fields of ministry. It is important that the mission of Catholic higher education remain a high priority among religious communities. The nurturing of tomorrow's leadership through service in Catholic colleges and universities is an effective way of building the Christian community and of preparing the next generation of leaders for our society.

---

29   Cf. John Paul II, Address at the Catholic University of America.

30   "To Do the Work of Justice," 5.

Parents

We join with Pope John Paul II to offer "gratitude and appreciation . . . to the parents . . . who, sometimes at the price of great personal and financial sacrifice, look toward the Catholic universities and colleges for the training that unites faith and science, culture and the gospel values."[31]

Combinations of federal, state and institutional student-aid programs make it possible, although not without sacrifice, for parents to encourage and support the attendance of their sons and daughters at Catholic institutions. These programs narrow the tuition gap between the independent college and the state institution, which is heavily subsidized by all taxpayers. Consequently, some exercise of choice is possible for many students. In helping a son or daughter select a college, parents should give a priority, where feasible, to the Catholic institution. Adult Catholic leaders need adult Catholic education. The religious learning of the child will not suffice for the religious needs and demands of the adult.

The American Church at Large

We appeal, finally, to the entire American church for support of Catholic higher education. Catholic foundations, as well as Catholic individuals and families, should see generous and long-term support of Catholic institutions as one of the top priorities in our church. The stability of institutions of higher learning in America in our time is based on a firm underpinning of endowment funds. The Catholic colleges and universities have relied throughout their history on the "living endowment" of religious and clergy, as well as on the generous assistance of lay persons. The day has now come when we American Catholics of the present must reciprocate the gifts we have received from the past.

To all Catholics who believe with us that Catholic higher education is important for the life of the church, we appeal for financial support, so that the benefits we have enjoyed will be preserved for the next generation of Catholic Americans.

We conclude by noting once again the historic interest of the Catholic Church in higher education. We thank the clergy and religious, and laity in ever-increasing numbers, who staff the colleges and universities of our country. We commend all who are undertaking the renewal of Catholic higher education as part of that renewal to which the Holy Spirit through the Vatican Council has called the whole church.[32]

---

31   At the Catholic University of America, no. 2.

32   Since this message has addressed exclusively Catholic higher education, we were unable to speak of the excellent intellectual and pastoral leadership of many Catholics engaged as teachers, administrators and campus ministers in the colleges and universities which are not Catholic. We hope for a future opportunity to speak of their invaluable contribution to the intellectual life of our country.

Empowered by the Spirit: Campus Ministry Faces the Future

November 15, 1985

Following the bishops' November 1982 general meeting, the Committee on Education was commissioned to draft a pastoral letter on campus ministry. The first draft of this letter was submitted to the bishops in June 1985. The Administrative Committee placed the subsequent draft, *Empowered by the Spirit: Campus Ministry Faces the Future*, on the bishops' November 1985 agenda. Approval of the text was given during the plenary meeting of the National Conference of Catholic Bishops in Washington, D.C., November 15, 1985. Accordingly, publication of this pastoral letter is authorized by the undersigned.

Msgr. Daniel F. Hoye
General Secretary, NCCB/USCC

INTRODUCTION

1. "I pray that he will bestow on you gifts in keeping with the riches of his glory. May he strengthen you inwardly through the working of his Spirit. May Christ dwell in your hearts through faith and may charity be the root and foundation of your life" (Eph 3:16-17). For over a century, Catholic campus ministry in our country, empowered by the Spirit, has been forming communities of faith which witness to the presence of the risen Christ. Now we are at the beginning of a new era filled with opportunities to build up the faith community on campuses and to promote the well-being of higher education and society as a whole. In this pastoral letter addressed to the Catholic Church in the United States and especially to the church on campus, we offer our prayerful support, encouragement and guidance to the men and women who are committed to bringing the message of Christ to the academic world. In preparing this letter we have consulted with many of them and have come to a deeper appreciation of their dedication and achievements, as well as their concerns and frustrations. This new era, which is filled with promise, challenges campus ministry to respond creatively to the promptings of the Spirit for the well-being of the church and higher education.

2. Our 1981 statement on Catholic higher education concluded by noting "the excellent intellectual and pastoral leadership of many Catholics engaged as teachers, administrators and campus ministers in the colleges and universities which are not Catholic."[1] We said at that time that "we hope for a future opportunity to speak

---

1   "Catholic Higher Education and the Pastoral Mission of the Church," in *Pastoral Letters of the United States Catholic Bishops*, 4 vols., ed. Hugh J. Nolan (Washington, D.C.: USCC Office of Publishing and Promotion Services, 1983-84), vol. 4, 1975-1983, no. 64, footnote 32. (Hereafter all pastoral letters will be cited from the Nolan text.)

of their invaluable contribution to the intellectual life of our country."[2] In this pastoral letter we fulfill that hope and turn our attention primarily to the ministry of the church on these public and private campuses, where each year millions of Catholics are being prepared as future leaders of society and church.[3] We are mindful of our previous comments on the crucial importance of Catholic higher education, especially the distinctive task of campus ministry on Catholic campuses to call the total institution to spread the Gospel and to preserve and enrich its religious traditions.[4] In addition, the suggestions for this document made by those who serve at Catholic institutions affirmed that all who minister in the world of higher education have certain common concerns and similar desires for cooperation. Collaboration among all colleges and universities within a diocese enhances the church's ministry to higher education. Mutual support, joint sponsorship of programs and sharing of resources improve the total efforts of campus ministry. Many of the perspectives, suggestions and directions in this pastoral letter should be helpful to those who serve so well in our Catholic institutions of higher education.

3. Campus ministry is best understood in its historical, sociological and theological context. Thus, the first section discusses our hopes for the church on campus in the light of its previous history. The next section locates campus ministry within the relationship between the church and the world of higher education, highlighting the need for renewed dialogue. Campus ministry derives its life from the persons who bring the Gospel of Christ to the academic world. Therefore, the third section focuses on the members of the church on campus, emphasizing the call of all the baptized to collaborate in the work of the church as well as the special responsibility of professional campus ministers to empower others for this task. The fourth section examines six aspects of campus ministry that flow from the nature of the church and the situation on campus. Here we state principles and suggest strategies for carrying out this ministry. The epilogue notes our own responsibilities as bishops to serve the church on campus and calls the church to an exciting new phase in the history of campus ministry in our country.

I. HISTORY AND CURRENT OPPORTUNITIES

A. History and Contemporary Developments

4. The church's response to current opportunities on campus will benefit from an awareness of the history of the Newman movement in the United States.[5] This ministry began in 1883 at the University of Wisconsin with the founding, through lay

---

2   Ibid.

3   There are over 3,300 institutions of higher learning in the United States. The 1985 fall enrollment was 12,247,000, of which approximately 9.6 million attend public colleges and universities and 2.7 million attend private institutions. In the total student population 43 percent are 25 or older and 45 percent attend part time. In recent times Catholics have constituted around 39 percent of the freshman class. For these statistics, see *Chronicle of Higher Education*, Sept. 4, 1985.

4   "Catholic Higher Education," nos. 45-46.

5   See John Whitney Evans, *The Newman Movement* (Notre Dame: Notre Dame Press, 1980).

initiative, of the Melvin Club, which was designed to keep Catholics on campus in touch with their religious heritage. A decade later the first Newman Club was established at the University of Pennsylvania with much the same purpose. It was named after Cardinal John Henry Newman, who was the English leader in the 19th-century intellectual renewal in the church and later was chosen the great patron of campus ministers in our country. During this initial stage, farsighted leaders recognized that the growing number of Catholic collegians attending public institutions needed support and instruction in their religious heritage. They responded by establishing clubs for Catholic students with their own chaplains and residence halls.

5. In 1908 the second stage began with the establishment of the first association of Catholic clubs in state universities. What would become the National Newman Club Federation replaced this first effort about the time of World War I. This phase, which lasted until 1969, was often characterized by a defensive and even hostile attitude on the part of Catholic students and their chaplains toward the academic world, which was perceived as dominated by a secularist philosophy. During this period, many students and chaplains in the Newman movement felt estranged from the rest of the church and decried the lack of support from the hierarchy.

6. The third stage, begun in 1969 in response to the Second Vatican Council and continuing until the present, has produced some healthy new developments. First, the church as a whole has grown in appreciation and support of campus ministry. It is true there are still problems: Some colleges and universities lack officially appointed campus ministers, and many others are understaffed and suffer from financial problems. At times there are misunderstandings between the church on campus and local parishes and diocesan offices. However, progress has clearly been made in integrating campus ministry into the life of the church. Today there are over 2,000 Catholics ministering on campuses throughout the country—a significant increase over a couple of decades ago. There is an increased commitment to providing well-trained campus ministers who appreciate the need for continued professional and theological development. Student groups at all levels collaborate with official representatives of the church. Diocesan directors of campus ministry help keep campus concerns before the whole church. More Catholics appreciate the importance of campus ministry and support diocesan funding of this work. Through this pastoral letter, we affirm these positive developments and pledge to work with others to build on them. We bring to the attention of the whole church the importance of campus ministry for the future well-being of the church and society. Our goal is to foster a closer relationship and a greater spirit of cooperation between campus ministry and the rest of the local church. Campus ministry is an integral part of the church's mission to the world and must be seen in that light.

7. Second, we endorse the improving relationship between the church on campus and the academic community. While problems remain, Catholics have developed a greater understanding of the positive values and legitimate concerns of higher education. Many campus ministers have established good working relationships with administrators, faculty and staff. There is greater appreciation of the way the church benefits from the teaching, research and service carried on by colleges and universities. Similarly, many administrators view campus ministry as an ally in the common effort to provide an integrated learning experience for the students. Faculty members frequently value the presence of campus ministers who

demonstrate an appreciation of the spiritual life and can articulate their Catholic heritage. In our consultations we found that many leaders in the academic community welcome a word from the church on matters of mutual concern.[6] Our hope in this letter is to build on this fund of good will and to heal any wounds which linger from past mistakes and misunderstandings. With respect for the freedom and autonomy of the academic community, we believe it is time to foster a renewed dialogue between the church and higher education to the benefit of society as a whole.

8. Third, we affirm the development of ecumenical and interfaith relationships. There are, of course, problems in resolving longstanding differences, and at some colleges and universities dialogue and cooperation have been difficult to establish and maintain. However, on many campuses the Catholic community and other religious groups, who share a common vision of ministry and who are interested in ecumenical and interfaith cooperation, have developed strong working relationships. This occurs especially with other Christian churches, with whom we share a common commitment to Jesus Christ, and with the Jewish community, with whom we hold a common heritage and shared Scriptures. In some situations Catholic campus ministers share an interfaith center and collaborate in some ministerial tasks. In other places the Catholic community cooperates with other religious groups through regular meetings, joint study and shared prayer. Mutual trust has grown as members of various religious traditions work together on common programs, such as projects to promote social justice. We commend this ecumenical and interfaith progress and give full support to greater and more creative efforts in this direction. Catholics who are deeply rooted in their tradition and who maintain a strong sense of identity with their religious heritage will be better prepared to carry out this mission. We appreciate the contributions and cooperative attitudes of most of the various religious communities on campus. The Catholic community on campus might also seek to engage those who are concerned with human ethical values of our society but do not directly relate their concerns to a faith tradition. To those who demonstrate less tolerant attitudes, we extend an invitation to join in the dialogue. In this pastoral message we address the Catholic campus community and discuss its particular challenges and opportunities. While we will not treat directly the ecumenical and interfaith dimensions of campus ministry today, we hope that the Catholic communities on individual campuses will be prompted by this letter to renewed dialogue and collaboration in serving the common good.

9. Finally, this third stage in the history of the Newman movement has produced a remarkable diversity of legitimate styles and approaches to campus ministry designed to match available resources with the unique situations at particular colleges and universities. These creative responses range from well-organized teams serving the needs of a large university parish to an individual ministering part time in a small community college. The styles include ministries that are primarily sacramental and those that rely mainly on the ministry of presence. Some campus ministers work on Catholic campuses where they can influence policy decisions, while others serve in public institutions where they have little or no access to the centers of power. In

---

6   Among the many consultations with administrators, faculty, students, selected experts and others, we found especially helpful the close to 300 responses received from presidents and elected faculty leaders representing institutions of higher education from all 50 states who informed us of their hopes and concerns.

some situations priests are working full time, while in others the ministry is carried out almost entirely by members of religious orders and lay people. Ministers on residential campuses can offer many set programs for students, while those who serve on commuter campuses must be attentive to the creative possibilities demanded by such a fluid situation. Most serve on one campus, although some are responsible for several colleges and universities. While we cannot discuss in detail all styles of ministry, we will offer principles and strategies designed to encourage all those concerned with the church on campus to make vigorous and creative applications to their own situations.

B. Current Challenges and Opportunities

10. We believe this is the opportune time to address a challenging word to the church on campus. Catholics are attending colleges and universities in numbers that far exceed their percentage of the general population.[7] It is crucial that these emerging leaders of church and society be exposed to the best of our Catholic tradition and encounter dedicated leaders who will share their journey of faith with them. Thus the time is right to encourage campus ministers to renew their own spiritual lives and to facilitate the faith development of the Catholics on campus.

11. Today there is a growing interest among many Catholics in various ministries. On campus there is a great reservoir of energy and talent that could be utilized in the service of the church and the world. Therefore, the time is right to challenge faculty members, administrators, support staff and students to contribute their time and gifts to the common effort to help the academic community achieve its goals and to build up the church on campus.

12. The academic world is in the midst of an important debate on how to improve the quality of higher education in our country.[8] Fundamental questions about the purpose, methods and direction of higher education must be addressed as colleges and universities continue to define their mission and to improve their performance. Therefore, the time is right to encourage Catholics on campus to participate in these local debates and thus to contribute their insights and values to this crucial national discussion.

---

7   In both 1983 and 1984, 39.3 percent of college freshmen were Roman Catholic. See Alexander W. Astin, *The American Freshman National Norms for Fall 1983* (and *1984*), published by the American Council on Education and the University of California at Los Angeles. Catholics constitute about 25 percent of the general population in the United States.

8   Cf. "Involvement in Learning: Realizing the Potential of American Education" (National Institute of Education, 1984); William J. Bennett, "To Reclaim a Legacy" (National Endowment for the Humanities, 1984); and "Integrity in the College Curriculum: A Report to the Academic Community" (Association of American Colleges, 1985); and "Higher Education and the American Resurgence" (Carnegie Foundation for the Advancement of Teaching, 1985).

II. CAMPUS MINISTRY AND THE RELATIONSHIP BETWEEN THE CHURCH AND HIGHER EDUCATION

A. History

13. Campus ministry is an expression of the church's special desire to be present to all who are involved in higher education. Throughout its history, the church has been instrumental in cultivating the intellectual life. During the period of the Fathers, great centers of learning at Antioch and Alexandria instructed the faithful and promoted the integration of faith and culture. The church contributed her resources to the task of forming medieval universities and founded many of them, including the great schools of Bologna, Paris, Oxford and Cambridge. In the modern world, government increasingly has taken over the responsibility for higher education, with a resulting split between the church and the university. This has occurred in our own country with the establishment of a massive system of public higher education that has its own autonomy. Shortly after 1900 it was evident that enrollments in this system were growing faster than those in the Catholic and Protestant colleges which for so long had constituted higher education in the United States. From the perspective of faith, Christians often detected in public institutions a growing secularism that celebrated the autonomy of reason and left little room for consideration of religious questions or moral values. This situation intensified after World War I, and the church responded not only by increasing her traditional commitment to higher education, but also by trying to protect Catholic students from the anti-religious elements perceived on public campuses. During this period the church and higher education experienced a good deal of mutual misunderstanding. Some people in the academic world feared that the church would try to reassert, in more subtle ways, its control over higher education. On the other side, members of the church at times regarded secular higher education as a threat to the Christian way of life. The time has come to move beyond these misunderstandings and to forge a new relationship between the church and higher education that respects the unique character of each. We remain convinced that "cooperation between these two great institutions, church and university, is indispensable to the health of society."[9]

B. The Contribution of Higher Education

14. We respect the autonomy of the academic community and appreciate its great contributions to the common good. Higher education benefits the human family through its research, which expands our common pool of knowledge. By teaching people to think critically and to search for the truth, colleges and universities help to humanize our world. The collegiate experience provides individuals with attitudes and skills that can be used in productive work, harmonious living

---

9   "To Teach as Jesus Did: A Pastoral Message on Catholic Education," in *Pastoral Letters*, vol. 3, 1962-1974, no. 63.

and responsible citizenship. Since higher education in the United States has taken on public service as one of its tasks, society has received significant assistance in solving human and technical problems. The Second Vatican Council placed this contribution in a personal context when it said that people who apply themselves to philosophy, history, science and the arts help "to elevate the human family to a more sublime understanding of truth, goodness and beauty and to the formation of judgments which embody universal values."[10]

15. The church, as well as society as a whole, benefits from the contributions of higher education. The members of the church hold a common faith in Jesus Christ, a faith that seeks understanding. When the academic world produces new knowledge and encourages critical thinking, it assists Christians in the process of deepening and articulating their faith. When higher education fosters fidelity toward truth in scientific research and collaborative efforts to improve the quality of life in our world, it helps to prepare for the acceptance of the gospel message.[11]

16. There is no doubt that the world of higher education has its own problems that must be addressed and dehumanizing practices that must be challenged. Fidelity to the Gospel demands critical judgment as well as affirmation. It is, however, vital that campus ministry maintains a fundamental appreciation of the contributions made by higher education to society and the church.

C. The Contribution of the Church

17. The church brings to the dialogue with higher education its general mission to preach the Gospel of Christ and to help the human family achieve its full destiny.[12] Thus the church seeks to help higher education attain its lofty goal of developing a culture in which human beings can realize their full potential.[13] In providing this assistance, the church joins its voice with others in promoting the ideal of educating the whole person. From our perspective this means keeping the dignity and worth of human beings in the center of our reflections on the purpose of higher education. Education is the process by which persons are "assisted in the harmonious development of their physical, moral and intellectual endowments."[14] It aims at the formation of individuals who have a sense of ultimate purpose and are moving toward greater freedom, maturity and integration. At the same time, genuine education nurtures a sense of responsibility for the common good and provides skills for active involvement in community life.

18. We think that it is important to keep the problems of higher education in a larger societal and educational context. Thus family life must be seen as central to the process of educating the whole person, since "the family is the first and

---

10   Pastoral Constitution on the Church in the Modern World, in *The Documents of Vatican II*, ed. Walter M. Abbott, SJ (New York: America Press, 1966), no. 57. (Hereafter all documents from Vatican II will be cited from the Abbott text.)

11   Ibid.

12   Ibid., no. 92.

13   "The Church of the University," *The Pope Speaks*, vol. 27, no. 3, (Fall 1982), 252.

14   Declaration on Christian Education in *Documents of Vatican II*, no. 1.

fundamental school of social living."[15] Moreover, improvement in the quality of higher education is dependent on primary and secondary schools doing a better job of cultivating the intellect, passing on the cultural heritage and fostering constructive values. If students are better prepared by a healthy family life and solid primary and secondary education, institutions of higher learning can attend to their primary purpose, "the passionate and disinterested search for the truth," which makes human beings free and helps them achieve their full humanity in accord with their dignity and worth.[16] The search for truth should also include the ability to handle ethical issues and to achieve a harmonious integration of intellect and will.

19. The church also brings to the dialogue its traditional understanding of wisdom. We believe that the faith community and the institutions of higher learning are involved in a common pursuit of the life of wisdom.[17] There are various interpretations of wisdom, but we agree with those who hold that its pursuit includes discovering the highest principles that integrate all knowledge; uncovering the deepest secrets that constitute human nature; and achieving a personal synthesis in which knowledge and love are ultimately united. For us, the mystery of human existence is fully revealed in Jesus Christ. He reminds us of our profound dignity and our immense potential. He provides us with perspective and teaches by example how love illumines knowledge. The wisdom that we learn from Christ includes the cross, which confounds the wisdom of the world (1 Cor 1:18-24). From the perspective of the cross, we are called to challenge the limitations and contradictions of the world (1 Cor 3:18-23). At the same time, our wisdom tradition includes an understanding of God's mysterious plan to bring all things in the heavens and on earth into unity under the headship of Christ (Eph 1:9-10). The risen Lord has poured out his Spirit on all creation and so we are moved to celebrate truth, goodness and beauty wherever they are to be found. Since no single community can monopolize the gift of wisdom, the church joins with the university and others in the search for wisdom. But when the quest for wisdom is forgotten or diminished, then the church must keep the ideal alive for the good of society. When the so-called wisdom of the world is employed in support of injustice, the church must proclaim the wisdom of the cross, which challenges all oppressive structures. In the church the practical wisdom enunciated by the Hebrew sages is celebrated; the traditional philosophical wisdom is remembered; and the integrating wisdom of faith is proclaimed. For Christians, this whole quest for wisdom finds its summation and final fulfillment in Jesus Christ, who is the wisdom of God (1 Cor 1:24). We are convinced that the Christian wisdom synthesis, merely sketched out here, is a valuable resource in the continuing dialogue between the church and higher education.

20. In a new relationship the church can work with higher education in improving the human community and establishing a culture that enables all human beings to reach their full potential. While admitting our failures in the past, we are concentrating on the future and a new era of cooperation. In the dialogue we expect to

---

15   John Paul II, *On the Family*, (Washington, D.C.: USCC Office of Publishing and Promotion Services, 1982), no. 37.

16   "The Church of the University," 250.

17   Ibid., 252.

learn and benefit from the work of higher education and will contribute our support, experience and insights.

D. Campus Ministry Described and Defined

21. Campus ministry is one of the important ways the church exercises her mission in higher education. Its goals include promoting theological study and reflection on the religious nature of human beings "so that intellectual, moral and spiritual growth can proceed together; sustaining a Christian community on campus, with the pastoral care and liturgical worship it requires; integration of its apostolic ministry with other ministries of the local community and the diocese; and helping the Christian community on campus to serve its members and others, including the many non-students who gravitate toward the university."[18] Campus ministry gathers the Catholics on campus for prayer, worship and learning in order that they might bring the light of the Gospel to illumine the concerns and hopes of the academic community. All the members of the church on campus are called, according to their own gifts, to share in this ministry, guided by the professional campus ministers. "The work of campus ministry requires continual evaluation of traditional methods of ministry and also new approaches which are licitly and responsibly employed. These latter can be highly appropriate in the campus setting, where there exists an audience receptive to the kind of sound innovation which may in the future prove beneficial to the larger Catholic community."[19] Such creativity has produced great diversity in organization, style and approach, as campus ministers strive to form a searching, believing, loving, worshiping Catholic presence on campus. With this diversity in mind, campus ministry can be defined as the public presence and service through which properly prepared baptized persons are empowered by the Spirit to use their talents and gifts on behalf of the church in order to be sign and instrument of the kingdom in the academic world. The eye of faith discerns campus ministry where commitment to Christ and care for the academic world meet in purposeful activity to serve and realize the kingdom of God.

III. PERSONS WHO SERVE ON CAMPUS

A. The Baptized

22. The church carries out its pastoral mission to the academic world both through its communal life and through the Christian witness of its individual members. "The baptized by the generation and anointing of the Holy Spirit are consecrated as a spiritual house and a holy priesthood" (cf. 1 Pt 2:4-5), in order that through all their works they may "proclaim the power of him who has called them out of darkness into his marvelous light."[20] All the faithful on campus, by virtue of their baptism, share

---

18   "To Teach as Jesus Did," no. 67.

19   Ibid., no. 69.

20   Dogmatic Constitution on the Church, in *Documents of Vatican II*, no. 10.

in the task of bringing the humanizing light of the Gospel to bear on the life of the academic community. They are called to live out Christian values while engaging in the teaching, learning, research, public service and campus life that constitute the academic world. They are united with other believers in this work but make their own unique contributions, according to their personal talents and specific circumstances." As generous distributors of God's manifold grace, put your gifts at the service of one another" (1 Pt 4:10). The Second Vatican Council further specified this scriptural teaching: "From the reception of these charisms or gifts, including those which are less dramatic, there arise for each believer the right and duty to use them in the church and in the world for the good of (humankind) and for the upbuilding of the church."[21] Thus, all the baptized members of the academic community have the opportunity and the obligation, according to their unique talents and situations, to join with others to help higher education reach its full potential.

23. The faithful are called not only to bring Christian witness to the academic world, but also to exercise their baptismal prerogatives by helping to build up the church on campus. While many persons today generously contribute their time, talent and experience to the faith community, Catholic faculty, staff and administration have a unique opportunity and calling to lead and direct campus ministry programs, according to their gifts. These individuals are particularly needed on the many campuses throughout the country where no campus ministry programs presently exist. This contribution is enhanced when individuals take time to prepare themselves through prayer and study for this work. In Section 4 of this letter, perspectives and strategies will be enunciated to guide the various aspects of campus ministry. We hope that students, including the large number of older students,[22] administrators, faculty members and all who are concerned with higher education will be able to make creative applications to their own situations based on the conviction that the Spirit moves among all the people of God, prompting them, according to their own talents, to discern anew the signs of the times and to interpret them boldly in the light of the faith.[23]

B. Professional Campus Ministers

24. Some members of the church on campus are called to lead the faith community. Ideally these men and women are professionally trained and exercise the kind of leadership that serves and empowers others. As officially appointed campus ministers, they are sent to form the faith community so that it can be a genuine sign and instrument of the kingdom. Their task is to identify, call forth and coordinate the diverse gifts of the Spirit possessed by all the members of the faith community. Their challenge is to educate all the baptized to appreciate their own calls to service and to create a climate where initiative is encouraged and contributions are appreciated. One of the most important functions of campus ministers is to provide a vision and a sense of overall direction that will encourage and guide the other members to

---

21 Decree on the Apostolate of the Laity, in *Documents of Vatican II*, no. 3.

22 Over two-fifths of the current student population are 25 years of age or over. See footnote 3.

23 "Called and Gifted: The American Catholic Laity," in *Pastoral Letters*, vol. 4, 1975-1983, no. 19.

contribute to the well-being of the academic community and the church on campus. If they understand their own family relationships in a faith perspective, they will be able to help others who are trying to improve the quality of their family lives. Setting up programs that embody this vision is a concrete way of encouraging others and of demonstrating what can be done with cooperative efforts. The goal of this style of leadership is to multiply the centers of activity and to unleash the creative power of the Spirit so that the community of faith can be an authentic sign and instrument of the kingdom.

25. Some professional campus ministers exercise the universal priesthood based on baptism, and others are ordained priests or deacons through the sacrament of holy orders. It is a sign of hope that a growing number of lay people serve as leaders in the faith community on campus. We commend members of religious orders who continue to make important contributions by gathering and encouraging the faithful. It is of historical significance that women, "who in the past have not always been allowed to take their proper role in the church's ministry"[24] find greater opportunities on campus to exercise their leadership abilities. Deacons often possess special talents and important life experiences that enhance their leadership skills. We encourage the priests who help form the faith community in a great variety of ways. Their prayerful celebration of the Eucharist, which invites active participation and manifests the unity of the congregation, as well as their compassionate celebration of the sacrament of reconciliation are especially important. All those officially appointed to lead the church on campus have a great responsibility to form vibrant communities of faith and an exciting challenge to bring forth the gifts of individual believers.

26. In order to meet these challenges, campus ministers often form teams which provide a broader base of leadership to the faith community. Individual members bring their unique personalities and gifts to the team and work cooperatively to set direction and carry out some programs. The team members are co-responsible for the well-being of the faith community and accountable in their own areas of activity and competency. At the same time they have the support of their colleagues when needed. Praying together helps the men and women on the team to keep in mind the true source and goal of their mission and to experience a sense of solidarity. We encourage the formation of such team ministries, which serve as models of ministry and community for the rest of the church.

27. There are certain general challenges faced by all campus ministers. To be effective, ministers must attend to their own spiritual development. Campus ministers who are serious about their prayer life and can speak openly about their relationship to God will be able to direct others. Ministers who have wrestled with the great questions of meaning, purpose and identity can offer helpful guidance to other genuine searchers. Those who have appropriated the faith and mined the riches of the Catholic heritage will be in a better position to invite others to join the faith community. If they genuinely care about the weak and the oppressed, they will inspire others to work for social justice. Finally, campus ministers who have achieved an integration of faith and culture will naturally serve as role models for

---

24   Ibid., no. 27.

students and faculty members who are trying to achieve a similar synthesis. In summation, the leaders of the faith community must be perceived as persons who know the struggles of life and who are working to develop themselves spiritually.

28. Campus ministers are also called to empower the faith community and its individual members in the task of helping their colleges or universities to reach their full potential. Ministers who have a genuine respect for academic life and for institutions of higher education will see clearly the importance of this work and find creative ways to respond. A healthy self-confidence will enable them to relate openly with faculty members and administrators and to empathize with students who are struggling with their personal growth. By gaining the respect and confidence of the various members of the academic community, they will find many ways to get involved on campus and promote human values in the institution. Campus ministers with solid training and good credentials will have more opportunities to enter into the mainstream of academic life on campus. Today it is clear that campus ministers must not remain on the margins of the academic community, but must accept the call to bring the light of the Gospel to the very center of that world.

29. To prepare for meeting all these challenges, we encourage campus ministers to take responsibility for their own personal and professional development. Clear contractual arrangements that include carefully defined expectations and procedures for accountability and evaluation help to set a proper framework for their personal enrichment. Membership in appropriate professional organizations, participation in activities on diocesan, regional and national levels, involvement in support groups with other campus ministers and regular interaction with a spiritual director can provide motivation and direction for improving their performance. If campus ministers are to remain flexible in response to the rapidly changing needs of the campus community, they need to study contemporary developments in scripture and theology while deepening their knowledge of the Christian tradition. Attaining an advanced degree or achieving competency in a particular area not only contributes to professional development, but helps gain respect in the academic world. Today skills in counseling and spiritual direction, as well as knowledge of family systems and life cycles, group dynamics and adult education, are especially valuable for leaders of the faith community. An understanding of the nature and dynamics of the academic world enables campus ministers to apply Christian teachings and values more effectively.

30. In addition to these common challenges, campus ministers find that the unique situations of their particular campuses create their own concerns and opportunities. For example, campus ministers at community colleges must respond to the needs of students who live at home and have jobs. They often need assistance in defining their roles and responsibilities in the home. Many students are married and are present on campus only for their classes. Some ministers have been able in these situations to form small faith communities around shared prayer or social action projects. At these two-year colleges, the ministry of presence is especially important, as is securing the support and active involvement of interested faculty members. These institutions are often open to the addition of religious courses into the curriculum. Skills in marriage and career counseling are especially valuable. It is important for these campus ministers to maintain close relationships with

neighboring parishes because that is where many students will find their primary faith community.

31. It is possible also to identify other particular challenges. Campus ministers on private denominational campuses must be especially attentive to the ecumenical dimension. Those who work primarily with minority students, including recently arrived immigrants, refugees and international students, must be in touch with their cultural background and family experiences, as well as the unique challenges they face in the academic world. Large state schools produce logistical problems for campus ministers in handling so many students. On commuter campuses, making contact with students is difficult in itself. All of these particular challenges represent opportunities for creative ministry.

32. Professional campus ministers are crucial to the work of the church on campus. They bear the heavy responsibility of guiding the faith community and empowering others to assist in the task of helping higher education reach its full potential. The extent and intensity of these demands remind them that they must gather others to assist them. They should expect support and guidance from the diocesan director of campus ministry, who is the usual liaison with the bishop and the local diocese. The director can help facilitate their personal growth, call for a proper accountability and possible diocesan-wide programming. As the diocesan bishop's representative, the director encourages the interaction among campus ministers in the diocese who serve on public, Catholic and other private campuses. We recognize our responsibility as bishops to offer all campus ministers moral support, to provide financial assistance to the degree this is needed and possible, and to help them achieve the competency they need to be effective witnesses of the Gospel.

IV. ASPECTS OF CAMPUS MINISTRY

33. After situating campus ministry in the relationship between the church and higher education and discussing the persons who perform this service, we now turn our attention to six aspects of campus ministry. These ministerial functions reflect the general mission of the church on campus and the distinctive situation of higher education today. In its ministry the faith community on campus must be faithful to the essential teachings of the church and, at the same time, read the signs of the times and accordingly adapt the message of the Gospel to meet the needs of the academic community.[25]

A. Forming the Faith Community

1. COMMUNITY AND ALIENATION ON CAMPUS

34. Campus ministry attempts to form faith communities in an academic environment that knows both a healthy sense of solidarity and a good deal of alienation. Ideally, colleges and universities gather teachers and students together into a community of shared values and common dedication to the pursuit of truth. In fact, on

---

25   The Church in the Modern World, no. 44.

campuses there is a good deal of collaborative effort. Organizations abound, close friendships are formed, interest groups gather the like-minded. Many administrators, faculty members and students move easily in this world and find that it satisfies their needs for companionship and involvement. Many Christians freely gather into communities of faith in which they share their strengths and gifts with others.

35. On the other hand, lonely voices on campus cry out for intimacy, and mildly estranged individuals express a desire for more personal interaction. Students who leave home and come to large universities often feel lost in the vast impersonal world. The world of research and scholarship can seem cold and demeaning to graduate students. Commuter students who are on campus only briefly for classes do not have the opportunity to form close bonds with others. Some sense of alienation seems inevitable for international students who must cope with a new culture. Recently arrived immigrant and refugee students experience the isolation and loneliness of being separated from family and homeland. Older students worry about fitting in and being accepted and, at times, have the added complication of marital and family pressures. Even students in small private colleges can experience a lack of depth in their relationships and a consequent sense of estrangement. Complaints are also heard from faculty members about the superficiality of their relationships with close colleagues and the lack of opportunities for interaction with those in other departments. Some feel cut off from the centers of power, as important academic decisions are made without their input. The difficulty of gathering students for anything except social events and concerts is a continuing problem for student-affairs leaders. Administrators speak openly about the fragmentation of campus life and search for ways to overcome it. The voices of estrangement are many and varied. Campus ministers who listen well know that there is a genuine hunger for community in the academic world, as well as a strong sense of solidarity.

2. THE IMPORTANCE OF CHRISTIAN COMMUNITY

36. The call to form communities of faith flows both from the very nature of the Gospel itself and from the pastoral situation on campus. Christianity is ecclesial by its very nature. The communal character of salvation is already clear in the Hebrew Scriptures: "It has pleased God, however, to make (human beings) holy and save them not merely as individuals without any mutual bonds, but by making them into a single people, a people which acknowledges him in truth and serves him in holiness."[26] This truth was exemplified in the life of Jesus Christ who, led by the Spirit, gathered together a community of followers. The Twelve served as official witnesses of his saving mission and symbolic representation of the new people of God. Through his striking parables and miraculous signs he proclaimed the kingdom in which all human beings, animated by the Spirit, were to live in peace and harmony. The death and resurrection of Jesus brought a new outpouring of the Spirit which "makes the church grow, perpetually renews her and leads her to perfect union with her Spouse."[27] Under the influence of the Spirit, the church

---

26   Dogmatic Constitution on the Church, no. 9.

27   Ibid., no. 4.

remembers the prayer of Jesus that "all may be one, Father, as you are in me and I am in you, so that the world may believe" (Jn 17:21). All the baptized, empowered by the Spirit, share responsibility for forming the church into a genuine community of worship and service. Guided by the Holy Spirit, the church is called, with all of its limitations and sinfulness, to wend its way through history as the visible sign of the unity of the whole human family and as an instrument of reconciliation for all.[28]

37. Today the church on campus is challenged to be a credible sign of unity and a living reminder of the essential interdependence and solidarity of all people. Thus, the faith community seeks to gather those who wish to serve others and to bring healing to those in the academic world who are restricted by artificial barriers and wounded by alienating practices. The church gains credibility when the dream of community produces genuine commitment and intelligent effort. In the ideal community of faith, the mystery that rules over our lives is named and worshiped. Dedication to Christ is fostered, and openness to all truth, goodness and beauty is maintained. The life of the Spirit is nourished and discussed. Positive images of God, Christ, Mary and the afterlife warm the heart and structure the imagination. The common good is emphasized and personal development encouraged. Individuals experience true freedom and at the same time accept responsibility for the well-being of the group. Traditional wisdom is available, and the best contemporary insights are valued. Prayerful liturgies enable us to praise God with full hearts and create a sense of belonging, as well as nourish people for a life of service. Members are known by name and newcomers are welcomed. Unity of faith is celebrated, while legitimate pluralism is recognized. Individuals find both support and challenge and can share their joys and sorrows. The members hunger for justice and have the courage to fight the dehumanizing tendencies in the culture. The community knows the sorrows of life, but remains a people of hope. In this ideal community of faith, the members are of one heart and mind (Acts 4:32) and receive the spirit of wisdom which brings them to full knowledge of Jesus Christ, who is the head of the church (Eph 1:17-23).

38. By working toward the dream of genuine community, campus ministry unleashes human potential and contributes to the common struggle against the forces of alienation. A church serious about building community reminds others of the beauty and nobility of a life lived in harmony and peace. The baptized who experience acceptance, healing and empowerment in the faith community are better prepared to bring an understanding ear, a reconciling touch and an encouraging voice to alienated persons on campus.

3. THE CHALLENGE OF FORMING THE FAITH COMMUNITY

39. When the dream of a genuine faith community is alive, then the search for effective strategies is intensified. Attitudes are crucial. Campus ministers whose personal outreach is warm and welcoming are likely to gain the active participation of others in the community. The ministry of presence, in which leaders of the faith community make themselves available by being on campus regularly and getting

---

28   Ibid., no. 48.

involved in activities and events, is a valuable way of making initial contact with potential members of the faith community and of enhancing existing relationships. Administrators, faculty members and students who sense that they are valued as persons and that their talents and initiatives are appreciated will find involvement more attractive.

40. On many campuses Mass and communion services have proven to be powerful means of building community. Ministers who put a great deal of effort into preparing liturgies that are in accord with the church's liturgical directives and are prayerful, coherent and aesthetically pleasing generally find an enthusiastic response. If they keep in mind the sensibilities of the academic community and strive for wide participation, the broad use of legitimate liturgical options and a flexible style, the inherent community-building power of the Eucharist is enhanced. There is a greater recognition today that stimulating homilies that apply the Gospel realistically and convey positive religious images are especially important in fostering genuine religious conversion and a sense of closeness to the worshiping community and the church as a whole.[29] It is a sign of hope for the future that so many collegians are gaining a deeper appreciation of the power of the Eucharist to raise the mind and heart to God and to serve as "a sacrament of love, a sign of unity, a bond of charity."[30]

41. In many sacramentally oriented campus ministries, the adult catechumenate process has become an especially valuable means of incorporating new members into the Catholic Church and strengthening the faith of those who are already members. As a result, the Catholic faith community becomes stronger, more attractive and inviting. The presence of adults who have freely chosen to join the church moves some members to think more deeply about their own relationships to the church. Those who serve as sponsors often gain a new appreciation of their faith and a renewed sense of the church as a community of committed believers. A community will attract newcomers as more and more of its members demonstrate enthusiasm for the faith and an attractive style of Christian living.

42. On other campuses, different forms of community building predominate. For example, campus ministers at some commuter colleges form community through Bible study programs.

Through personal contact, they gather together faculty members and students for shared reading and discussion of the Scriptures. This leads into group prayer and joint projects to serve others. Such programs reveal the power of the Scriptures to call individuals out of their isolation and to give them a sense of solidarity as they struggle to live out the Christian life in the academic world.

43. The experience of Christian community on campus is important to the life of the whole church. Students who have such a positive experience and are taught their responsibilities to the larger church will continue to be a very valuable resource for family, parish and diocesan life when they leave school. Campus ministers can prepare for this by maintaining good ties with local parishes and giving students the opportunity to be of service there.

---

29   Fee et. al., *Young Catholics* (New York: William H. Sadlier, Inc., 1980), 154-55.

30   Constitution on the Sacred Liturgy, in *Documents of Vatican II*, no. 47.

44. Building up the community of faith on campus is the responsibility of all baptized persons. The desire to serve and the hunger for community must be tapped. Individuals who are personally invited to join in this task and given freedom and encouragement to use their gifts and talents for the benefit of the community are more likely to respond. It is the duty of leaders to provide vision and encourage others to accept their responsibilities. The task of forming Christian communities on campus encounters great difficulties but also brings deep satisfaction. This crucial aspect of campus ministry is worthy of vigorous and creative efforts so that the Catholic community can be an authentic sign and instrument of the kingdom on campus.

B. Appropriating the Faith

1. THE CHALLENGES TO FAITH ON CAMPUS

45. Campus ministry has the task of enabling Catholics to achieve a more adult appropriation of their faith so that they can live in greater communion with God and the church, give more effective witness to the Gospel and face the challenges to belief that exist in the academic world. In the classroom, students learn to question traditional assumptions and to tolerate diverse opinions on important questions that cause some to doubt their religious beliefs. Most students eventually encounter the modern critics of religion, who charge that belief is either infantile or dehumanizing. In some classes, the scientific method that has advanced human learning so effectively is presented as a total world view which supplants religion and renders obsolete other approaches to truth. Some professors give the impression that maturation involves rejection of religious beliefs. In these and other ways the academic world challenges the traditional belief systems of many students.

46. Campus life tends to reinforce these intellectual challenges. Catholic students at times find their faith shaken by encountering peers who profess widely divergent world views and lifestyles. Today a significant number of Catholics are attracted away from their religious heritage by fundamentalist groups that employ aggressive proselytizing tactics and promise clear answers and instant security in the midst of a frightening and complex world. When students learn more about the harsh realities of life and the monstrous evils that have been part of human history, they are at times forced to question their belief in a God who seems callous in allowing such human suffering. Finally, the whirl of campus life, with its exhilarating freedom and the pressure of making good grades, can so dominate the attention of students that they drift away from their faith without much real thought.

47. Many Catholics on campus, including faculty members, are unprepared to deal with intellectual challenges to the faith. They are unable to explain their belief to interested friends or to defend it against attacks by hostile critics. Their understanding of the faith has not kept pace with their knowledge in other areas. The legitimate pluralism of theology and spirituality in the church confuses them. They have not achieved an adult appropriation of their religion that would enable them to speak about it not only with conviction, but also with intelligence. At times this produces frustration and anger over the inadequacy of their religious training.

48. These problems are intensified by the general religious illiteracy in our culture. Public education is not committed to passing on the religious heritage. Many good people do not recognize the importance of religious knowledge for a well-rounded education. Most colleges and universities still do not have departments or programs of religious studies nor do they provide adequate opportunities to explore the religious dimension of various disciplines in the curriculum. In the academic world there are still those who think that teaching about religion necessarily involves proselytizing and that it cannot be done in an academically sound way. This attitude compounds the problems of campus ministers, who seek to promote a more mature appropriation of the faith among Catholics.

49. On the positive side, the challenges on campus prompt some Catholics to explore and deepen their belief. Doubts, which are frequently a part of faith development, at times lead to further study and renewed convictions. The academic world provides intellectual stimulation and helpful resources for those who want to explore their religious tradition. There is a growing interest in religious studies and an increase in programs and courses around the country. Some public institutions have excellent departments or programs in religious studies that demonstrate that this can be done legally and according to proper academic standards. Today within the academic community a few voices are heard insisting that a well-educated person should have a knowledge of religion. At some institutions, campus ministry has produced excellent programs in theological studies that supplement the offerings in the curriculum through a wide variety of credit and non-credit courses, seminars and lectures. The faculty members and students who have achieved a more mature appropriation of their faith provide important witness on campus and are a sign of hope in the struggle against religious illiteracy.

2. PRINCIPLES FOR APPROPRIATING THE FAITH

50. By its very nature, Christianity calls us to an ever-deeper understanding and appreciation of our faith. Baptism initiates us into a lifelong process in which we are gradually formed anew in the image of our Creator and thus grow in knowledge (Col. 3:10). The Scriptures remind us that this process means moving beyond childish ways to more mature approaches: "Let us, then, be children no longer, tossed here and there, carried about by every wind of doctrine that originates in human trickery and skill in proposing error. Rather, let us profess the truth in love and grow to the full maturity of Christ the head" (Eph 4:14-16). The Scriptures also call us to move beyond illusion to a deeper way of thinking and relating to God: "You must lay aside your former way of life and the old self which deteriorates through illusion and desire, and acquire a fresh, spiritual way of thinking" (Eph 4:22-23). Members of the faith community who achieve a more mature grasp of their Christian faith are in a better position to understand themselves and their world. Those who continue their theological education are better able to reflect on their experiences in the light of the Gospel. By assimilating the meanings and values in the Christian tradition, believers are better equipped to affirm the positive meanings and values in the culture and to resist those who are opposed to the Gospel. Individuals who are well grounded in their own Catholic heritage are better prepared to enter into

ecumenical and interfaith dialogue and cooperation. The Second Vatican Council reminded us that Christians have the task of achieving "a public, persistent and universal presence in the whole enterprise of advancing higher culture."[31] The council called upon Christians to "shoulder society's heavier burdens and to witness the faith to the world."[32] Those best qualified for this great work are the believers who have understood the implications of their faith and are able to articulate their deepest beliefs. The Scriptures offer us this advice: "Should anyone ask you the reason for this hope of yours, be ever ready to reply, but speak gently and respectfully" (1 Pt 3:15-16). To respond credibly, intelligently and sensitively to honest inquiry requires careful and systematic preparation. All the members of the community of faith have a right to the kind of theological education that prepares them to meet this responsibility.[33] When we consider the demands of the academic world, it is clear that the church on campus has a special responsibility to enable all of its members to appropriate the faith more deeply in order to give effective witness to the academic community.

51. The importance of achieving an intelligent appropriation of the faith can also be established by examining the nature and purpose of education. As we have noted elsewhere, "a truly liberating and elevating education is incomplete without the study of theology or religion."[34] We must continue to encourage the study of religion in our society as a whole because, as Cardinal Newman insisted, religious truth has an inherent value and is "not only a portion but a condition of general knowledge."[35] Educated persons should know something of the history, teachings and practices of the various world religions and be especially versed in the Judeo-Christian tradition, which shaped Western civilization in general and our own culture in particular. Furthermore, they should be aware of the religious aspects of other disciplines, such as literature, history and art, as well as the religious dimension of our contemporary culture.[36]

52. Traditionally, theology has been known to the church as the "queen of the sciences." Today we must emphasize its continuing power to keep alive the great questions of meaning, purpose and identity and to provide a coherent vision of life which serves as a framework and unifying principle for all learning. Theological study helps to produce the kind of intellect described by Cardinal Newman, "which cannot be partial, cannot be exclusive, cannot be impetuous, cannot be at a loss, cannot but be patient, collected and majestically calm, because it discerns the end in every delay; because it ever knows where it stands, and how its path lies from one

---

31   Declaration on Christian Education, no. 10.

32   Ibid.

33   Ibid., no. 2.

34   "Catholic Higher Education," no. 22. In this regard it is important to distinguish theology, which involves a faith perspective and commitment, from religious studies, which can proceed in a more neutral fashion.

35   Cardinal John Henry Newman, *The Idea of a University* (Garden City, N.Y.: Image Books, 1959), 103.

36   "Catholic Higher Education," no. 22.

point to another."[37] The study of theology not only helps us gain this kind of perspective, but also helps us to understand in greater depth Jesus Christ, who reveals to us the secrets of the Father. In a well-rounded Christian education, the teachings of the church are presented with fidelity to the magisterium and with the contemporary situation in mind. This kind of solid theological training enables the members of the faith community to achieve a genuine synthesis of their rich religious heritage and the best in the contemporary culture.

53. A Christian faith that fails to seek a more mature understanding is not faithful to its own inner dynamism. A culture that is unaware of its religious roots and substance is impoverished and weakened. Educated Christians who have not grown beyond an adolescent level of faith development are limited in their ability to achieve personal integration and to make a contribution to society. These dangers remind campus ministry to maintain its dedication to forming the best possible learning community. The goal is that all of the members of the community achieve a deep understanding of their faith so that they are better prepared to witness to the kingdom of truth in the world.

3. STRATEGIES FOR APPROPRIATING THE FAITH

54. In order to move toward these goals it is vital that campus ministry creates a climate in which theological learning is respected. Campus ministers help to produce this climate by reminding all the members that they need an adult appropriation of the faith that matches their learning in other areas in order to function as effective Christians in the world. This message is strengthened if the campus ministers are perceived as being serious about continuing their own theological education. The presence of faculty members and students who are already finding enlightenment and satisfaction in theological studies is a powerful motivation for others. A tradition of pursuing theological learning must be established, in which all the members sense their responsibility to achieve a more mature understanding of their faith.

55. If the faith community shares this broad appreciation of the importance of religious studies, then individual programs are more likely to be successful. Program planners should be aware of the courses on campus that deal with religious matters, as well as the current needs and interests of faculty and students. For example, the existence on campus of an increasing number of fundamentalist groups has intensified the need for Scripture courses that combine the historical-critical method with opportunities for personal application and shared prayer. Such courses tap the current interest in relating the Scriptures to everyday life and prepare members of the faith community to deal with the aggressive recruiting methods employed by some fundamentalist groups. In general, campus ministry should supplement the religious offerings in the curriculum and provide a wide variety of opportunities for Catholics to study and appropriate their religious heritage and to reflect critically on their experiences in the light of the Gospel.

56. Effective strategies must deal realistically with the situations of the targeted audiences. Theological studies can be made more attractive for students by arranging

---

37   Newman, *The Idea of a University*, 159.

credit for courses offered by the campus ministry program. For example, through a theologian-in-residence program, students on a state university campus could gain academic credit from a nearby Catholic college for theology courses taught at the campus ministry center on the state campus. Programs for faculty members and administrators must respect their vast experience while, at the same time, taking into account their general lack of systematic theological training.

57. Campus ministry has the responsibility not only to provide theological education for Catholics, but also to work with others to improve the response of higher education to the problem of religious illiteracy in our culture. The key to making progress in this area is to overcome the unfortunate assumption that the study of religion cannot be a genuine academic discipline. The academic community must be shown that religion is worthy of careful and systematic study because it is central to human existence and is an important wellspring of our culture. Professors who deal with religious questions in their courses can help to overcome this bias by teaching this material according to rigorous academic standards of objectivity and with obvious respect for op-posing opinions. If the bias against religion as an academic subject can be overcome, then a variety of positive steps might be possible, such as establishing a religious studies program, organizing a lectureship devoted to religious questions and founding an endowed chair for Catholic thought. If the climate on campus were more open, then campus ministers with advanced degrees might find opportunities to teach part time in appropriate departments or programs. Even if some of these larger initiatives are not possible, campus ministers still can provide a valuable service for students by identifying the courses on campus in which the religious aspect is treated well and fairly.

58. In the faith community it is understood that religious literacy is for the well-being of society and that theological learning is for the sake of a deepened faith. The goal is an adult appropriation of the faith that fosters personal commitment to Christ and encourages intelligent witness in the world on behalf of the Gospel.

C. Forming the Christian Conscience

1. MORAL RELATIVISM ON CAMPUS

59. The church on campus must facilitate the formation of a Christian conscience in its members so that they can make decisions based on gospel values and thereby resist moral relativism. Many questions of personal values and ethics inevitably arise for individuals in the academic community. Students are concerned with the moral dimension of such matters as relating to family members, abortion, sexual conduct, drinking and drugs, forming friendships, honesty in their studies and pursuing a career. At times faculty members experience a conflict of values as they try to balance their research and teaching and attempt to remain objective in the classroom while expressing their personal opinions. Their integrity can be tested as they fight against grade inflation and struggle to maintain academic freedom, while accepting external funding for research. Individual courses often produce particular ethical and value questions. This occurs in obvious ways in philosophy, literature and the life sciences, and in more subtle ways in the physical sciences and technology

courses. For example, a computer course may be based on assumptions about human nature that need to be discussed. Ethical questions also arise in relation to institutional policies and practices, such as whether a particular college or university is demonstrating a proper respect and care for the athletes it recruits and utilizes.

60. As members of the academic community deal with these questions, they unavoidably come under the influence of the moral climate that dominates their particular college or university. The eyes of faith discern in the academic world as a whole the predictable mixture of grace and sin that characterizes all institutions. On the one hand, the climate is shaped by high idealism, dedicated service, a long tradition of civil discourse, great tolerance for opposing views, sensitive care for individuals, hard work and a deep love for freedom. Examples of personal virtue are evident in students who resist intense peer pressure and maintain their high moral standards; in faculty members who make financial sacrifices to stay in the academic world and who carry on their teaching and research with responsibility and integrity; in administrators who consistently speak the truth and treat all members of the academic community humanely. Organizations and groups often help raise the moral tone of the campus by being involved in charitable activities and espousing high ideals. In some fields such as business, medicine, law and the life sciences, more courses are being offered that deal with ethical questions. Periodically a wave of idealism sweeps our campuses which reminds us of the great potential for goodness in the academic community.

61. On the other hand, Christians recognize in the academic world a strong strain of moral relativism that tends to reduce genuine freedom to license and an open-minded tolerance to mindlessness. Rational discourse about ethical questions degenerates into nothing more than sharing personal feelings. Sin is reduced to neurosis or blamed on societal pressures. The project of forming a healthy conscience is neglected in favor of a selfish individualism. In this climate some persons assume that it is impossible or useless to make judgments about whether particular actions are right or wrong, whether some values are better than others and whether certain patterns of behavior are constructive or destructive.

62. If this philosophy predominates on campus, Catholics are hard pressed to maintain their values and principles. They find it harder to mount an effective critique of institutional practices that violate the high ideals of higher education and fail to respect the dignity of human beings. Young adults who are moving through various stages of moral development are often confused by mixed messages and conflicting philosophies. Students must contend with peer pressures to enter into the drug scene, to cheat on exams, to engage in promiscuous sexual activity, to have abortions and, in general, to adopt a hedonistic lifestyle. Some older students find that their commitments to spouses and families are called into question. Faculty members and administrators at times experience subtle pressures to go along with morally questionable institutional policies and practices.

2. CONSCIENCE IN A CATHOLIC PERSPECTIVE

63. In this situation, campus ministry has the crucial task of assisting in the formation of Catholic consciences so that individuals who will continue to face very

complex ethical issues throughout their lives are prepared to make good moral judgments according to gospel values. The Scriptures remind us: "Do not conform your-
self to this age but be transformed by the renewal of your mind so that you may judge
what is God's will, what is good, pleasing and perfect" (Rom 12:2). Conscience formation involves just such a transforming renewal of mind in accord with the will of
God.[38] For conscience is that "most secret core and sanctuary of a person where one
is close with God."[39] There we hear the voice of God echoing in the depths of our
being and calling us to heed the law written on our hearts. As Cardinal Newman
wrote in the last century: "Conscience does not repose on itself, but vaguely reaches
forward to something beyond itself and dimly discerns a sanction higher than self
for its decisions, as is evidenced in that keen sense of obligation and responsibility
which informs them."[40] "Conscience then, though it is inviolable, is not a law unto
itself."[41] It is rather through our conscience that we detect a call from God, sum-
moning us to love the good and avoid evil. It is in response to this call, heard in the
secret recesses of our hearts, that we make the judgments of conscience required by
the concrete circumstances of our daily lives. This requires an informed conscience,
one nourished in prayer, enlightened by study, structured by the Gospel and guided
by the teachings of the church. Self-deception is all too easy; blindness and illusion
can easily mislead us. "Beloved, do not trust every spirit, but put the spirits to a test
to see if they belong to God" (1 Jn 4:1). Thus we need the community of faith to
challenge our illusions and to call us to greater self-honesty.

64. In emphasizing the objective call from God, mediated through the church,
we do not want to lose sight of the fact that the divine summons must be answered
freely and intelligently. "Morality, then, is not simply something imposed on us
from without, but is ingrained in our being; it is the way we accept our humanity
as restored to us in Christ."[42] Thus all human beings are bound to follow their conscience faithfully in order that they may set the course of their lives directly toward
God.[43] We are freely responsible for ourselves and cannot shift that burden to anyone else. We come to the full measure of freedom by putting on the mind of Christ.
When Christ freed us, he meant us to remain free (Gal. 5:1). By preaching Christ
and his message of freedom, the community of faith seeks to inform the consciences
of all of its members. The Christian who possesses a conscience structured by the
Gospel of Christ and who is guided by the continuing presence of Christ's spirit in
the church is better prepared to deal with the rapidly changing complexities of the
world today. When genuine virtue is acquired, then good actions flow more spon-
taneously and new strength is found to live according to one's ideals. Individuals
whose conscience has been tutored by the Gospel understand that their task is not
only to resist evil but to help transform the world.

---

38   The Church in the Modern World, no. 16.

39   Ibid.

40   Cited in "The Church in Our Day," in *Pastoral Letters*, vol. 3, 1962-1974, no. 205.

41   Ibid., no. 206.

42   "To Live in Christ Jesus," in *Pastoral Letters*, vol. 4, 1975-1983, no. 22.

43   Declaration on Religious Freedom, in *Documents of Vatican II*, no. 3.

65. This portrayal of the informed Christian conscience stands in stark contrast to moral relativism. If morality is based on the call of God, then it cannot be totally arbitrary. Moral relativism betrays the essential structure of human persons, who are ultimately dependent on a God who calls all of us to account. A conscience that remembers its source and is nourished and supported by the community of faith is the best resource for dealing with the complex questions of personal values and ethics.

3. METHODS OF CONSCIENCE FORMATION

66. Campus ministry is called to bring the Gospel of Christ to bear on the moral problems faced by members of the academic community. This can be done by personal encounters such as spiritual direction and counseling, as well as through homilies, classes and seminars. When campus ministers address these questions, it is vital that they are perceived as being in touch with the texture and complexities of the moral problems generated by campus life. They also must have a working knowledge of the wisdom found in the Catholic tradition on particular moral questions. A good way for campus ministers to multiply their effectiveness is by facilitating peer-ministry programs in which individuals who have successfully dealt with particular moral problems can help others in similar situations. For example, a senior athlete who managed to keep a healthy perspective on sports and maintain good grades could be prepared to speak with other athletes struggling to keep their values intact in highly pressurized situations. Students who have freed themselves from the drug scene could help others interested in breaking their drug habits. For older students struggling to keep their marriages together, conversations with faculty members who kept their commitments in similar circumstances could be mutually beneficial in enriching their married lives. In all such peer-ministry approaches, it is important that those serving others are well prepared through a proper grounding in gospel ideals and church teachings on these moral questions. Engaging members of the faith community in such peer-ministry programs is a valuable way of extending the effort to form Christian consciences.

67. Courses or seminars provide a more structured approach to the formation of conscience. For example, undergraduate students can be gathered for a seminar on the question of premarital sex, contraception and abortion. An open atmosphere is needed so that the students can speak freely about the prevailing attitudes and peer pressures on campus, as well as about their own outlooks and modes of decision making. A skillful leader can use the discussion as a basis for bringing out the Christian teaching that insists that sexuality is best understood in terms of personal relationships and that intercourse is a sign of the total commitment associated with marriage. In dealing with this and all areas of personal morality, the Catholic tradition must be presented as containing a wisdom that illuminates the mystery of human existence and encourages behavior that is in the best interest of the individual and society.

68. A good deal of conscience formation must be done on an individual basis. Counseling, spiritual direction and the celebration of the sacrament of reconciliation provide excellent opportunities to apply Christian teachings to an individual's

precise situation and current stage of moral development. Through these means, persons can gradually discover the illusions and destructive patterns that impede the development of a conscience fully attuned to the Gospel.

Such settings also provide the occasion to proclaim the great mercy of our God, who deals patiently with our weaknesses and guides us gradually to full growth in Christ.

69. If campus ministry hopes to deal effectively with questions of personal values and ethics, it must be concerned with the general moral climate on campus. When individuals maintain high moral standards despite pressures, they make an important personal contribution to the moral tone of the academic community. Since colleges and universities have the task of fostering critical thinking and transmitting our cultural heritage, they should include questions of values and ethics in this general mission. Members of the faith community who understand the importance of the moral dimension of life are called to join with others in promoting a more extensive and informed discussion of ethical issues on campus. This can be done in a great variety of ways, such as facilitating an appreciation of the need for courses on ethics in each department and program, encouraging professors to treat the questions of ethics and values that arise in their courses, and sponsoring lectures and seminars on particular moral questions. It is especially helpful to get the whole academic community involved in concentrated discussions. For example, campus ministers could join with other interested groups in sponsoring a "Values and Ethics Week" on campus, designed to deal directly with moral issues. During this week, all professors are encouraged to spend class time discussing the ethical implications of their courses. Informal discussions and structured seminars are arranged throughout the week. In order to give the whole program momentum and status, major speakers are brought in to address current ethical concerns. The important element in these strategies is to move the academic community to carry on its proper task of promoting critical thinking in the area of values and ethics.

D. Educating for Justice

1. THE SEARCH FOR JUSTICE ON CAMPUS

70. Campus ministry is called to make the struggle for social justice an integral part of its mission. The academic world generates questions not only of personal morality but also of social justice, which includes issues of peace and war, as well as reverence for life in all phases of its development. Some questions arise as colleges and universities determine their internal policies and practices. How, for instance, should they balance their concern for quality education with a policy of open access that gives disadvantaged students the opportunity for higher education?[44] Issues also emerge as higher education interacts with other institutions. A prime example is whether universities can maintain their integrity, freedom and a balanced research program while accepting massive funding from the Department of Defense for research

---

44   See the report by the Southern Regional Education Board's Commission for Educational Quality, "Access to Quality Undergraduate Education," *Chronicle of Higher Education*, July 3, 1985, 9 ff.

on weapons systems. Periodically a social justice issue captures the imagination of a significant number of students on campus, producing demonstrations and an appeal for direct action. A more sustained commitment to particular justice issues is demonstrated by some individuals, such as those who remain active in the peace movement over a long period of time and those who maintain the effort to gain legal protection for unborn human life. Such persons of conscience often encounter apathy, misunderstanding and rejection and therefore deserve the special support and encouragement of the church.

71. The academic community could generate intense debate over all these issues. In general terms, some want the university to remain detached from social issues, while others look for more active involvement to achieve a more just society. Most agree that higher education makes a valuable contribution by providing a forum for discussing the great questions of the day in a civil and reasoned fashion so that constructive solutions can be worked out.

72. Finally, it must be admitted that there is a great deal of apathy in evidence on campus today. Many are caught up in their own concerns and have little if any interest in social matters. Others who have been actively involved are now weary of the battles and have retreated into less demanding activities. Most students do not even think in terms of altering unjust structures through political action or social involvement. In general, alongside striking examples of personal commitment to justice, we sense a strong current of individualism that undercuts concern for the common good and eclipses the urgency of social concerns.

2. PRINCIPLES OF CATHOLIC SOCIAL TEACHING

73. Campus ministry is called to be a consistent and vigorous advocate for justice, peace and the reverence for all life. All the baptized should understand that "action on behalf of justice is a significant criterion of the church's fidelity to its missions. It is not optional nor is it the work of only a few in the church. It is something to which all Christians are called according to their vocations, talents and situations in life."[45] With this in mind, campus ministers have the responsibility of keeping alive the vision of the church on campus as a genuine servant community that is dedicated to the works of justice, peace and reverence for life in all stages of its development.

74. As we noted in our pastoral letter on peace, "At the center of all Catholic social teaching are the transcendence of God and the dignity of the human person. The human person is the clearest reflection of God's presence in the world; all of the church's work in pursuit of both justice and peace is designed to protect and promote the dignity of every person. For each person not only reflects God, but is the expression of God's creative work and the meaning of Christ's redemptive ministry."[46] In our day the sanctity of the life of the unborn calls everyone to pro-

---

45 United States Catholic Conference, *Sharing the Light of Faith: National Catechetical Directory for Catholics of the United States* (Washington, D.C.: USCC Office of Publishing and Promotion Services, 1979), no. 160.

46 "The Challenge of Peace: God's Promise and Our Response," in *Pastoral Letters*, vol. 4, 1975-1983, no. 15.

tect vigorously the life of the most defenseless among us. When we reflect further upon Christ's redemptive ministry, we see that he demonstrated a special care for the poor and the outcasts of his society. He came "to bring glad tidings to the poor, to proclaim liberty to the captives" (Lk. 4:18). In identifying himself with suffering persons, he provided us with the strongest motivation to work for justice for all (Mt. 25:31-46). In word and deed Jesus taught us the essential unity between love of God and love of neighbor. His followers understood that if you claim to love God and hate your neighbor, you are a liar (1 Jn 4:20). The Gospel he proclaimed and the Spirit he sent were to transform and renew all of human existence, the social and institutional dimensions as well as the personal.[47] This analysis suggests a rationale for the commitment to justice, a rationale that should be known and understood by all members of the church.

75. In the struggle for justice we need Christians who understand that "knowledge of economics and politics will not in itself bring about justice, unless it is activated by human and religious ideals. However, religious ideals without the necessary secular expertise will not provide the kind of leadership needed to influence our complex society."[48] The faith community on campus, which includes individuals with significant academic achievements, is especially well-equipped to achieve the integration of an informed faith with knowledge and skill in the social arena. To accomplish this there must be great emphasis on "teaching and learning the tradition of Catholic social thought, the creation of an environment for learning that reflects a commitment to justice and an openness on the part of all Catholics to change personal attitudes and behavior."[49] We call special attention to the coherent body of Catholic social thought developed during the past century in papal encyclicals and reflected in our pastoral letters.[50] It is especially important for Catholics on campus to assimilate these teachings and to use them in their work for justice.

76. As the faith community carries on this educational task, it must remember that the goal is not learning alone, but constructive action to eradicate injustice and to transform society.

Christians must learn how to empower individuals and groups to take charge of their own lives and to shape their own destinies. The sin that infects the social order must be not merely analyzed, but attacked. Unjust structures and institutions must be changed, as must policies and laws that fail to respect human life. To be a credible partner in this task, the church on campus should remember that "any group which ventures to speak to others about justice should itself be just and should be

---

47   The Church in the Modem World, no. 26.

48   Catholic Higher Education, no. 39.

49   "To Do the Work of Justice," in *Pastoral Letters*, vol. 4, 1975-1983, no. 8.

50   For important papal documents, see David J. O'Brien and Thomas A. Shannon, eds., *Renewing the Earth: Catholic Documents of Peace, Justice, and Liberation* (Garden City, N.Y.: Doubleday, 1977). Among our more recent pastoral letters and statements on social justice and peace we call attention to: *The Challenge of Peace: God's Promise and Our Response; Brothers and Sisters to Us; To Do the Work of Justice;* and our forthcoming pastoral letter on the economy. Finally we note the valuable insights in the pastoral letter *What We Have Seen and Heard: A Pastoral Letter on Evangelization from the Black Bishops of the United States* (Cincinnati: St. Anthony Messenger Press, 1984).

seen as such. It must therefore submit its own policies, programs and manner of life to continuing review."[51]

3. WORKING FOR JUSTICE

77. Considering the apathy on campus, the faith community has the vital task of raising consciousness on social issues and providing motivation for study and action. Leaders in the faith community who are already actively committed to the struggle for justice are a valuable resource in this effort. Drawing on their own experience, they can try to recruit others to work on specific justice issues. The very presence in the faith community of a core group dedicated to justice serves as an example and invitation to others to contribute their own talents and gifts to create a more humane society. Since apathy and excessive individualism are such pervasive problems, it is important for all those who are concerned about social justice to sustain their efforts even in the midst of limited successes.

78. Education for justice can be carried out in a variety of ways, ranging from Scripture studies and liturgies with a justice orientation to seminars and guided readings on a particular justice issue. Education for justice is enhanced by including an action component. For example, a seminar on hunger that raises consciousness on the issue should include suggested actions, such as joining an appropriate organization, writing congresspersons or helping out in a local food distribution center. Given the gravity of the nuclear threat, it is especially important to study the issue of peace and war. Such studies should include a discussion of ways to implement the summons to peacemaking contained in our pastoral letter *The Challenge of Peace: God's Promise and Our Response.*

79. Since the struggle for social justice demands involvement and not simply objective analysis, the church on campus should provide ample opportunities for all of its members to work directly in programs and projects designed to create a more just social order in which peace and reverence for life are possible. Students who are involved in service projects, such as visiting nursing homes, tutoring disadvantaged children or helping out during vacations in impoverished areas of the country, often grow in appreciation of the people they serve, as well as discover more about the complexity of institutional problems. Systematic reflection on such experiences in the light of the Gospel and the social teachings of the church enhances their learning and prepares them to be lifelong seekers after justice.

80. Campus ministry has the responsibility to work with others to enable higher education to live up to its commitments and ideals in the area of social justice. Individuals have many opportunities to speak on behalf of those who are powerless. For instance, administrators and faculty members who are helping to set admissions policies or who are involved in hiring decisions can raise up the concerns of the disadvantaged and underrepresented. Students in various organizations can be vigilant so that the rights and sensibilities of international and minority students are respected. Individuals and groups who are attuned to the social dimension of the Gospel can raise ethical questions about institutional policies.

---

51   *Sharing the Light of Faith,* no. 160.

81. Periodically issues arise that call for a more public response by the church on campus. Campus ministers, for instance, may be asked to be advocates for a group of students who are seeking redress of legitimate grievances or to provide leadership on a particular issue, such as combating the problems of racism and sexism. These are important opportunities, and campus ministers should respond by drawing on the social teaching of the church and giving public witness to the church's concern for justice and peace.

82. Finally, the faith community can touch the conscience of the academic world by sponsoring programs on campus designed to raise consciousness and to promote justice and peace. For example, the church could organize a day of fasting on campus, with the meal money saved going to help feed hungry people. This is a means of alerting individuals to the magnitude of the problem, of offering concrete help to the hungry and of witnessing to the social dimension of the Gospel.

E. Facilitating Personal Development

1. SELF-FULFILLMENT IN THE ACADEMIC WORLD

83. Campus ministry has the task of promoting the full personal development of the members of the academic community in a setting that is filled with rich, if often neglected, resources for self-fulfillment. Colleges and universities provide marvelous opportunities for healthy personal growth. Classes, lectures and seminars provide intellectual stimulation. Cultural and social events broaden horizons and facilitate emotional growth. The greatest catalyst for development comes from interaction with the concerned people who make up the academic community. There are campus ministers who can provide guidance for the spiritual quest; administrators who possess broad visions and sensitive hearts; faculty members who are generous in sharing the results of their scholarship; international students who bring the richness of different cultures; and peers who are willing to share friendship and the common struggle for greater maturity. With all of these resources, many individuals find the academic world to be an ideal setting for establishing their identities, forming relationships, developing their talents, preparing for leadership, discerning their vocations and charting the direction of their lives.

84. On the other hand, this vast potential for growth is often ignored or impeded. Some students think of college only in terms of opening the door to a good job and a secure future. They attend classes, gain credits and manage to graduate. Learning to think critically and achieving a well-rounded personality through involvement on campus are not part of their program. For these students the call to self-fulfillment either falls on deaf ears or is interpreted exclusively in terms of a lucrative career and material success. The great potential of higher education to promote personal development can also lie dormant because of the policies and practices of colleges and universities themselves. The traditional task of producing well-rounded individuals who are prepared to serve the common good can recede into the background, as policy decisions are made on the basis of declining enrollments and financial pressures. Recently voices from within the academic community have been raised claiming that higher education has not remained faithful to

its traditional goals and is not living up to its potential. Some say this is because students are not involved enough in the whole learning process.[52] One report claims that administrators and faculty have lost their nerve in the face of cultural trends and student pressures. It charges that leaders, by failing to insist on the systematic study of the humanities, have effectively deprived students of the cultural heritage that is needed for a well-rounded education.[53] Others decry the lack of a coherent curriculum and call for diverse learning experiences that foster critical thinking and help produce integrated persons who can live responsibly and joyfully as individuals and democratic citizens.[54] Among the critics, there is general agreement that reform is needed so that colleges and universities can achieve their proper goal of facilitating the full personal development of students.

2. CHRISTIAN PERSPECTIVES ON SELF-FULFILLMENT

85. The church has the task of distinguishing and evaluating the many voices of our age.[55] Campus ministry must be attuned to the voices of reform in the academic community and be prepared to function as the friend of genuine personal development and as an ally in the quest for healthy self-fulfillment. Our Scriptures remind us that the Spirit calls us to put aside childish ways and to live with greater maturity (1 Cor 14:20). For us Christians, Jesus Christ is the perfectly fulfilled human being.[56] In him, we see the depth of our potential and sublime character of our call. "He blazed a trail, and if we follow it, life and death are made holy and take on a new meaning."[57] By following this path of truth and love, we can grow to full maturity in Christ (Eph 4:15). The Spirit of Jesus, poured out through his death and resurrection, energizes us for the task of developing our potential. The same Spirit enables us to recognize and overcome the selfishness in our hearts and the contradictions in the culture that distort the quest for healthy self-fulfillment. When individuals pursue personal development within the community of faith, they are constantly challenged to use their talents in the service of others and to stay open to the Spirit, who accomplishes surprising things in us (Jn 3:8).

86. The Second Vatican Council has given contemporary expression to these biblical insights.[58] Human dignity demands that persons act according to intelligent decisions that are motivated from within. We should pursue our goals in a free choice of what is good and find apt means to achieve these laudable goals. The Christian vision of human existence safeguards the ideal of full human development by rooting it in the sacredness of the person. All persons are worthy of respect and

---

52   See "Involvement in Learning."

53   See Bennett, "To Reclaim a Legacy."

54   See "Integrity in the College Curriculum."

55   The Church in the Modern World, no. 44.

56   Ibid., no. 22.

57   Ibid.

58   Ibid., no. 17.

dignity and are called to perfection because they are "a living image of God"[59] and possess a "godlike seed" that has been sown in them.[60] This intrinsic relationship with God, far from limiting the drive for personal development, frees human beings to pursue their fulfillment and happiness with confidence.[61] Furthermore, life in community teaches us that personal freedom acquires new strength when it consents to the requirements of social life, takes on the demands of human partnership and commits itself to the service of the human family.[62]

87. These principles remind us that Christians must proclaim an ideal of self-fulfillment that is solidly rooted in the sacredness of persons, is placed in the service of the common good and stays open to the God who is the source of all growth.

88. When campus ministry brings the light of the Gospel to the educational process, the search for personal development leads to a Christian humanism that fuses the positive values and meanings in the culture with the light of faith.[63] Genuine Christian humanists know that the heart is restless until it rests in God and that all persons are unsolved puzzles to themselves, always awaiting the full revelation of God.[64] Thus, for them, personal development is perceived as a lifelong adventure, completed only in the final fulfilling union with the Lord. Christian humanists know that history and all cultures are a mysterious mix of grace and sin[65] and that where sin exists, there grace more abounds (Rom 5:20). Thus, while rejecting the sinful elements in the culture, they are able to assimilate the grace-inspired meanings and values in the world into a comprehensive and organic framework built on faith in Jesus Christ. As individuals pursue their personal development, the ideal of Christian humanism lights the path and sets the direction.

3. ACHIEVING PERSONAL DEVELOPMENT IN A CHRISTIAN CONTEXT

89. Campus ministry can facilitate personal development through vibrant sacramental life, courses, seminars and retreats that enable Catholics on campus to integrate their collegiate experience with their Christian faith. Through pastoral counseling and spiritual direction, campus ministers can encourage individuals to make use of the resources on campus and guide them on the path toward a Christian humanism. This important work is enhanced when the ministers are perceived as persons of prayer who are serious about their own personal growth.

---

59   "Pastoral Letter on Marxist Communism," in *Pastoral Letters*, vol. 4, 1975-1983, no. 14.

60   The Church in the Modern World, no. 3.

61   Ibid., no. 21.

62   Ibid., no. 31.

63   This term *Christian humanism* has been used in the church to suggest the ideal of integrating positive cultural values and meanings in a faith perspective. For a recent usage of this term, see "Catholic Higher Education," no. 19.

64   The Church in the Modern World, no. 21.

65   Ibid.

90. It is helpful to multiply these efforts by bringing together in a personal encounter those who share the journey toward Christian maturity. A program that enables an individual faculty member to meet on a regular basis outside the classroom with a particular student for friendly conversation and serious discussion provides great opportunities for the kind of exchange that is mutually enriching. Faculty members who are inspired by gospel ideals and undergo training for this kind of program are in an excellent position to be role models for students and, perhaps, spiritual mentors. Students, in turn, bring to the relationship their distinctive experience and challenging questions, which can be a catalyst for mutual growth. A great variety of such programs is possible. The key is to increase the opportunities for more personal contact between members of the faith community so that they can assist one another in the quest for a genuine Christian humanism.

91. Since there is a temptation to reduce self-fulfillment to a selfish individualism, campus ministry provides a valuable service by keeping alive the ideal of Christian humanism, which recognizes that personal growth must be open to the transcendent and in service to the common good. Through prayer groups and liturgical celebrations that link life and worship, in lectures and seminars that relate current questions and the Christian tradition, by service projects and actions for justice that put personal gifts at the service of others, the community of faith publicly manifests the Christian ideal of self-fulfillment. The sacrament of reconciliation is a powerful means for personal development since it enables individuals to confront the sins and destructive patterns that inhibit their progress and to hear again the compassionate summons to grow into greater maturity in Christ. Communal penance services that encourage an examination of the distinctive challenges and opportunities for personal development presented by campus life are especially effective in making the ideal of Christian humanism more concrete.

92. Inspired by this ideal, individual members of the faith community have the responsibility to assist their colleges or universities in the task of educating whole persons for lifelong growth and responsible citizenship. This is done in obvious ways by students who study hard and take advantage of cultural opportunities on campus and by faculty members who teach well and take a personal interest in students. In addition, there is the challenge of establishing institutional policies and practices that better facilitate these goals. Today there is a general consensus that undergraduate education must be improved by various means, such as setting higher standards for classroom work, establishing a more coherent curriculum and improving teacher performance through better preparation and proper incentives.[66] As the precise shape of the reforms is debated on particular campuses, it is vital that the voices of Christian humanists be joined with others of good will on behalf of reform, which makes possible the education of the whole person. Trustees, administrators and deans, as well as faculty members and students who serve on appropriate committees, can promote policies that clearly place the well-being of students in the center of the academic enterprise. The opportunities are many and varied for members of the faith community to work with others in an effort to improve the quality of higher education so that a healthy personal development is facilitated. What is

---

66   We recall the three reports cited in footnote 8.

needed is the conviction that this is an essential aspect of bringing Christian witness to the campus.

F. Developing Leaders for the Future

1. POTENTIAL LEADERS ON CAMPUS

93. Campus ministry has the great opportunity to tap the immense pool of talent in our colleges and universities and to help form future leaders for society and the church. Large numbers of intelligent and ambitious young people are on campuses, gaining the knowledge and skills needed to launch them into eventual positions of leadership in the world. Many of the older students at our colleges and universities are acquiring new knowledge and skills that will enhance their opportunities to influence their world for the good. The intense course of studies pursued by graduate students equips them with specialized knowledge that can be used for the common good. When international students, trained on our campuses, return to their own countries, they carry with them knowledge and skills that can be extremely valuable in promoting progress in their own societies. While not all of the students on campuses today will assume prominent leadership positions, everyone will have opportunities to provide some leadership in their various communities.

94. The large numbers of Catholics attending colleges and universities are potential leaders not only of society, but of the church as well. Parishes require women and men who, in actively proclaiming the Gospel, combine commitment and good will with knowledge and skills. The Catholic community is in great need of more priests who will dedicate themselves to serving the needs of others. The religious orders are looking for new members who will live a life of dedicated service. In searching for this kind of church leadership for the future, we naturally turn to our colleges and universities, where so many of our talented young people are being educated.

95. The search for church leaders on campus should also extend to Catholic administrators and faculty. The local church should make every effort to train individuals to carry out campus ministry on campuses where there are no professional campus ministry personnel. These men and women, who are blessed with extensive education, perform an important Christian service in the academic world and constitute an immense resource for church leadership. Not all of these individuals have the time or calling to assume leadership positions within the faith community. However, as a whole, they constitute a valuable pool of leadership talent that could be better utilized for the benefit of the church.

2. LEADERSHIP IN THE CHRISTIAN PERSPECTIVE

96. From the perspective of faith, the Scriptures present a distinctive understanding of leadership. Jesus told his followers, "You are the light of the world . . .your light must shine before all so that they may see goodness in your acts and give praise to your heavenly father" (Mt. 5:14-19). This suggests that all the disciples of Jesus carry the responsibility of offering personal witness in order to make a difference in

the world and of using their influence to bring others to a greater appreciation of the goodness of God. This kind of leadership is to be carried out according to one's own unique talents. As the Apostle Paul indicated: "Just as each of us has one body with many members, and not all the members have the same function, so too we, though many, are one body in Christ and individually members one of another. We have gifts that differ according to the favor bestowed on each of us" (Rom 12:4-6). Paul also reminds us of the deep purpose involved in such gifts when he says, "To each person the manifestation of the Spirit is given for the common good" (1 Cor 12:7). In the Christian community genuine leadership is based not on coercive power or high status, but on loving service that leads to the empowerment of others (Mk. 10:42-45). Thus the clear teaching of Scripture is that gifts and talents are not given simply for personal advantage; they are to be used generously for the benefit of others and for the good of society and the church.

97. The Second Vatican Council recognized the great opportunities for this kind of Christian leadership and called on all adult Christians to prepare themselves for this task. "Indeed, everyone should painstakingly ready himself (or herself) personally for the apostolate, especially as an adult. For the advance of age brings with it better self-knowledge, thus enabling each person to evaluate more accurately the talents with which God has enriched (each) soul and to exercise more effectively those charismatic gifts which the Holy Spirit has bestowed on (all) for the good of (others)."[67] Thus, from the perspective of faith, it is clear that effective leadership in the contemporary world is connected both with a sense of loving service and with a more mature development in self-knowledge.

98. The nature of Christian leadership can also be understood from the viewpoint of the vocation we all receive from God. Through baptism, "all the faithful of Christ of whatever rank or status are called to the fullness of the Christian life and to the perfection of charity. By this holiness a more human way of life is promoted even in this earthly society." [68] This baptismal vocation gives to every Christian the special task "to illumine and organize" temporal affairs of every sort "in such a way that they may start out, develop and persist according to Christ's mind."[69] Individuals may choose to live out this general vocation as single persons, as members of the clergy or religious orders, or as married couples. In all of these states of life there are opportunities large and small for exercising a leadership that is based on service and helps to humanize our world.

3. STRATEGIES FOR FORMING CHRISTIAN LEADERS

99. Campus ministers can facilitate the development of Christian leaders by encouraging members of the faith community to identify their gifts and to use them for the common good. Individuals must be helped to overcome their fears and to gain confidence in their abilities. They need proper training and opportunities to improve their leadership skills. For example, retreats for liturgical ministers can help them

---

67 Decree on the Laity, no. 30.

68 Dogmatic Constitution on the Church, no. 40.

69 Ibid., no. 9.

sense the importance of their roles at Mass and enable them to perform these roles prayerfully and competently. A leadership training session for officers in Catholic student organizations at the beginning of the academic year can give them added confidence and practical skills. Campus ministers who work with student organizers of a social justice project can provide them with Christian principles and practical advice that will enhance their effectiveness as current and future leaders.

100. In addition to developing leaders within the faith community, campus ministers should also encourage students to exercise their influence in other groups and activities. It helps to remind them that involvement in the life of their college or university is a significant factor in getting more out of the collegiate experience and that all Catholics on campus have the responsibility to work for the betterment of the academic community.

101. The development of leaders involves helping students to discern their vocations in life and to prepare for them. Most young people on campus today need guidance in preparing for marriage and family life. The preparation should include programs that encompass the following elements: the sacrament of marriage as an interpersonal relationship; the identity and mission of the family; the role of human sexuality and intimacy; conjugal love as union and as sharing in the creative power of God; responsible parenthood; and the couple's responsibilities to the larger community.[70] A significant number of collegians seriously consider vocations to the priesthood or religious life.[71] Campus ministers are in an excellent position to promote these vocations. A program in which campus ministers gather interested students together regularly for discussions and prayer is a valuable way of helping them discern the promptings of the Spirit. Students moving in the direction of the single life often need personal assistance in order to deal with societal pressures and cultural stereotypes.

102. In order to get more faculty members and administrators to exercise leadership in the faith community, campus ministers need to establish personal contact with them, offer them opportunities that fit their particular expertise and provide them with training, if necessary. For example, counselors on campus could run marriage preparation and enrichment programs for the faith community after studying the church's teachings on marriage. It would also be helpful to gather the Catholic faculty and administrators together on occasion to give them a sense of group identity and to encourage their active participation in the church on campus. This could be done through a retreat in which they explore ways of integrating their faith with their professional concerns. The more this integration takes place, the better role models they will be for students, who are the emerging leaders of society and the church.

EPILOGUE

103. In this pastoral letter we have placed campus ministry in its historical and cultural context and have examined it from the viewpoint of the persons who carry it

---

70   John Paul II, *On the Family*, no. 66.

71   Fee et. al., *Young Catholics*, 154-55.

out, as well as the tasks they perform. We are convinced that this ministry is vitally important for the future of church and society. As bishops, we recognize our responsibility to "see to it that at colleges and universities which are not Catholic there are Catholic residences and centers where priests, religious and (lay persons) who have been judiciously chosen and trained can serve as on-campus sources of spiritual and intellectual assistance to young college people."[72]

104. The revised Code of Canon Law has reinforced this responsibility by reminding us that the diocesan bishop is to be zealous in his pastoral care of students, even by the creation of a special parish or at least by appointing priests with a stable assignment to this care.[73] We know it is important to find dedicated persons for this ministry who have a solid faith, a love for the academic world and the ability to relate well to both inquiring students and an educated faculty. They need proper training, which includes personal development, practical experience and theological study. Advanced degrees are helpful in order to gain credibility in the academic world. We are committed to providing the best professional campus ministers possible and intend to hold them accountable for dedicated and creative service to the academic community. Our responsibilities extend to ensuring that within each diocese adequate funding is available for campus ministry and that there is an overall plan for allocating resources.

105. Our hope is that this pastoral letter will mark the beginning of a new phase in the history of Catholic campus ministry in the United States. In our vision of the new era, campus ministry will succeed more than ever before in forming the faithful into vibrant communities of faith and in empowering them to bring the light of the Gospel to the academic world. Campus ministry will be better understood and supported by the church as a whole and will therefore be strengthened to make its voice heard in the center of campus life. The spiritual life of the church on campus will be renewed so that it can be a more potent force, enabling the academic community to live up to its own ideals. The faith community will be more in touch with its Catholic roots so that it can confidently enter into deeper dialogue and more productive relationships with other religious groups on campus. A contemporary Christian humanism will flourish which will demonstrate to all the value of an adult faith that has integrated the best insights of the culture. The church on campus will be seen more clearly as a genuine servant community dedicated to social justice and therefore will be a more effective sign and instrument of the kingdom of peace and justice in the world. In the new era the church and higher education will find more productive ways of working together for the well-being of the whole human family. In our vision, campus ministry, empowered by the Spirit, faces a future bright with promise.

---

72 Declaration on Christian Education, no. 10.

73 Code of Canon Law, (Washington, D.C.: Canon Law Society of America, 1983), cc. 813-814.

Doctrinal Responsibilities: Approaches to Promoting Cooperation and Resolving Misunderstandings Between Bishops and Theologians

June 17, 1989

Doctrinal Responsibilities initially began with the work of a joint committee composed of representatives from the Catholic Theological Society of America and the Canon Law Society of America. It was passed unanimously by both learned societies in June and October of 1983. This document was then presented to the National Conference of Catholic Bishops which remitted it to the Committee on Doctrine in the Fall of 1983. This final text was approved by the body of bishops in June 1989 as an independent document of the National Conference of Catholic Bishops and is so published.

Reverend Robert N. Lynch
General Secretary
NCCB/USCC

Abbreviations

The following abbreviations are used in this document:

AAS   *Acta Apostolicae Sedis*
AG   *Ad Gentes* (Vatican II)
CD   *Christus Dominus* (Vatican II)
CLSA   Canon Law Society of America
CTSA   Catholic Theological Society of America
DH   *Dignitatis Humanae* (Vatican II)
DS   Denzinger-Schoenmetzer, *Enchiridion Symbolorum, Definitionum et Declarationum de Rebus Fidei et Morum*, 32 ed. (Freiburg: Herder, 1963)
DV   *Dei Verbum* (Vatican II)
GS   *Gaudium et Spes* (Vatican II)
ITC   Document of the International Theological Commission, *Theses on the Relationship between the Ecclesiastical Magisterium and Theology* (Washington, D.C.: United States Catholic Conference, 1977)
LG   *Lumen Gentium* (Vatican II)
NCCB   National Conference of Catholic Bishops
PO   *Presbyterorum Ordinis* (Vatican II)

PREFACE

The present document constitutes a part of the continuing work by the Committee on Doctrine concerning the teaching mission of the Church. While the material was first prepared by a joint committee of the Canon Law Society of America and the Catholic Theological Society of America, with extensive consultation among bishops and scholars, this current text represents a revision drafted by the Committee on Doctrine in the winter of 1986-1987 and then emended in view of suggestions from the Administrative Committee in September 1987 and amendments or suggestions proposed before and during the general meeting of November 1987.[1] After further consultation with the full body of bishops from April through June of 1988 and with the Holy See in 1989, and subsequent revisions, *Doctrinal Responsibilities* has been clarified and strengthened as an instrument for promoting cooperation and for helping to resolve theological questions between bishops and theologians.

The document is in three parts.

I. The Context of Ecclesial Responsibilities presents a general statement of the ecclesial framework, the operative principles, and the responsibilities and rights of bishops and theologians. This section does not propose a full, much less a definitive, theological treatment. Rather it speaks in a summary and descriptive way to provide a context for the rest of the report.

---

1   In June 1980 an Ad Hoc Committee on Cooperation between Theologians and the Church's Teaching Authority reported to the Catholic Theological Society of America and recommended that the CTSA and the Canon Law Society of America jointly form a committee "to develop a proposed set of norms to guide the resolution of difficulties which may arise between theologians and the magisterium in North America." (*Catholic Theological Society of America Proceedings*, 35 [1980] 331.) The two societies agreed and, in September 1980, they formally constituted The Joint CLSA-CTSA Committee on Cooperation between Theologians and the Ecclesiastical Magisterium.

The committee divided its task into two phases. In the first, the members prepared six background studies and published them for scholarly discussion and criticism as *Cooperation between Theologians and the Ecclesiastical Magisterium*, edited by Leo J. O'Donovan, SJ (Washington, D.C.: CLSA, 1982). In the second phase, the committee worked to develop procedures for cooperation and circulated them for reaction from representative bishops, canonists, and theologians. Further, Bishop James R. Hoffman (Toledo), Bishop John F. Kinney (Bismarck), and Archbishop Daniel E. Pilarczyk (Cincinnati) accepted the committee's invitation to join its meetings and contribute to the formulation of its final document.

The joint committee completed its procedural document, *Doctrinal Responsibilities*, and presented it to the annual meetings of the two societies in June and October 1983 where it received unanimous votes of approval. The societies then presented it to the NCCB, which remitted it to the Committee on Doctrine. After a preliminary review by the committee under the chairmanship of Archbishop John R. Quinn, *Doctrinal Responsibilities* was taken up again in 1986 by the reorganized Committee on Doctrine chaired by Bishop Raymond W. Lessard. This committee accepted the document as a working draft and collaborated with representatives of the Joint CLSA/CTSA Committee to develop it in its present form.

Previous to this entire project, the National Conference of Catholic Bishops had adopted two other procedural documents. In 1972, the conference adopted *On Due Process*, (rev. ed., Washington, D.C.: NCCB, 1972) as a model for due process in dioceses. In 1979, the conference issued its procedures for conciliation and arbitration, *Committee on Conciliation and Arbitration*, (Washington, D.C.: NCCB, 1979). However, in contrast with *Doctrinal Responsibilities*, those procedures dealt only with administrative conflicts.

II. Promoting Cooperation and Informal Dialogue recommends ways in which bishops and theologians can enhance cooperation in their common service of the gospel and the Church, especially through personal contacts and informal dialogue. This section focuses on positive efforts to promote cooperation, and also makes suggestions for actions by which bishops or theologians can screen complaints from third parties so that unnecessary disputes might be avoided.

III. A Possibility for Formal Doctrinal Dialogue sets out a suggested procedure designed specifically to deal with doctrinal disputes between bishops and theologians in dioceses. Since the circumstances in the nearly 200 dioceses of the United States vary widely, the approach given here is intended to be flexible and adaptable to local needs.

The recommended structures for promoting cooperation and for resolving doctrinal disputes draw upon experience already acquired by the Church in the United States for building a spirit of collaboration and resolving conflicts. They are designed to address the special problems of disputes of a doctrinal nature. It must be stressed that these guidelines can only serve if they are *adapted* to the particular conditions of a diocese, its history, and its special needs. The document presents a full complement of procedures as something from which bishops and theologians can draw. The adaptability of the procedures to local conditions by mutual consent of bishops and theologians should promote collaboration and conflict resolution. Although this report is concerned with theologians who are members of the Catholic Church, its approach may also prove useful with other theologians in Catholic institutions.

Both bishops and theologians are called to serve the word of God (cf. DV no. 10; CD no. 12). In the exercise of their office, bishops serve through authoritative teaching (LG no. 25). On the basis of scholarly competence illumined by faith (DS no. 3016), theologians serve through disciplined reflection seeking an understanding of the gospel for humanity today (GS no. 62). As they fulfill their distinctive but complementary duties, both bishops and theologians are sustained by the faith of the Church in God's revelation and by their participation in the Church's life of prayer, especially the Sacred Liturgy.

Moreover, in a time of philosophical and theological pluralism, much of which is good and enriching, the task of building cooperation between bishops and theologians becomes more urgent than ever so that Catholic doctrine may be effectively taught and intractable disputes avoided. A common commitment of bishops and theologians to the integrity of the word of God and a common sensitivity to the pastoral implications of theological teaching within the Church can make the structures suggested effective both in promoting cooperation and in resolving disputes.

The approach outlined here is offered to bishops and theologians in the United States for their use, though it does not have the status of law. Obviously, when used, these guidelines are to be interpreted in a manner consistent with the *Code of Canon Law*. Likewise they presuppose, as will be indicated in the pages that follow, the teaching of the Second Vatican Council and the subsequent statements of the magisterium on the nature of episcopal office and authority in the Church.

This document is not intended to offer suggestions for handling specific cases of dissent. Neither is it primarily to provide an approach to clarifying Catholic doctrine, although this may be one benefit of the process. Finally it does not in any way presuppose a situation of tension or envisage adversarial relations between bishops and theologians in the United States, as if the rights of one had to be protected against the other. On the contrary, the purpose of this document is to encourage increased communication and collaboration between bishops and theologians, to forestall disputes, and, if such disputes arise, to promote their resolution for the good of the faithful. Its guidelines will be reevaluated and, if necessary, refined in the light of these goals and the experience in using them.

I. THE CONTEXT OF ECCLESIAL RESPONSIBILITIES

A. Context and Principles

The ecclesial context is critical for understanding the relationship between bishops and theologians, for encouraging cooperation, and for constructing an adequate approach to prevent or to address disputes related to the Church's teaching.

Before considering the different services which bishops and theologians render to the Church, it is important to recognize what they have in common as members of the Body of Christ. In virtue of their faith, baptism, and communion with the Church, bishops and theologians alike—however distinct their ministries, charisms, and authority—are dedicated to the active proclamation of the gospel and its transformative power for contemporary society. Both participate in the community's experience of faith and both seek to promote greater understanding of the word of God. In their common effort, both recognize the importance of communicating the faith with sensitivity to the cultural pluralism of today's world. Their common fidelity to the word of God permeates the particular responsibilities and rights of bishops and theologians; revelation is the good which both serve in analogous ways according to their distinctive ecclesial roles (DV no. 10; ITC Thesis 2). Thus, in different ways, rooted in the sacramental life of the Church, theologians and bishops discharge the mission of the Church "to show forth in the world the mystery of the Lord in a faithful though shadowed way, until at last it will be revealed in total splendor" (LG no. 8).

In his address to leaders of Catholic higher education at Xavier University in New Orleans on September 12, 1987, Pope John Paul II stressed this ecclesial context which bishops and theologians share in common and which helps clarify the right relations between them. These words and the practice of *communio* they embody, we make our own:

> Theology is at the service of the whole ecclesial community. The work of theology involves an interaction among the various members of the community of faith. The bishops, united with the Pope, have the mission of authentically teaching the message of Christ; as pastors they are called to sustain the unity in faith and Christian living of the entire People of God. For this they need the assistance of Catholic theologians, who perform an inestimable service to the Church. But theologians also need

the charism entrusted by Christ to the bishops and, in the first place, to the Bishop of Rome. The fruits of their work, in order to enrich the lifestream of the ecclesial community, must ultimately be tested and validated by the Magisterium. In effect, therefore, the ecclesial context of Catholic theology gives it a special character and value, even when theology exists in an academic setting.[2]

Thus, diverse gifts, ministries, and authority exist for the full development of the Church's unity in life and mission. They require an ecclesiological application of shared responsibility, legitimate diversity, and subsidiarity. Upon the bishops devolves the responsibility to encourage this diversity and to unify the various contributions of members of the Church. It is inevitable that misunderstandings about the teaching of the gospel and the ways of expressing it will arise. In such cases, informal conversation ought to be the first step towards resolution. If this proves unproductive, a reasonable, clear, and fair process must protect fundamental human and sacramental responsibilities and rights of all parties concerned. Any guidelines developed for such cases should encourage that free and responsible theological inquiry in service to the gospel which is faithful to Catholic tradition, in accord with the teaching authority of bishops, and responsive to the needs of the Church and the world. Similarly, any guidelines should promote the informed judgment of the bishops and hence their freedom to act responsibly as guardians and authoritative teachers of the faith.

Hence, the ultimate goal and importance of these procedures are to foster collaboration between bishops and theologians for the good of the entire Church, recognizing the vocation of theologians to study, clarify, and mediate the truth of the gospel which the magisterium authoritatively proposes.[3] The recommendations given in sections II and III deal with the diocese. It is advisable that attempts to resolve doctrinal disputes be made first at the local level before an appeal is made to the Holy See. Of course, any bishop or theologian can contact the Holy See

---

2   *Origins*, vol. 17, no. 16 (October 1, 1987): 270, paragraph 7.

3   Cf. International Theological Commission, *Theses on the Relationship between the Ecclesiastical Magisterium and Theology* (Washington, D.C.: USCC, 1977) Theses 2 and 4:

Thesis 2: The element common to the tasks of both the magisterium and theologians, though it is realized in analogous and distinct fashions, is "to preserve the sacred deposit of revelation, to examine it more deeply, to explain, teach and defend it," for the service of the people of God and for the whole world's salvation. Above all, this service must defend the certainty of faith; this is a work done differently by the magisterium and by the ministry of theologians, but it is neither necessary nor possible to establish a hard and fast separation between them.

Thesis 4: Common to both, although also different in each, is the manner, at once collegial and personal, in which the task of both the magisterium and the theologian is carried out. If the charism of infallibility is promised to "the whole body of the faithful," to the College of Bishops in communion with the Successor of Peter, and to the Supreme Pontiff himself, the head of that College, then it should be put into practice in a co-responsible, co-operative, and collegial association of the members of the magisterium and of individual theologians. And this joint effort should also be realized as much among the members of the magisterium as among the members of the theological enterprise, and also between the magisterium on the one hand and the theologians on the other. It should also preserve the personal and indispensable responsibility of individual theologians, without which the science of faith would make no progress.

directly, but in terms of subsidiarity, every effort should ordinarily be made to initiate the process within the local church.[4]

The terms *magisterium, theologian,* and *responsibilities and rights* are frequently used in this report. There is considerable variation in the current use of these words, but for the sake of clarity, the following specific meanings are stipulated here.

Magisterium will be used to refer to the ecclesiastical magisterium, i.e., to the unique teaching authority exercised in the name of Christ by the pope and other bishops united with the pope. Throughout, this document affirms the final pastoral authority of the episcopal office in the Church and the tasks of sanctifying, teaching, and ruling which are conferred by the Sacrament of Orders (cf. LG 21; ITC Thesis 6). By their ordination and hierarchical communion, bishops are members of the college of bishops and authoritative teachers in their local churches. By virtue of their divine and ecclesial mission and with a discerning awareness of the needs of contemporary society, bishops have the pastoral duty in the name of Christ to proclaim the word of God with authority, to teach the truth of the faith, and to maintain the authentic interpretation of the word of God as it has been handed down in the course of history (cf. LG 25; DV 10). For this reason, the *Directory on the Pastoral Ministry of Bishops* stated for every bishop:

> In order that he (the bishop) may be found a faithful minister and supporter of the orthodox faith that has been handed on to him, protecting it from errors and dangers, he must diligently cultivate theological science and daily increase it with new yet proven doctrine (*Directory*, Part I, chapter 4, no. 24).

---

4   Subsidiarity as used in this text was introduced into ecclesiology by Pius XII in his address to the newly created cardinals of February 20, 1946:

   That is why the Apostle of the Gentiles, speaking of Christians, proclaims they are no more "children tossed to and fro" by the uncertain drift in the midst of human society. Our predecessor of happy memory, Pius XI, in his Encyclical Quadragesimo Anno on social order, drew a practical conclusion from this thought when he announced a principle of general application, viz: that what individual human beings can do by themselves and by their own forces, should not be taken from them and assigned to the community.

   It is a principle that also holds good for smaller communities and those of lower rank in relation to those which are larger and in a position of superiority. For—as the wise Pontiff said, developing his thought—every social activity is of its nature subsidiary (*subsidiaria*); it must serve as a support to members of the social body and never destroy or absorb them. These are surely enlightened words, valid for social life in all its grades and also for the life of the Church without prejudice to its hierarchical structure.

   Now Venerable Brethren, over and against this doctrine and practice of the Church, place in their real significance the tendencies of imperialism. (AAS 38 [1946], 144-5).

   In his letter to the presidents of the Episcopal conferences throughout the world, Francis Cardinal Seper, Prefect of the Sacred Congregation for the Doctrine of the Faith, used this same principle in his formulation of the mandate for the recently established doctrinal commissions of these conferences. His Eminence connects this principle with the mind of the Second Vatican Council:

   Episcopi opera Commissionis doctrinalis uti possunt in quaestionibus quae territorium Conferentiae seu Coetus Episcopalis tangent. Ad determinandum vero quaenam negotia ad hanc Sacram Congregationem mittenda sint, prae oculis habeatur "principium subsidiarietatis," ad mentem Concilii Occumenici Vaticani II, ita nimirum ut ordinarie ipsae Conferentiae seu ipsi Coetus per se expedient ea quae suos territoriales limites non excedunt, neque ob aliam rationem peculiarem Sanctae Sedis interventum requirere videantur (July 10, 1968, Prot. N. 214/67).

   Also see Thesis 12 in ITC.

The term *theologian* in these pages is used to designate the Catholic who seeks to mediate, through the discipline of scholarship, between a living faith and the culture it is called to transform (GS 44, 62).[5] Thus, within the ecclesial community, theologians fulfill certain specific tasks. Like other Catholics, theologians live lives of faith within the community and in fidelity to the teaching authority of the Church (LG 25). Grounded in the commitment of their ecclesial faith and trained in the skills of scholarship, theologians systematically explore the nature and foundations of God's revelation and the teaching of the Church. They examine the interrelationships of Christian truths and offer interpretations of God's word in response to the challenges of contemporary society. Though theologians as such share in the Church's mission to serve the Gospel as effectively as possible and do so through their scholarly work, they are not primarily preachers or catechists. Typically, they hold a doctorate or comparable degree in one of the sacred sciences, have had extensive exposure to the Catholic tradition in their particular area of expertise, and are engaged in teaching and research in a seminary, college, or university.

The contribution and cogency of a theologian's work, therefore, depend upon scholarly competence that is rooted in faith and is faithful to the Church's teaching under the guidance of the Holy Spirit (ITC Thesis 6:2). That competence can be assessed from the quality of the evidence theologians adduce and the soundness of the arguments they advance for the sake of Christ's truth. Such competence can be shown, for example, when theologians ask searching and serious questions as they seek to discern and communicate the abiding truth of Christ. The constructive critical quality of theological scholarship does not compromise its fidelity to the Church and its magisterium, but indicates the disciplined reflection characteristic of genuine scholarly investigation.

Responsibilities and rights are used variously in law and ethics. We mean *by right* a moral or legal power to act or to be immune from injury. Responsibilities, and the rights with which they are correlative, have their source in one's human dignity, in one's standing in the Church, or from one's functions within the Catholic community. Commonly the possession of a right is distinguished from its exercise, because the exercise of a right may be circumscribed in order to protect the common good or the rights of others, even though the right itself remains intact. In the Catholic heritage, individual rights are always to be promoted within the context of the common good.[6]

---

5   From another point of view and concerned more with theology's function ad intra, the International Theological Commission recalls the assertion of Pope Paul VI and speaks of the theologians as "in some way mediat(ing) between the magisterium and the People of God." Thesis 5, no. 2. This thesis also recalls the urgent question of culture addressed in GS no. 62.

6   The term *interests* sometimes occurs in discussions of responsibilities and rights. In such cases, it designates other and more elusive factors in a conflict situation. *Interests* relate to particular and concrete concerns involved in the exercise of personal or official discretion. *Interests* arise in the pursuit of one's rights or obligations, or more generally, from the freedom appropriate to all the people of God. Within this ecclesial context, the procedures designed to resolve conflicts must determine facts, the responsibilities and rights of the parties, and the interests of the parties which are at issue.

B. The Responsibilities and Rights of Bishops

The guidelines proposed in this document reflect a concern to recognize and foster the responsibilities and rights of both bishops and theologians.[7]

The responsibilities and rights of bishops flow from their pastoral office of teaching, sanctifying, and governing in the Church. These tasks (*munera*) cannot be fully separated one from the other; they form a single pastoral office. Of the responsibilities and rights of bishops which arise from their pastoral task of authoritative teaching, we call attention to the following.

Preeminent among the responsibilities of bishops is preaching the word of God. Bishops are also charged to preserve and protect the truth of faith, i.e., to transmit the authentic gospel of Christ. Moreover, in the particular church where he serves, the bishop is to teach in the name of Christ and the Church; he is to make the pastoral judgment as to how the faith of the community will be publicly expressed at a given time and place. For that reason, the bishop is called upon to judge whether some opinions endanger or are contrary to faith and the Christian life. But it is also the responsibility of bishops to discharge their office so as to respect the gifts imparted by the Holy Spirit to various members of the Church. It follows that in the exercise of their pastoral role, bishops should encourage theologians to pursue a deeper understanding of the gospel and its meaning for contemporary life (LG no. 25; CD nos. 12, 13, 14; PO no. 19; GS no. 62; ITC Thesis 5:1). In order to encourage theology and to make provisions for the consultation he needs in his teaching, the bishop should select the most suitable candidates for theological studies and should encourage these studies among religious communities and lay men and women within his diocese.

In addition to these responsibilities, certain rights of bishops are rooted in their task as teachers. Thus, the bishops of particular churches have the right to exercise their care for the truth of the gospel in the Church over which they preside. The bishops teach in the name of Christ and his Church, in union with the head and other members of the episcopal college. What they teach should meet with that religious reception proportionate to the degree of authority with which it is presented (LG no. 25; Canon 753).

But bishops also have the right to draw upon the contributions and the gifts of all who share the Church's saving mission, which includes the heralding of the faith (LG nos. 12-13; AG nos. 10-18). In their particular church communities bishops have the right to the cooperation and support of the priests who form one presbyterate with the bishop. Bishops also have a right to the collaboration of theologians: bishops draw on their scholarly competence and support as well as rely upon them as one necessary resource for their own ongoing theological study. Bishops consult theologians for aid in scrutinizing the signs of the time and in evaluating new issues and questions. Bishops look to theologians for aid in keeping their own formulations of Catholic belief and practice faithful to the word of God. Further,

---

7   Because those responsibilities and rights have been discussed elsewhere, they are recalled here only schematically to provide the general context for the sections that follow. See, for example, the articles by John P. Boyle, Robert J. Carlson, Jon Nilson, and John A. Alesandro in O'Donovan, ed., *Cooperation between Theologians and the Ecclesiastical Magisterium*.

bishops have a right to require in the name of the Church that theologians faithfully discharge their own responsibility for the integrity of the gospel. Bishops must also have the freedom to teach without interference from civil authority or unwarranted criticism by theologians or others in the Church. Finally, because their solicitude extends to the universal Church, bishops have a right to expect fraternal support from one another.

C. The Responsibilities and Rights of Theologians

The responsibilities and rights of theologians may be grouped according to the ways in which theologians participate in the life of the Church.

As members of the community of faith, theologians share the common responsibility of maintaining the unity and integrity of Catholic faith, reflected in the *sensus fidei* (cf. no. LG 12) and the documents of tradition in which it is set forth. They must keep in mind the pastoral and missionary effects of their work (ITC Thesis 3). Theologians also acknowledge that it is the role of bishops as authoritative teachers in the Church to make pastoral judgments about the soundness of theological teaching so that the integrity of Catholic doctrine and the unity of the faith community may be preserved. In other words, theological teaching always remains subject to testing in the life of the Church and to the teaching of its bishops.

As scholars, theologians discharge their responsibility in fidelity to apostolic faith by meditative appropriation of the faith and by critical inquiry according to the principles of that branch of theology in which their work is done.[8] As they fulfill that responsibility, theological scholars must expect to exchange constructive criticism with other scholars, other Christians, and other interested persons of good will. Fidelity to the faith and to the canons of sound scholarship requires

---

8   International Theological Commission, p. 6:

   Thesis 8: The difference between the magisterium and the theologians takes on a special character when one considers the freedom proper to them and the critical function that follows from it with regard to the faithful, to the world, and even to one another.

   1. By its nature and institution, the magisterium is clearly free in carrying out its task. This freedom carries with it a great responsibility. For that reason, it is often difficult, although necessary, to use it in such a way that it not appear to theologians and to others of the faithful to be arbitrary or excessive. There are some theologians who prize scientific theology too highly, not taking enough account of the fact that respect for the magisterium is one of the specific elements of the science of theology. Besides, contemporary democratic sentiments often give rise to a movement of solidarity against what the magisterium does in carrying out its task of protecting the teaching of faith and morals from any harm. Still, it is necessary, though not easy, to find always a mode of procedure which is both free and forceful, yet not arbitrary or destructive of communion in the Church.

   2. To the freedom of the magisterium there corresponds in its own way the freedom that derives from the true scientific responsibility of theologians. It is not an unlimited freedom, for, besides being bound to the truth, it is also true of theology that "in the use of any freedom, the moral principle of personal and social responsibility must be observed" (DH no. 7). The theologians' task of interpreting the documents of the past and present magisterium, of putting them in the context of the whole of revealed truth, and of finding a better understanding of them by the use of hermeneutics, brings with it a somewhat critical function which obviously should be exercised positively rather than destructively.

a willingness on the part of members of the theological community to exchange candid judgments on one another's work.

As members of diverse communities, theologians have the responsibility to seek suitable ways of communicating doctrine to people today. They should adapt the communication of their research to the audience of their lectures or publications, and take into account the effect their presentation may have. They should use pastoral discretion in dealing with the communications media in order to avoid any harm which might result from premature or inappropriate dissemination of their thought to the theologically untrained (ITC Thesis 3:4).

To the extent that theologians accept more specifically ecclesiastical activities, such as the formation of future priests, they must accept reasonable canonical ordering of their work.

Correlative to the responsibilities of theologians in the life of the Church are certain rights. Paramount among them is lawful freedom of inquiry and expression of scholarly opinion (Canon 218; GS no. 62). As they discharge their responsibilities, theologians have the right to moral support from the Church, though they must also expect and even welcome objective criticism of their work.

Closely related to that right is another: the right of the theologian to a good reputation (Canon 220; GS no. 26), and, if needed, the defense of that right by appropriate administrative or judicial processes within the Church. In cases of dispute, the theologian has the right to expect access to a fair process, protecting both substantive and procedural rights. In addition, as professional scholars, theologians have the right to employ the usual means of research and publication and to associate freely in private and professional groups.

II. PROMOTING COOPERATION AND INFORMAL DIALOGUE

A. The Purposes and Climate of Cooperation

Authoritative teaching and theological inquiry are distinct but inseparable tasks. For this reason, bishops and theologians need to cooperate with one another in accordance with their respective responsibilities to enhance the quality of their diverse service to the Church. This cooperation is intended to realize the ideals of mutual encouragement, support, and assistance which are proposed by Vatican II, as well as to promote the efficacy of the episcopal office, the soundness of theological scholarship, and that unity without which the Church's mission in the world becomes weak and diffuse (LG nos. 4, 13; DV no. 8; GS no. 44).

Cooperation between theologians and bishops ought to play a significant, indeed indispensable, role as context and prelude to the employment of formal doctrinal dialogue for resolving doctrinal disputes. Bishops and theologians involved in ongoing collaboration are likely to grow in respect and trust for one another and thus to assist and support their respective service to the gospel. As they appreciate each other's struggles to be faithful to the demands of the gospel according to their different functions in the Church, their mutual respect and trust should grow.

This may serve to prevent theological disagreements and differences in viewpoint from degenerating to such an extent that formal doctrinal dialogue must be used to resolve the conflict.

Even in cases where formal doctrinal dialogue is employed, structured cooperation will already have established a climate in which all the parties are motivated to act prudently, patiently, and in charity (DH no. 14). Regular and meaningful cooperation provides the opportunity for each party to discern and clarify the responsibilities, rights, and interests of the other. Thus, if and when formal doctrinal dialogue is requested, both bishops and theologians can be aware of the necessary distinctions and of the possibilities and limitations of formal procedures used to deal with them.

Cooperation has a long history in the Church. In our own century prior to Vatican II, there were well established ways for theologians to cooperate with bishops in their tasks of teaching, sanctifying, and governing in the Church. In the 1917 *Code of Canon Law*, theologians (who were, in almost all cases, clerics) were envisaged as members of seminary faculties, as censors of books, as synodal examiners, and as conciliar and curial experts. In the revised *Code of Canon Law*, even more cooperative roles for theologians are envisaged, at least by implication.[9]

Bishops do rely upon theologians, explicitly or implicitly. Every bishop has been educated by theologians. So has every priest who cooperates with him in his ministry. Bishops have been encouraged, even charged, to study theology regularly to inform their preaching and to make their exercise of the pastoral office more effective.[10] So the appropriate questions are: How should bishops select theologians for consultation? When do they rely upon them? How is that reliance enacted?

Some bishops have appointed theologians as advisors and vicars for theological affairs, or have established boards of theological consultants.[11] The NCCB regularly calls upon theologians to cooperate in its work. While collaborative efforts like these are surely encouraging, much more needs to be done.[12]

Theologians, too, could profit from reinvigorated cooperation. Their relationship to the Church, which is an essential element in their identity and work as Catholic theologians, may take a further vital form in the course of collaboration with bishops. Cooperation would thus enable theologians better to understand and to fulfill their specific responsibilities in the Church.

While the focus of this section of the report is on structured cooperation between bishops and theologians, not all cooperation need or should take place

---

9 Cf. John A. Alesandro, "The Rights and Responsibilities of Theologians: A Canonical Perspective," in O'Donovan, ed., *Cooperation between Theologians and the Ecclesiastical Magisterium*, 101-102.

10 LG no. 25. See also Bishop John Cummins, "The Changing Relationship Between Bishops and Theologians," *Origins* 12 (June 17, 1982): 65-71, and Archbishop James Hickey, "The Bishop as Teacher," *Origins* 12 (July 29, 1982): 140-4.

11 "One method I find most helpful is to have the assistance of a personal theologian. . .We would not think of leading a diocese without someone trained in canon law. How much more then the presence of someone well trained in the authentic theology of the Church?" Hickey, 141-42.

12 See Cummins, 69, for recent instances of cooperation between bishops and theologians; also, *Catholic Theological Society of America Proceedings* 35 (1980): 332-6.

in a formal mode. If bishops and theologians are convinced of the importance of the help they can render one another in carrying out the mission of the Church, they will be determined and creative in seeking ways to work together informally. Without the pressure of a crisis, they may find their conversations deeply nourishing and empowering. Together they need to foster regular and personal ways of contact.

The emergence of an important national issue, the promulgation of a papal document, the weeks preceding or following a meeting of the NCCB can be occasions for the bishop and theologians of a diocese to discuss materials, proposals, or concerns and to discern their local implications and applications. Further, bishops could invite Catholic faculties of theology to consider and evaluate theological issues which have arisen in the life of the Church. On the other hand, Catholic colleges, universities, and seminaries might make it a practice to invite the bishop to campus events of theological or pastoral significance. Catholic scholars at secular institutions could do the same. In some dioceses, it may be feasible for bishops and theologians to meet regularly for informal exploration of mutual concerns or simply for shared prayer.

B. Implementing Structured Cooperation

1. Suggested Areas of Implementation. Initiation and development of collaboration between bishops and theologians will not always require the establishment of new structures. Most dioceses already have offices, departments, and staffs which assist the bishop in meeting his varied and complex responsibilities. The issues and areas delegated to these offices often have important theological dimensions, e.g., health care, ecumenical relations, adult education, catechetics, liturgy, finances, and family life. It would be a relatively simple matter to invite competent theologians to serve as consultants to these offices or even as part-time staff members.

There are also other questions of concern and interest to both bishops and theologians in which a cooperative approach could yield very desirable results. The importance of these matters will motivate joint efforts to establish the appropriate collaborative structures to deal with them. Just as presbyteral councils and pastoral councils cooperate with their bishops, so ways could be developed for theologians and bishops to bring their expertise and talent to bear on concerns such as:

- the means and efficacy of the local church's proclamation of the gospel;
- diocesan goals, missions statements, and priorities;
- religious education materials in use or proposed for use in the diocese;
- health care policies and procedures;
- goals and policies of Catholic educational institutions in the diocese;
- policies and guidelines for lectures, conferences, and workshops held in the diocese;
- priorities and policies for the Church's charitable endeavors;
- continuing education for priests, religious, deacons, and catechists;
- the theological supports for diocesan statements, position papers, and testimony to be presented in various civic and legal fora;
- the theological background for pastoral letters;

- ecumenical relations;
- diocesan employment policies and procedures.

Although bishops and theologians teach in very different ways, nevertheless the position of either can become the target of complaints and charges which have no substance or merit. Although the accuser(s) might be well-intentioned, these situations are potentially volatile and enervating for everyone involved. In some dioceses, it may prove desirable to the diocesan bishop to establish a procedure which prevents groundless charges from occupying more time and attention than they deserve.

An individual or a small committee recognized by the bishop and the theological community for theological expertise, tact, and pastoral sensitivity could be appointed by the bishop to screen these complaints. All complaints about theological teaching in the diocese could be referred here, after they have been presented to the bishop as well as the theologian in question. The screening task, while respecting and protecting the dignity of the complainant, is to keep a groundless complaint from becoming a dispute which needlessly distracts the bishop and/or the theologian from their more important services to the Church.

Another area that calls for cooperation is the provision contained in Canon 812 of the revised *Code of Canon Law*. This requires theologians teaching in institutes of higher learning to have *habeant oportet* a mandate granted by the competent ecclesiastical authority. It is important that bishops and the theological community work together to formulate a constructive way of ensuring the pursuit of truth in teaching Catholic doctrine, observing church law, and respecting the legitimate concerns of the American system of higher education.

2. Means of Implementation. The first steps toward structured cooperation can be taken by the bishop or by theologians in his diocese. The bishop himself can request the theologians to provide him with the names and areas of expertise of theologians who are willing and competent to offer their services to the local church in a collaborative way. Theologians themselves could also develop such information and offer it to the bishop. Either way, the local church would have more substantial theological expertise available to it.

With a view to appointing a theological advisor, the bishop could also consult widely with theologians inside and outside the diocese. In larger dioceses, this advisor could be of great assistance for theological affairs and serve as the bishop's liaison to the theologians in the diocese. The theological advisor could facilitate contact between the bishop and the theologians. Such a person should not be the bishop's only spokesperson on theological issues, nor substitute for the personal contact of the bishop with theologians.

In large urban centers or wherever there is a sufficient number of theologians, the bishop might well consider establishing a board of theological advisors. Among other functions, the board could serve in cases of dispute as the mediating, screening, or fact-finding body, prior to the initiation of any formal procedures.

Most dioceses in the United States do not have enough theologians to implement structured cooperation very extensively on their own. While this factor presents particular difficulties, it also provides the bishops and theologians of a province or region an opportunity to realize the vision of mutual support and cooperation among dioceses set forth by Vatican II (LG no. 23; CD nos. 6, 36, 37).

The theologians and bishops of a region could come together informally in the ways suggested above. They could also consider ways in which formal and regular cooperation could be established among them. For example, some dioceses have coordinated regional resources to develop more effective tribunals. Efforts have already been made in the United States with a view to sharing the theological and canonical resources of a region. The document On Due Process proposed a regional pooling of resources for more effective resolution of doctrinal conflicts.[13] Some state Catholic conferences have established medical-moral commissions.

Granted that the geographical distances involved make such cooperation more difficult to develop and maintain, still the advantages to be gained far outweigh the difficulties involved. Perhaps a demonstration project in a particular region could develop guidelines to facilitate regional structures for cooperation elsewhere.

Structured cooperation between bishops and theologians should, and to some extent already does, exist on the national level.[14] Prospects for developing it further, however, deserve serious consideration.

3. Principles Regarding Theological Consultants. Most theologians hold full-time positions in colleges, universities, or seminaries. As a result, in most instances of structured cooperation their role will be consultative. This means that they will serve in a part-time capacity as consultants or advisors to bishops or to diocesan departments and staffs which assist the bishop in carrying out his service to the Church.

If this form of structured collaboration is to function effectively and to realize the purposes for which it is established, certain principles should be followed.

First, theological consultants should be persons in full accord with the faith of the universal Church and aware of the ways that faith is known and lived in the particular church which they serve as consultants. The bishop is always free to choose his own advisors, but the competence of theologians who serve in any consultative capacity should be recognized by their peers. They should be selected from as many segments as possible on the spectrum of acceptable theological opinion, so that the Church can reap the benefits of the fullest range of theological resources available on particular issues or problems.

Second, there are often advantages to making public the names of consultants and perhaps even the selection process. Unnecessary secrecy can lead to suspicion and mistrust.

Third, whenever possible, consultants should serve for a fixed term. A policy of orderly succession among consultants will foster the benefits of both continuity and freshness of perspective on the issues. It will also realize the ideal of common effort which is at the heart of authentic unity in the Church.

Fourth, everyone involved centrally or marginally in the process should remember that the theological consultant, through faithfulness to the truth of the gospel and the demands of theological science, serves not only the local bishop, but also

---

13   On Due Process, 10.

14   Ibid.

the entire local Church. Otherwise, the complementary but distinct and irreducible roles of the bishop and the theologian may be confused and the anticipated results of real cooperation may not be fully realized.[15]

C. Cooperation as Aiding Doctrinal Dialogue

As their conversation and collaboration become more common, bishops and theologians are likely to gain a greater sense of the distinct but inseparable services they perform in the one Church through, for example, authoritative teaching and pastoral leadership (on the part of the bishops) and ethical reflection, theological education, and research (on the part of the theologians). This alone should eliminate many misunderstandings between them.[16]

Regular and active cooperation will also establish a mutual personal knowledge and trust between bishops and theologians which can lessen the occasions when formal doctrinal dialogue is required to resolve a dispute. As bishops and theologians come to know each other not merely in official roles but as faithful persons, recourse to formal procedures to resolve conflicts between them should become less and less frequent.

If formal doctrinal dialogue is necessary, however, the mutual knowledge and trust established by previous cooperation will help to ensure that it works to the benefit of everyone involved. The dispute is also less likely to become an arena for an adversary relationship between the bishop and the theologian. Mutual knowledge and trust will help to maintain the unity of love throughout the course of the procedures, when tempers may be short, sensitivities acute, and feelings high. Each will more likely be concerned to protect the other's good name and reputation and to employ the formal doctrinal dialogue so as to preserve and enhance the service each offers to the Church. Both bishops and theologians will be solicitous for the maintenance and exercise of each other's responsibilities and rights.

III. A POSSIBILITY FOR FORMAL DOCTRINAL DIALOGUE

A. Purposes of the Dialogue

Collaboration and structured cooperation help to clarify doctrinal positions. Throughout such contacts there is a presupposition of sound doctrine, a presumption which holds unless it is refuted by contrary evidence. Nevertheless, there may be differences of opinion, disagreements, or questions concerning doctrinal matters. The bishop may have already deemed it necessary to speak or act publicly in an

---

15 See ITC, 17.

16 "The magisterium and theology have two different tasks to perform. That is why neither can be reduced to the other. Yet they serve the one whole. But precisely on account of this configuration they must remain in consultation with one another." John Paul II, *L'Osservatore Romano* [English], no. 50 (662), December 15, 1980, 17.

effort to provide pastoral guidance to the faithful. If these differences or actions lead to conflict or dispute, formal doctrinal dialogue may be used, always respecting the differing roles of bishops and theologians in the Church (cf. Canons 753, 218).

Such dialogue is not a judicial or administrative proceeding (cf. ITC Theses 10, 11, 12 with commentary). Its scope is to determine the facts and their theological and pastoral implications, and thereby to resolve any misunderstandings between bishops and theologians. It would precede any judgment which the bishop as authoritative teacher might eventually feel himself obliged to make for the sake of the faith of the Church. A dialogue about doctrine would also ordinarily take place before any consideration of a possible administrative response to a doctrinal matter. This distinction between doctrinal discussion and administrative action is basic. A doctrinal dialogue does not entail new obligations for bishops in their authoritative teaching or for theologians in their scholarly reflection, but offers adaptable means for both to exercise their roles as effectively as possible. By entering such a dialogue no theologian acquires the authority of a bishop, nor is a bishop expected to be a theological scholar. Each would participate according to his or her respective role in the Church, but each also as desiring greater understanding of the question at issue. If a bishop is to make a final determination of his view of a theologian's teaching, his judgment should be well informed and reasonable. While not expected to justify his decision in the manner of a scientific theologian, he should ordinarily present reasons for his judgment. If theologians are to sustain or modify their positions, they should do so through dialogue with bishops as well as with their theological colleagues. For example, if a bishop has questioned the teaching of a theologian, the theologian might request such a dialogue. On the other hand, if a bishop is concerned about the reported opinions of a theologian, he might be the one to request the initiation of formal doctrinal dialogue. In such cases, initiation of a private formal dialogue would serve the unity of the Church far better than public disagreement.

Neither a bishop nor a theologian may be *required* to use this process, and public pressure should not be brought to bear upon their choice. If they choose to do so, the dialogue would proceed through adopting or adapting any of the procedures that follow. A formal dialogue does not imply equality of roles in the Church but a structured pattern for doctrinal discussion.

Briefly stated, the purpose of formal doctrinal dialogue is to determine the nature and gravity of the issue at dispute as well as its pastoral significance and to achieve an agreement between the parties. The process will normally involve meetings, although much can be accomplished by written statements. As a sign of unity and charity, an atmosphere of prayer should mark the dialogue in all its stages.

B. Participants

For the purpose of these guidelines, the dispute in need of resolution is presumed to be between a theologian and a bishop. The theologian or bishop who requests the use of this formal dialogue is termed the *initiating party*. The other partner who agrees to this formal dialogue is termed the *second party*. Several bishops or several theologians may be acting as initiating party or second party.

Other persons may assist the principals in the formal dialogue. These may be involved in regard to one or more of the following functions.

1. *Advice*. Advisors may assist the initiating party or the second party by their advice and counsel. Advisors are selected freely by the party whom they will be serving as advisor.

2. *Expertise*. Experts may be called upon to assist the parties in reaching mutual understanding about their respective positions, to offer an evaluation of the relationship of theological statements with Catholic tradition, and to give advice about the pastoral effect of such teaching. Experts, therefore, should be knowledgeable about the matter under discussion, should be representative of the variety of views within Catholic tradition, and should participate in the process in a manner acceptable to both parties. Normally such experts will themselves be professional theologians or persons versed in pastoral ministry. While the opinion of experts, even if unanimous, is not binding on either of the parties, it should be given serious weight in proceeding with the dialogue and should not be rejected without good reason.

3. *Facilitation*. At the request of both parties, a facilitator may assist at any of the various stages of formal dialogue. The facilitator helps the process to move forward by bringing the principals to a better understanding of what each means, by setting specific questions for them, and by providing at various stages in the dialogue *a state of the question* to clarify what points are truly at issue at that particular moment.

4. *Delegation*. Dialogue is carried out most effectively in a face-to-face exchange, through which each party comes to a more personal appreciation of the other's position. Although this is the preferred method, there may be occasions when either party considers it necessary to delegate another person to assist in the various tasks of formal doctrinal dialogue. A bishop, for example, may choose to participate directly throughout this dialogue or to have his concerns represented by a theologian. In every case, however, the final statement of agreement for each task in the formal dialogue should be signed by the principal parties themselves.

C. Procedures for Formal Doctrinal Dialogue

1. BEGINNING THE DIALOGUE

Either a theologian or a bishop may request formal doctrinal dialogue. But the decision to begin such a dialogue must be freely agreed upon by both.

a. Direct contact between the two parties. The initiating party should first have approached the second party in an informal manner to determine whether the apparent dispute may be immediately resolved without formal dialogue. If formal dialogue is needed, the initiating party makes a written request to the second party to enter into formal doctrinal dialogue. The written request outlines the doctrinal points at issue, the manner in which the dispute has arisen, the attempts to resolve the issue which have already been made, the specific request to employ formal doctrinal dialogue to settle the question, and initial suggestions concerning ways to resolve the doctrinal dispute.

b. Indirectly, through a contact person. A contact person may be appointed within a diocese to process requests for the use of formal doctrinal dialogue. The contact person is appointed by the bishop and should be qualified to evaluate and process such requests, generally acceptable also to the theological community and easily available for contact.

The first function of the contact person would be to determine whether the request for formal dialogue is legitimate. If the request is judged to be inappropriate, the contact person informs the initiating party, indicating the reasons for rejecting the request. If the initiating party then resubmits the request, the contact person submits it to the second party for a response.

If the request at the outset is judged to be appropriate, it is sent to the second party for a response and the initiating party is informed immediately of the date of this action. Rejection of the request by the contact person or submission of the request to the second party for response should normally take place within one month of the receipt of the request by the contact person.

2. THE RESPONSE

Acknowledgment of a request for formal dialogue ordinarily should be given in writing within two weeks of the receipt of the request, and a formal response within one month of the receipt of the request.

a.   An affirmative response to the request should include an explicit commitment to formal doctrinal dialogue, a statement of the points about which both parties seem at the outset to be in agreement, the points which seem to be in dispute, and initial suggestions concerning ways to resolve the doctrinal dispute.

b.   A negative response should explicitly refuse to make use of formal doctrinal dialogue and state the reasons for refusal.

c.   If after six weeks from the date on which the formal request was sent to the second party no response has been received by the initiating party, a second request should be sent to the second party. Failure to respond to this second request within two weeks shall be interpreted as refusal to make use of formal doctrinal dialogue.

3. AGREEMENT ON PROCEDURE

The written request for dialogue and the response may have already clarified the disagreement and the desired goal in dialogue. Nevertheless, the next step should be a preliminary agreement on the statement of the issues, on the procedures to be followed, and on the goal to be achieved by their formal dialogue.

In determining procedures, the preliminary agreement should address matters such as the following:

    a.   level of confidentiality to be respected;
    b.   participation by other persons and how they are to be selected (see above, B, 1-4);
    c.   record keeping and, if appropriate, transcripts;
    d.   time limits;
    e.   responsibility for expenses.

Good order requires that this preliminary agreement be in writing and signed by both parties. It can be modified at any time by their mutual consent.

4. THE DIALOGUE

Disputes between theologians and members of the ecclesiastical magisterium are usually complex and may involve deep feelings. It is not easy to decide *a priori* on the best or simplest method to resolve the situation. At the beginning it is essential that both parties be committed to the procedure. As the dialogue progresses, the parties may find it helpful to alter by mutual consent the procedures they had agreed upon.

Although disputes may be considerably different, formal doctrinal dialogue proposes primarily to clarify the objective content of what is at issue and to accomplish this through the completion of four tasks:

    a.   gathering data;
    b.   clarifying meaning;
    c.   determining the relationship of the points at issue to Catholic tradition;
    d.   identifying implications in the life of the Church.

One of the main instruments for achieving agreement is the formulation of written statements with regard to each of the tasks. These statements, signed by both parties, express points of agreement, clarify reasons for disagreement, and specify further questions to be addressed.

FIRST TASK: GATHERING THE DATA

Since doctrinal disputes arise from public utterances or writings, the first task is to agree on what was actually said or written. There may be no disagreement as to the data at all, in which case a statement of agreement should immediately be drawn up and signed by both parties.

If the parties initially disagree about what was said or written, ways should be found to solve this difference of opinion. Examples include:

    1.   In written matters, copies of the actual materials should be made available to both parties.

2. In spoken matters, tape recordings, written reports, and other trustworthy records, if they exist, should be made available to both parties.

3. If no record exists, to settle the question of what was actually said or written it may be necessary to call upon witnesses.

Adequate access to the record by both parties is essential to effective dialogue. In cases in which a dispute has arisen because of complaints or accusations by other persons, the party accused or complained against has the right of access to the materials sent by the other persons—confidentiality in accord with church law, of course, always being respected. In such situations the burden of proof as to matters of fact rests on those bringing the complaint or accusation.

In determining what was said or written, it is important to specify the pertinent context, such as:

1. the literary genre: newspaper article, theological study, popular religious work, etc.;

2. the context of spoken communications: lecture, classroom, seminar, radio or television, etc.;

3. the audience addressed;

4. the level and extent of publicity.

In especially complicated matters the accomplishment of the task of gathering data may very well benefit from a facilitator who can settle factual questions to the satisfaction of both parties. The parties may also make use of advisors or, if necessary, delegates to expedite the process.

This task should be completed with a written statement of agreement, signed by both parties. It specifies the data gathered and the agreement of the parties on the essential points of what was said or written. In some cases agreement on accurate data may itself resolve the dispute and complete the dialogue.

SECOND TASK: CLARIFYING THE MEANING

While completion of the first task may determine clearly what was said or written, questions may still exist about the meaning of the data. Since words may admit of varying interpretations, the parties need to seek a common understanding of the meaning of what was said or written. The result of this effort should be an agreement either on a single meaning of these data or on their possible, differing interpretations.

In reaching this clarification, consideration should be given to various factors, such as:

1. the significance of the words in text and context;

2. the broader corpus of the author's work, philosophical and theological perspective, and method;

3. the author's intention in presenting the material, whether the position was being advocated, defended, described, etc.;

4. the pertinent context of the work at issue as determined in the first task (see above);

5. the degree to which the statement is presented as a personal opinion or as a teaching of the Church.

If agreement on meaning is not readily achieved, the parties may find it useful to rely on the advice of others or perhaps to submit the matter to a jointly acceptable facilitator.

This second task should be completed with a written statement of agreement, signed by both parties, expressing as clearly as possible the mutually accepted meaning of what was said or written. The statement may also specify any differing interpretations which remain. In some cases, agreement on the meaning may itself resolve the dispute and complete the dialogue.

THIRD TASK: DETERMINING THE RELATIONSHIP WITH CATHOLIC TRADITION

Every doctrinal dispute will initially involve at least an apparent divergence of opinion about the consonance of a public utterance or writing with Catholic tradition. The completion of the first two tasks may result in the conclusion that the disagreement was unfounded. Nevertheless, the first two tasks may simply serve to clarify the point at issue, that is, the consonance of what was said or written with Catholic tradition.

This stage of the doctrinal inquiry is complex. It is not the same as a final judgment about public teaching that the bishop may make at the end of the entire process. Nor is it a task that can be isolated from the parties themselves; their personal involvement is especially important. It is a learning process in which dialogue should assist both parties to develop a more precise understanding of the fullness of Catholic tradition. Thus, in approaching this task the parties should seek to discover points of agreement, particularly in regard to the questions which must be studied and the appropriate order for addressing those questions.

This stage of dialogue should begin with a written statement by the initiating party outlining the basis on which consonance with Catholic tradition is questioned. The second party should respond to this initial statement in writing. If no agreement is reached, these two documents form the basis for further dialogue.

The term *Catholic tradition* refers to the whole range of church teaching grounded in the word of God, especially in the Scriptures, and received in the Church through the centuries. The magisterium serves the word of God by proposing doctrine in solemn conciliar or papal pronouncements, in ordinary papal and episcopal teaching, and in other activities such as the approval of materials used in the instruction of the faithful and the worship of the Church. Catholic tradition is also reflected and furthered in the *sensus fidelium*, the works of approved authors, and in Catholic life, worship, and belief. Determining the consonance of a theological view with Catholic tradition will demand a careful consideration of the historical context and development of church teaching, an understanding of the hierarchy of truths, an evaluation of the various levels of teaching authority, appreciation of the distinction between the substance of the faith and its expression, and the degree to which the Church has committed itself in this matter.

At this stage in the dialogue the parties may be assisted by a facilitator, by personal advisors, and especially by consultation with theological experts.

This task should be completed with a written statement of agreement, signed by both parties. It specifies the steps taken to complete the task, the resulting points of agreement, and any remaining disagreement. Here, too, the written statement of agreement may suffice to resolve the dispute and complete the dialogue.

FOURTH TASK: IDENTIFYING THE IMPLICATIONS FOR THE LIFE OF THE CHURCH

The previous tasks have resulted in agreements on the public utterances and writings in question and possibly differing interpretations and disagreements about them. The fourth task is to determine the pastoral implications of these utterances and writings in the life of the Church. While actual or apparent implications precipitate most doctrinal disputes, they are frequently the most difficult to sort out and agree upon. This task requires not merely understanding, but prudence; not just learning, but wisdom. Concern for such implications is a responsibility of both bishops and theologians.

To begin this task, the initiating party should state in writing the nature and extent of the implications. The second party should respond to this statement in writing. If no agreement has been reached, these two documents form the basis for further dialogue on this matter.

A discussion about implications cannot be simply an exchange of personal impressions. It should clarify the criteria used by the parties to assess pastoral life. Conclusions should be based on adequate information required for prudential judgments. This may necessitate gathering additional evidence. The discussion might be assisted by the opinion of persons noted for prudence and experience in pastoral and theological matters. The parties may rely on advisors or may mutually agree on a facilitator to assist in this task.

This task is concluded with a written statement of agreement signed by both parties, specifying the steps taken to determine the implications in the life of the Church and their mutual and individual conclusions. It may include actions agreed upon for the future. This written statement may suffice to resolve the dispute and conclude the dialogue, or even provide for continued review of the issue.

D. Possible Results of Formal Doctrinal Dialogue

Formal doctrinal dialogue may conclude in a variety of ways. It is important to identify the conclusion of the dialogue process and the outcome of the dispute itself. The degree of publicity to be given to the results of the dialogue should be carefully adapted to the particular situation. In every case, even if complete agreement has not been reached, both parties should discuss these matters so that both are aware of proposed actions.

These are some possible results of the dialogue:

1. The theological and pastoral issues may be resolved to the satisfaction of both parties at any stage in the formal dialogue.
2. At the conclusion of the formal dialogue the theological issue may be unresolved, but both parties may agree that the issue may remain so without the need for further action. Agreement to disagree may be a recognition of legitimate pluralism or of a situation in which pastoral responsibility requires no further action.
3. There may be no agreement concerning the theological and pastoral issues nor acceptance of the disagreement as a form of legitimate pluralism. In light of pastoral considerations, various responses on the doctrinal level are then possible. Such responses vary in purpose, intensity, and publicity. They will also depend on the qualification of the theological issue in question. The following are some possibilities:

   a. Call for continued critical theological study.
   b. Expand the context of the dialogue to a regional or national level.
   c. Restate in a positive fashion authoritative church teaching.
   d. Issue a doctrinal *monitum*, i.e., a clear warning of danger to the faith in what is being taught.
   e. Declare publicly the apparent error of a position.
   f. Classify certain positions as one of the following:

      1) a private position which may be presented by itself, provided it is not represented as official Catholic teaching;
      2) a private opinion which, when presented, must be accompanied by other more acceptable positions;
      3) unsuitable for teaching as Catholic doctrine.

   g. Make an accurate presentation of views to the media.

E. Subsequent Administrative Action

The foregoing procedure has been a doctrinal dialogue. The best response to bad teaching is good teaching. A doctrinal response which convincingly expresses the authoritative teaching of the Church is, therefore, the most desirable response to a doctrinal dispute. Nonetheless, when doctrinal differences begin to affect the common good and doctrinal dialogue has failed to resolve them, administrative action on the part of bishops or canonical recourse on the part of theologians may be appropriate or even necessary. (On the limits of dialogue, cf. ITC Thesis 12 with commentary.)

Administrative procedures do not of themselves resolve doctrinal issues; they are intended primarily to address pastoral situations. The kind and degree of administrative action should be proportionate to the pastoral requirements of the common good and should be no more severe than those requirements demand.

The degree of understanding reached in the doctrinal dialogue should help all parties to appreciate their mutual concern for the good of the Church and will influence the decision about any subsequent action or recourse. In addition, the signed agreements of the formal doctrinal dialogue will provide a valuable record for subsequent action on the part of bishops or recourse on the part of theologians. Differences of responsibility and authority, of course, can become especially apparent at this point. But this should not obscure the fact that doctrinal truth is not decided or assured by juridical decisions alone. In all cases, bishops and theologians alike should recognize that administrative action is always in service to the truth of a gospel that is meant to free us to love God and one another.

AFTERWORD

The Church's witness and mission in the world are seriously conditioned by its own internal care for truth and justice. Disputes about doctrines and the manner of their resolution seldom remain purely internal affairs. On the contrary, our understanding and practice of faith today concern Christians and non-Christians alike. Bishops and theologians should all be conscious that unavoidable publicity is a fact of modern life. They should take care that media involvement not render ineffective the opportunity and structure for cooperation and dialogue. They should be concerned to avoid scandal. The attitude of participants and atmosphere for process should blend civility and charity with restraint and, where necessary, that dimension of confidentiality conducive to trust, understanding, and, perhaps, reconciliation.

We believe that, with the guidance of the Spirit, the many different parts of the body of Christ can be knit together in justice and love and thereby become more truly themselves before God. In seeking clear and equitable ways to resolve disagreements about our faith, we recommit ourselves to being a Church that is one and open, a genuine community of grace sharing the truth freely given to it. Thus we choose again the life that has been offered to us, that there truly may be "one body and one Spirit, as you were also called to the one hope of your call; one Lord, one faith, one baptism, one God and Father of all, who is above all and through all and in all" (Eph 4:4-6).

A Letter to College Students

November 1995

The Letter to College Students on the tenth anniversary of the pastoral letter on campus ministry *Empowered by the Spirit* was developed by the Committee on Education of the United States Catholic Conference. The text was reviewed and approved by the full body of bishops in November 1995, and is hereby authorized for publication by the undersigned.

Monsignor Dennis M. Schnurr
General Secretary
NCCB/USCC

Dear College Students,

We write to you as your co-workers in Christ and we congratulate you on all you have done to arrive at this point in your life. Already you are leaders, because in a very real sense you have begun to lead, especially if you are an older student with family and work responsibilities.

Your college years are a very significant time for you. In these few years you will greatly expand both your knowledge and your skills. At the same time, you will be making many important choices— about vocation, relationships, and career.

These years will also provide a wonderful opportunity for you to grow in your faith, a faith that is rooted in your own personal relationship with Jesus and is nourished by prayer, reading of the Scriptures and your participation in the sacraments. As you grow in faith, you will recognize the important responsibility of sharing your faith with others.

We realize that foremost among the many priorities in your life is the time devoted to study. Your study is not unrelated to your life of faith. Through your exploration of history, language, science and art, you can also deepen your faith and your understanding of our religious tradition. In the future, what you study now can help transform business, academia, culture and the mass media into places where the Spirit of God truly lives and works. And there is always the possibility of a career of ministry and leadership in the church.

But you do not have to wait. Think of the impact you can have even now as a Catholic college student on others who may not know the rich tradition of Catholicism. Working with students of other faiths and religious traditions on campus, you can make important contributions toward peace and justice, reminding the whole academic community of the presence of those whom society neglects or marginalizes. By your involvement as a Catholic, you can help others to see the face of Christ in the faces of the poor.

It is a fact of campus life and life everywhere that many people today experience a deep sense of uncertainty and confusion. It seems that for some the world is filled with questions and even discouragement. While we have to admit that the future, as always, is uncertain, we also have to recognize that it is full of possibilities. And as Catholics, we have the added certainty and hope that comes from our faith in the victory of Jesus' death and resurrection. You can be witnesses of that hope for everyone you meet, sharing with them the hope that is based on the Gospel and the abiding presence of the Spirit. By your care and concern, you can also reassure other people that they are really loved and that Christ's love is always present for them.

There are many specific ways that you can minister on campus to create a climate of hope and a community of welcome. Begin by inviting your friends and neighbors to join you at Sunday Mass, the most important celebration of the Catholic community. It is easier for them to respond to the prompting of the spirit when someone else is willing to go with them. Also, offer to be a reader, server, eucharistic minister, cantor or musician, according to your gifts.

Strengthen your own spirituality by searching for answers and by becoming more knowledgeable about your faith. Start with the Scriptures, God speaking to us. Then the Catechism of the Catholic Church is a wonderful reference that can help to answer both your questions and those others might have. And campus ministers, with their special training, want to be a help to you with your questions, spiritual growth and religious identity.

There are so many other ways to serve. Volunteer to help out in the local community or improve the quality of life on campus by becoming involved in peer ministry or by tutoring your fellow students. Working together with campus ministers, you can organize or participate in small prayer or faith groups in your residence hall or local community. By your efforts on behalf of life, you can remind others that a lived Christian faith begins with a profound respect for human life from conception to natural death. By simplifying your lifestyle, you can be a reminder that our resources are not without limit and ought to be used wisely.

Jesus commissioned us to be witnesses by the testimony of our lives when he said, "You will receive power when the Holy Spirit comes upon you, and you will be my witnesses in Jerusalem, throughout Judea and Samaria, and to the ends of the earth" (Acts, 1:8). We bishops of the United States enumerated in our pastoral letter on campus ministry of 1985, "Empowered by the Spirit," six ways by which the church on campus can be a faithful witness to the message of the Gospel: forming the faith community, appropriating the faith, forming the Christian conscience, educating for justice, facilitating personal development and developing leaders for the future.

Since 1985, many campus ministries have reported increased student involvement in liturgy, community service, retreat opportunities and justice concerns. Now as the church approaches the 2,000-year mark in its history, we challenge you to reflect, using these categories from "Empowered by the Spirit," on the ways in which you have revealed the church on campus to be a faithful witness to the truth of the Gospel, a "servant community, dedicated to social justice, and a more effective sign and instrument of the kingdom of peace and justice in the world." This will be especially challenging for you who do not have the help of an organized campus ministry program.

You have so many gifts to offer the church: your faith, your desire to serve, your spiritual hunger, your vitality, your optimism and idealism, your talents and skills. We can all learn from you, so we ask you to expand your leadership role in witnessing to the Gospel on campus. We promise you our prayerful support and encourage your future involvement in the mission of the church through a parish faith community. We look forward to working more closely with you to make the church ever more effective in announcing the reign of God. We ask for your prayers for us in our work of shepherding the church.

The Application of *Ex corde Ecclesiae* for the United States

1999

In November 1999, Most Reverend Joseph A. Fiorenza, president of the National Conference of Catholic Bishops, petitioned the Apostolic See that these executive norms of the apostolic constitution *Ex corde Ecclesiae*, approved according to the norm of law by a plenary session of the Conference, be duly granted recognition. In May 2000, the Congregation for Bishops, after consultation with the Congregation for Catholic Education and the Pontifical Council for the Interpretation of Legislative Texts, found these norms in conformity with universal canon law and declared them valid. These norms are printed here as *The Application of Ex corde Ecclesiae for the United States*, which is authorized for publication by the undersigned.

Monsignor Dennis M. Schnurr
General Secretary
NCCB/USCC

DECREE OF PROMULGATION

On November 17, 1999, the Catholic Bishops of the United States, meeting in Plenary Session of the National Conference of Catholic Bishops, approved *The Application of Ex corde Ecclesiae for the United States* implementing the Apostolic Constitution *Ex corde Ecclesiae*, according to the norm of law.

The action was granted *recognitio* by the Congregation for Bishops in accord with article 82 of the Apostolic Constitution *Pastor Bonus* and issued by Decree of the Congregation for Bishops signed by His Eminence Lucas Cardinal Moreira Neves, Prefect, and His Excellency Most Reverend Francisco Monterisi, Secretary, and dated May 3, 2000.

As President of the National Conference of Catholic Bishops, I hereby decree that *The Application of Ex corde Ecclesiae for the United States* will be in force as particular law for the United States on May 3, 2001.

Given at the offices of the National Conference of Catholic Bishops in Washington, DC, on June 1, 2000.

Most Reverend Joseph A. Fiorenza
Bishop of Galveston-Houston
President, National Conference of Catholic Bishops

INTRODUCTION

Catholic higher education in the United States has a unique history. The opening of Georgetown in 1789 and subsequent growth into 230 Catholic colleges and universities is a remarkable achievement for the Church and the United States.

Catholic colleges and universities are related to the ecclesial community, to the higher education enterprise of the United States and to the broader society. Founded and developed principally by religious communities of women and men, they now involve lay administrators, professors and trustees who are Catholic and not Catholic—all committed to the vision of Catholic higher education.

Catholic colleges and universities, where culture and faith intersect, bring diversity to American higher education. Diversity is present among the institutions themselves: two-year colleges and graduate program universities; liberal arts colleges and research universities; schools for the professions and schools for technical education.

To all participating in Catholic higher education, the Bishops of the United States express their admiration and sincere gratitude, knowing that both the nation and ecclesial community are affected by their commitments and talents. Bishops want to maintain, preserve and guarantee the Catholic identity of Catholic higher education, a responsibility they share in various ways with sponsoring religious communities, boards of trustees, university administration, faculty, staff and students.

PART ONE: THEOLOGICAL AND PASTORAL PRINCIPLES

1. *EX CORDE ECCLESIAE*

On August 15, 1990, Pope John Paul II issued an apostolic constitution on Catholic higher education entitled *Ex corde Ecclesiae*.[1] The Apostolic Constitution described the identity and mission of Catholic colleges and universities and provided General Norms to help fulfill its vision.

The General Norms are to be applied concretely by episcopal conferences, taking into account the status of each college and university and, as far as possible and appropriate, civil law. Accordingly, recognizing that the Apostolic Constitution *Ex corde Ecclesiae* is normative for the Church throughout the world, this document seeks to apply its principles and norms to all Catholic colleges, universities, and institutions of higher learning within the territory encompassed by the United States Catholic Conference of Bishops.

---

1   Pope John Paul II, Apostolic Constitution on Catholic Universities *Ex corde Ecclesiae* (ECE), August 15, 1990, AAS 82 (1990) 1475-1509. English translation: *Origins*, CNS Documentary Service, October 4, 1990. In accordance with canon 455, §1, the United States Conference of Bishops promulgates this Application as a response to the special mandate of the Apostolic See (cf. ECE, II, Art. 1, §2). The Application refers to Catholic universities and other institutes of higher learning (cf. canons 807-814); excluded from the Application's treatment are ecclesiastical universities and faculties (cf. canons 815-821), which are governed by the Apostolic Constitution, *Sapientia Christiana* (see footnote 19).

2. THE ECCLESIOLOGICAL CONCEPT OF COMMUNION

The Church is made up of individual faithful and communities linked with one another through many active ecclesial relationships. A true understanding of these dynamic relationships flows from the faith-conviction that God the Father, through His incarnate Son, Jesus Christ, has revealed His desire to incorporate all people into the life of the Trinity. It is in the Church, through the indwelling of the Holy Spirit, that this relationship of all persons and communities with the Triune God takes place. This body of dynamic relationships held together by the unity of faith is aptly described in the theological concept of communion.[2]

The dynamic of communion unites on a deeper and more productive level the various communities in the Church through which so much of her mission of salvation, and consequently human progress, is carried out. More specifically, ecclesial communion furnishes the basis for the collaborative relationships between the hierarchy and Catholic universities contemplated in *Ex corde Ecclesiae*: "Every Catholic University is to maintain communion with the universal Church and the Holy See; it is to be in close communion with the local Church and in particular with the diocesan bishops of the region or the nation in which it is located."[3] The Catholic university is a vital institution in the communion of the Church and is "a primary and privileged place for a fruitful dialogue between the Gospel and culture."[4]

The richness of communion illuminates the ecclesial relationship that unites the distinct, and yet complementary, teaching roles of bishops and Catholic universities. In the light of communion, the teaching responsibilities of the hierarchy and of the Catholic universities retain their distinctive autonomous nature and goal but are joined as complementary activities contributing to the fulfillment of the Church's universal teaching mission. The communion of the Church embraces both the pastoral work of bishops and the academic work of Catholic universities, thus linking the bishops' right and obligation to communicate and safeguard the integrity of Church doctrine with the right and obligation of Catholic universities to investigate, analyze and communicate all truth freely.

The communion of all the faithful with the Triune God and with one another is a theological reality expressing the will of God. It is by understanding and living this communion that bishops and Catholic universities can most effectively collaborate to fulfill their proper mission within the Church. In carrying out its mission to search for truth, the Catholic university is uniquely situated to serve not only the

---

2   See Vatican Council II, Dogmatic Constitution on the Church (*Lumen Gentium*) nos. 4, 7, 9-29 (Chapter II: the People of God) and *passim*; Congregation for the Doctrine of the Faith, "Letter to the Bishops of the Catholic Church on Some Aspects of the Church Understood as Communion," *Origins* 22 (1992), 108-112; *Catechism of the Catholic Church*, nos. 787-801 and *passim*; 1985 Extraordinary Synod of Bishops, "A Message to the People of God," *Origins* 15 (1985), 441-444, and "The Final Report," *Origins* 15 (1985), 444-450.

3   ECE, II, Art. 5, §1.

4   ECE, I, no. 43. See also ECE, I, no. 49. For purposes of stylistic simplicity, this document, in both the "Theological and Pastoral Principles" and "Particular Norms," uses the word "university" as a generic term to include universities, colleges and other institutions of higher learning.

people of God but the entire human family "in their pilgrimage to the transcendent goal which gives meaning to life."[5]

3. THE CATHOLIC UNIVERSITY'S TWOFOLD RELATIONSHIP

Catholic universities are participants in the life of the universal Church, the local Church, the higher education community of the United States and the civic community. As such, they "are called to continuous renewal, both as 'universities' and as 'Catholic.'"[6] This twofold relationship is described in the May 22, 1994, joint document of the Congregation for Catholic Education and the Pontifical Councils for the Laity and for Culture, which states that the Catholic university achieves its purpose when

> . . . it gives proof of being rigorously serious as a member of the international community of knowledge and expresses its Catholic identity through an explicit link with the Church, at both local and universal levels—an identity which marks concretely the life, the services and the programs of the university community. In this way, by its very existence, the Catholic university achieves its aim of guaranteeing, in institutional form, a Christian presence in the university world. . . .[7]

One of the ways this relationship is clarified and maintained is through dialogue that includes faculty of all disciplines, students, staff, academic and other administrative officers, trustees, and sponsoring religious communities of the educational institutions, all of whom share responsibility for the character of Catholic higher education. The bishop and his collaborators in the local Church are integral parties in this dialogue.

The Catholic university is related to the local and universal ecclesial community[8] as well as to the broader society[9] and the higher education academy.[10] In this document we are directing special attention to the relationship between universities and Church authorities. *Ex corde Ecclesiae* provides one of the ecclesiological principles to address this specific relationship.

> Bishops have a particular responsibility to promote Catholic Universities, and especially to promote and assist in the preservation and strengthening of their Catholic identity, including the protection of their Catholic identity in relation to civil authorities. This will be achieved more

---

5   ECE, I, 13, quoting from "The Catholic University in the Modern World," the final document of the Second International Congress of Delegates of Catholic Universities, Rome, November 20-29, 1972, Sec. 1.

6   ECE, Introduction, no. 7.

7   "The Church's Presence in the University and in University Culture," II, §2, *Origins*, June 16, 1994, 74-80.

8   ECE, I, nos. 27-29, 31.

9   Ibid., I, nos. 32-37.

10   Ibid., I, nos. 12, 37; II, Art. 7, §§1-2.

effectively if close personal and pastoral relationships exist between University and Church authorities, characterized by *mutual trust, close and consistent cooperation and continuing dialogue*. Even though they do not enter directly into the internal government of the University, Bishops "should be seen not as external agents but as participants in the life of the Catholic University." [italics added][11]

Each of these elements in the pastoral relationship of bishops with Catholic universities warrants attention.

4. MUTUAL TRUST BETWEEN UNIVERSITY AND CHURCH AUTHORITIES

Mutual trust goes beyond the personalities of those involved in the relationship. The trust is grounded in a shared baptismal belief in the truths that are rooted in Scripture and Tradition, as interpreted by the Church, concerning the mystery of the Trinity: God the Father and Creator, who works even until now; God the Son and incarnate Redeemer, who is the Way and the Truth and the Life; and God the Holy Spirit, the Paraclete, whom the Father and Son send. In the spirit of *communio*, the relationship of trust between university and Church authorities, based on these shared beliefs with their secular and religious implications, is fostered by mutual listening, by collaboration that respects differing responsibilities and gifts, and by a solidarity that mutually recognizes respective statutory limitations and responsibilities.

5. CLOSE AND CONSISTENT COOPERATION BETWEEN UNIVERSITY AND CHURCH AUTHORITIES

Collaborating to integrate faith with life is a necessary part of the "close personal and pastoral relationships"[12] to which universities and bishops are called. Within their academic mission of teaching and research, in ways appropriate to their own constituencies and histories, including their sponsorship by religious communities, institutions offer courses in Catholic theology that reflect current scholarship and are in accord with the authentic teaching of the Church.

Many cooperative programs, related to Gospel outreach, already flourish throughout the country. It is highly desirable that representatives of both educational institutions and Church authorities jointly identify, study, and pursue solutions to issues concerning social justice, human life and the needs of the poor.

Allocation of personnel and money to assure the special contributions of campus ministry is indispensable. In view of the presence on campus of persons of other religious traditions, it is a concern of the whole Church that ecumenical and inter-religious relationships should be fostered with sensitivity.

A structure and strategy to insure ongoing dialogue and cooperation should be established by university and Church authorities.

---

11   Ibid., I, no. 28. The citation at the end is from John Paul II, *Address to Leaders of Catholic Higher Education*, Xavier University of Louisiana, USA, September 12, 1987, no. 4: AAS 80 (1988) 764.

12   ECE, I, no. 28.

6. CONTINUING DIALOGUE AMONG UNIVERSITY REPRESENTATIVES AND CHURCH AUTHORITIES

Dialogues occasioned by *Ex corde Ecclesiae* may be graced moments characterized by

  a. a manifest openness to a further analysis and local appropriation of Catholic identity;
  b. an appreciation of the positive contributions that campus-wide conversations make; and
  c. a conviction that conversation can develop and sustain relationships.

A need exists for continued attention and commitment to the far-reaching implications—curricular, staffing, programming—of major themes within *Ex corde Ecclesiae*. These include Catholic identity, *communio*, relating faith and culture, pastoral outreach, the New Evangelization, and relationship to the Church.

7. CATHOLIC IDENTITY

Catholic identity lies at the heart of *Ex corde Ecclesiae*. In 1979, Pope John Paul II, in an address to the Catholic academic community at The Catholic University of America, stressed the importance of the Catholic character of Catholic institutions of higher learning:

> Every university or college is qualified by a specified mode of being. Yours is the qualification of being Catholic, of affirming God, his revelation and the Catholic Church as the guardian and interpreter of that revelation. The term 'Catholic' will never be a mere label either added or dropped according to the pressures of varying factors.[13]

Catholic universities, in addition to their academic commitments to secular goals and programs, should excel in theological education, prayer and liturgy, and works of charity. These religious activities, however, do not alone make a university "Catholic." *Ex corde Ecclesiae* highlights four distinctive characteristics that are essential for Catholic identity:

  a. Christian inspiration in individuals and the university community;
  b. Reflection and research on human knowledge in the light of the Catholic faith;
  c. Fidelity to the Christian message in conformity with the magisterium of the Church;
  d. Institutional commitment to the service of others.[14]

---

13   Pope John Paul II, Address "*Ad prope et exstantes sedes Studiorum Universitatis Catholicae profectus hanc allocutionem fecit ad moderatores et doctores eiusdem Athenaei atque ad legatos Collegiorum Universitatumque Catholicarum totius Nationis,*" October 6, 1979, AAS 71:13 (1979) 1260.

14   ECE, I, no. 13 [quoting "The Catholic University in the Modern World," the final document of the Second International Congress of Delegates of Catholic Universities, Rome, November 20-29, 1972, Sec. 1].

Catholic universities cherish their Catholic tradition and, in many cases, the special charisms of the religious communities that founded them. In the United States, they enjoyed the freedom to incorporate these religious values into their academic mission. The principles of *Ex corde Ecclesiae* afford them an opportunity to re-examine their origin and renew their way of living out this precious heritage.

Catholic universities enjoy institutional autonomy: as academic institutions their governance "is and remains internal to the institution."[15] In order to maintain and safeguard their freely-chosen Catholic identity, it is important for Catholic universities to set out clearly in their official documentation their Catholic character and to implement in practical terms their commitment to the essential elements of Catholic identity, including the following:

e.   Commitment to be faithful to the teachings of the Catholic Church;

f.   Commitment to Catholic ideals, principles and attitudes in carrying out research, teaching and all other university activities, including activities of officially-recognized student and faculty organizations and associations, and with due regard for academic freedom and the conscience of every individual;[16]

g.   Commitment to serve others, particularly the poor, underprivileged and vulnerable members of society;

h.   Commitment of witness of the Catholic faith by Catholic administrators and teachers, especially those teaching the theological disciplines, and acknowledgment and respect on the part of non-Catholic teachers and administrators of the university's Catholic identity and mission;

i.   Commitment to provide courses for students on Catholic moral and religious principles and their application to critical areas such as human life and other issues of social justice;

j.   Commitment to care pastorally for the students, faculty, administration and staff;

k.   Commitment to provide personal services (health care, counseling and guidance) to students, as well as administration and faculty, in conformity with the Church's ethical and religious teaching and directives; and

l.   Commitment to create a campus culture and environment that is expressive and supportive of a Catholic way of life.

Catholic universities should make every effort to enhance their communion with the hierarchy so that through this special relationship they may assist each other to accomplish the mission to which they are mutually committed.

In a secular world the strong Catholic identity of our institutes of higher learning is invaluable in witnessing to the relationship of truth and reason, the call of

---

15   See ECE, I, no. 12 and footnote 15; Vatican Council II, Pastoral Constitution on the Church in the Modern World (*Gaudium et Spes*) 59; Declaration on Catholic Education (*Gravissimum Educationis*) 10.

16   See ECE, II, Art. 2, §§4-5.

the revealed Word, and the authentic meaning of human life. "The present age is in urgent need of this kind of disinterested service, namely of proclaiming the meaning of truth, that fundamental value without which freedom, justice and human dignity are extinguished."[17]

PART TWO: PARTICULAR NORMS

The chief purpose of the following norms is to assist Catholic colleges and universities in their internal process of reviewing their Catholic identity and clarifying their essential mission and goals. They are intended to provide practical guidance to those committed to the enterprise of Catholic higher education as they seek to implement the theological and pastoral principles of *Ex corde Ecclesiae*. Accordingly, the norms follow the basic outline of the General Norms found in *Ex corde Ecclesiae* and provide concrete steps that will facilitate the implementation of the Holy Father's document in the context of the relevant sections of the *Code of Canon Law* and complementary Church legislation.[18]

ART. 1. THE NATURE OF THE PARTICULAR NORMS

1. These particular norms are applicable to all Catholic colleges, universities and institutions of higher learning within the territory encompassed by the National Conference of Catholic Bishops, contrary particular laws, customs or privileges notwithstanding.[19]

2. Catholic universities are to observe the general norms of *Ex corde Ecclesiae* and the following particular norms as they apply to their individual institutions, taking into account their own statutes and, as far as possible and appropriate, relevant provisions of applicable federal and state law, regulations and procedures.

    a.   Those universities established or approved by the Holy See, by the NCCB, by other hierarchical assemblies, or by individual diocesan bishops are to incorporate, by reference and in other appropriate ways, the general and particular norms into their governing documents and conform their existing statutes to such norms. Within five years of the effective date of these particular norms, Catholic universities are to submit the aforesaid incorporation for review and affirmation to the university's competent ecclesiastical authority.

    b.   Other Catholic universities are to make the general and particular norms their own, include them in the university's official documentation by reference and in other appropriate ways, and, as much as possible, conform their existing statutes to such norms. These steps to ensure their

---

17   ECE, I, no. 4.

18   See ECE, II, Art. 1, §§1 & 2.

19   ECE, II, Art. 11: "Any particular laws or customs presently in effect that are contrary to this constitution are abolished. Also, any privileges granted up to this day by the Holy See whether to physical or moral persons that are contrary to this present constitution are abolished." These Particular Norms are not applicable to ecclesiastical universities and faculties insofar as they are governed by the Apostolic Constitution *Sapientia Christiana*.

Catholic identity are to be carried out in agreement with the diocesan bishop of the place where the seat of the university is situated.[20]

c. Changes in statutes of universities established by the hierarchy, religious institutes or other public juridic persons that substantially affect the nature, mission or Catholic identity of the university require the approval of competent ecclesiastical authority.[21]

3. Those establishing or sponsoring a Catholic university have an obligation to make certain that they will be able to carry out their canonical duties in a way acceptable under relevant provisions of applicable federal and state law, regulations and procedures.[22]

ART. 2. THE NATURE OF A CATHOLIC UNIVERSITY

1. The purpose of a Catholic university is education and academic research proper to the disciplines of the university. Since it enjoys the institutional autonomy appropriate to an academic institution, its governance is and remains internal to the institution itself. This fundamental purpose and institutional autonomy must be respected and promoted by all, so that the university may effectively carry out its mission of freely searching for all truth.[23]

2. Academic freedom is an essential component of a Catholic university. The university should take steps to ensure that all professors are accorded "a lawful freedom of inquiry and of thought, and of freedom to express their minds humbly and courageously about those matters in which they enjoy competence."[24] In particular, "[t]hose who are engaged in the sacred disciplines enjoy a lawful freedom of inquiry and of prudently expressing their opinions on matters in which they have expertise, while observing the submission [obsequio] due to the magisterium of the Church."[25]

3. With due regard for the common good and the need to safeguard and promote the integrity and unity of the faith, the diocesan bishop has the duty to recognize and promote the rightful academic freedom of professors in Catholic universities in their search for truth.[26]

4. Recognizing the dignity of the human person, a Catholic university, in promoting its own Catholic identity and fostering Catholic teaching and discipline,

---

20 See ECE, II, Art. 1, §3.

21 See ECE, II, Art. 3, §4.

22 See canon 807 and ECE, Art. 3; Congregation for Catholic Education, *Directives to Assist in the Formulation of the Ordinances for the Apostolic Constitution "Ex corde Ecclesiae,"* not dated, no. B1.

23 See footnote 15.

24 Vatican Council II, Pastoral Constitution on the Church in the Modern World (*Gaudium et Spes*) no. 62. A university's commitment to Catholic ideals, principles and attitudes is not only consistent with academic freedom and the integrity of secular subjects, it requires "[f]reedom in research and teaching" and respect for "the principles and methods of each individual discipline." ECE, II, Art. 2, §5.

25 C. 218.

26 See ECE, II, Art. 2, §5.

must respect the religious liberty of every individual, a right with which each is endowed by nature.[27]

5. A responsibility of every Catholic university is to affirm its essential characteristics, in accord with the principles of *Ex corde Ecclesiae*, through public acknowledgment in its mission statement and/or its other official documentation of its canonical status[28] and its commitment to the practical implications of its Catholic identity, including but not limited to those specified in Part One, Section 7 of this document.

6. The university (in particular, the trustees, administration, and faculty) should take practical steps to implement its mission statement in order to foster and strengthen its Catholic nature and character.[29]

ART. 3. THE ESTABLISHMENT OF A CATHOLIC UNIVERSITY

1. A Catholic university may be established, or an existing university approved, by the Holy See, the National Conference of Catholic Bishops, other hierarchical assemblies, or individual diocesan bishops. It may also be established by a religious institute or some other public juridic person, or by individual Catholics, acting singly or in association, with proper ecclesiastical approval.[30]

---

27 Though thoroughly imbued with Christian inspiration, the university's Catholic identity should in no way be construed as an excuse for religious indoctrination or proselytization. See Vatican Council II, Declaration on Religious Liberty (*Dignitatis Humanae*) nos. 2-4.

28 See footnote 31 for a listing of canonical categories.

29 In this regard, the university may wish to establish a "mission effectiveness committee" or some other appropriate structure to develop methods by which Catholics may promote the university's Catholic identity and those who are not Catholic may acknowledge and respect this identity.

30 ECE, II, Art. 3, §§1-3, cf. Canon 808. Note that, under Canon 322, private associations of the faithful can acquire juridic personality by the issuance of a formal decree of competent ecclesiastical authority (§1) and approval of their statutes, retaining, all the while, their private character (§2).

2. At the time of its establishment the university should see to it that its canonical status is identified, including the ecclesiastical authority by which it has been established or approved or to which it otherwise relates.[31]

3. The statutes of Catholic universities established by hierarchical authority or by religious institutes or other public juridic persons must be approved by competent ecclesiastical authority.[32]

4. No university may assume the title Catholic without the consent of the competent ecclesiastical authority.[33]

ART. 4. THE UNIVERSITY COMMUNITY

1. The responsibility for safeguarding and strengthening the Catholic identity of the university rests primarily with the university itself. All the members of the university community are called to participate in this important task in accordance with their specific roles: the sponsoring religious community, the board of trustees,

---

31   A Catholic university may be established by various ecclesiastical authorities or entities (e.g., the Holy See) or by individual Catholics. Moreover, the university may be erected as a self-standing public juridic person or it may be simply a complex "activity" or "apostolate" of a public juridic person. The following alternatives outline different categories that describe a Catholic university from the canonical perspective:

   a) *The university as an apostolate of the Holy See.* The Holy See may erect a university or approve an already-established university as an apostolate of the Holy See itself. Such universities, which are sometimes granted the title of "pontifical," are erected or approved by a decree of the Holy See and their statutes must be approved by the Holy See. The "competent ecclesiastical authority" to which such universities are related is the Holy See through the Congregation for Catholic Education.

   b) *The university as an apostolate of the National Conference of Catholic Bishops.* An episcopal conference has the right to erect a university or approve an already-established university as an apostolate of the conference itself through the issuance of a decree and approval of its statutes. The "competent ecclesiastical authority" to which such a university is related is the National Conference of Catholic Bishops.

   c) *The university as an apostolate of a diocesan bishop or a group of diocesan bishops.* Diocesan bishops, acting individually or jointly, have the right to erect a university or approve an already-established university as a diocesan or inter-diocesan apostolate through the issuance of a decree and approval of its statutes. The "competent ecclesiastical authority" to which such a university is related is the individual diocesan bishop or the group of diocesan bishops establishing or approving it.

   d) *The university as an apostolate of a public juridic person.* A university may be established or approved as an apostolate of a public juridic person (such as a religious institute). In such cases the consent of the bishop of the diocese in which the seat of the university is situated (or of a group of bishops, the NCCB or the Holy See) and approval of its statutes are required. Such a university relates to the public juridic person that established or approved it and to the diocesan bishop (or group of bishops, the NCCB or the Holy See) as its "competent ecclesiastical authority."

   e) *The university as public juridic person.* A university may itself be erected as a public association of the faithful or some other type of public juridic person (*universitas rerum or universitas personarum*). Such juridic personality requires the issuance of a decree of erection and approval of the statutes by the Holy See, the National Conference of Catholic Bishops, or an individual or group of diocesan bishops.

   f) *The university established by individuals.* Individual Catholics may found a university or convert an existing university into a Catholic institution without its being established or approved by the Holy See, the National Conference of Catholic Bishops, individual diocesan bishops or a public juridic person. Nonetheless, in accordance with canon 808, such a university may refer to itself as Catholic only with the consent of the competent ecclesiastical authority.

32   ECE, II, Art. 3, §4.

33   C. 808.

the administration and staff, the faculty, and the students.[34] Men and women of religious faiths other than Catholic, on the board of trustees, on the faculty, and in other positions, can make a valuable contribution to the university. Their presence affords the opportunity for all to learn and benefit from each other. The university should welcome them as full partners in the campus community.

2. The Board of Trustees

a. Each member of the board must be committed to the practical implications of the university's Catholic identity as set forth in its mission statement or equivalent document.

b. To the extent possible, the majority of the board should be Catholics committed to the Church.

c. The board should develop effective ways of relating to and collaborating with the local bishop and diocesan agencies on matters of mutual concern.[35]

d. The board should analyze ecclesiastical documents on higher education, such as *Ex corde Ecclesiae* and this Application, and develop specific ways of implementing them appropriate to the structure and life of the university.

e. The board should see to it that the university periodically undertakes an internal review of the congruence of its mission statement, its courses of instruction, its research program, and its service activity with the ideals, principles and norms expressed in *Ex corde Ecclesiae*.

3. Administration and Staff

a. The university president should be a Catholic.[36]

b. The administration should inform faculty and staff at the time of their appointment regarding the Catholic identity, mission and religious practices of the university and encourage them to participate, to the degree possible, in the spiritual life of the university.

---

34 ECE, II, Art. 4, §1. In these norms the phrases "board of trustees," "president" and "administration" are used to denote the highest bodies of governance within the university's corporate and operational structure. If, in an individual case, the university's governance uses a different structure or other titles, the norms should be applied accordingly.

35 In individual situations, it may be possible and appropriate to invite the diocesan bishop or his delegate to be a member of the board itself. In other cases, arranging periodic meetings to address the university's Catholic identity and mission may prove more practical and effective.

36 Upon assuming the office of president for the first time, a Catholic should express his or her commitment to the university's Catholic identity and to the Catholic faith in accordance with canon 833, §7 (see also Congregation for the Doctrine of the Faith, Formula *Professio Fidei et Iusiurandum*, July 1, 1988, AAS 81 [1989] 104-106; and Congregation for the Doctrine of the Faith, *Rescriptum ex audientia SS. mi Quod Attinet*, September 19, 1989, AAS 81 [1989] 1169). When a candidate who is not a Catholic is being considered for appointment as president of a Catholic university, the university should consult with the competent ecclesiastical authority about the matter. In all cases, the president should express his or her commitment to the university's Catholic mission and identity.

    c.   The administration should be in dialogue with the local bishop about ways of promoting Catholic identity and the contribution that the university can make to the life of the Church in the area.

4. *Faculty*

    a.   In accordance with its procedures for the hiring and retention of professionally qualified faculty and relevant provisions of applicable federal and state law, regulations and procedures, the university should strive to recruit and appoint Catholics as professors so that, to the extent possible, those committed to the witness of the faith will constitute a majority of the faculty. All professors are expected to be aware of and committed to the Catholic mission and identity of their institutions.

    b.   All professors are expected to exhibit not only academic competence and good character but also respect for Catholic doctrine.[37] When these qualities are found to be lacking, the university statutes are to specify the competent authority and the process to be followed to remedy the situation.[38]

    c.   Catholic theology should be taught in every Catholic university, and, if possible, a department or chair of Catholic theology should be established. Academic events should be organized on a regular basis to address theological issues, especially those relative to the various disciplines taught in the university.[39]

    d.   Both the university and the bishops, aware of the contributions made by theologians to Church and academy, have a right to expect them to present authentic Catholic teaching. Catholic professors of the theological disciplines have a corresponding duty to be faithful to the Church's magisterium as the authoritative interpreter of Sacred Scripture and Sacred Tradition.

    e.   Catholics who teach the theological disciplines in a Catholic university are required to have a *mandatum* granted by competent ecclesiastical authority.[40]

        i.   The *mandatum* is fundamentally an acknowledgment by Church authority that a Catholic professor of a theological

---

37   The identity of a Catholic university is essentially linked to the quality of its professors and to respect for Catholic doctrine. The Church's expectation of "respect for Catholic doctrine" should not, however, be misconstrued to imply that a Catholic university's task is to indoctrinate or proselytize its students. Secular subjects are taught for their intrinsic value, and the teaching of secular subjects is to be measured by the norms and professional standards applicable and appropriate to the individual disciplines. *See* ECE, II, Art. 4, §1 and footnotes 24 and 27.

38   C. 810, §1.

39   *Gravissimum Educationis* no. 10.

40   C. 812 and ECE, II, Art. 4, §3.

      discipline is a teacher within the full communion of the
      Catholic Church.

ii.   The *mandatum* should not be construed as an appointment, authorization, delegation or approbation of one's teaching by Church authorities. Those who have received a *mandatum* teach in their own name in virtue of their baptism and their academic and professional competence, not in the name of the Bishop or of the Church's magisterium.[41]

iii.   The *mandatum* recognizes the professor's commitment and responsibility to teach authentic Catholic doctrine and to refrain from putting forth as Catholic teaching anything contrary to the Church's magisterium.

iv.   The following procedure is given to facilitate, as of the effective date of this Application, the process of requesting and granting the *mandatum*. Following the approval of the Application, a detailed procedure will be developed outlining the process of requesting and granting (or withdrawing) the *mandatum*.

(1)   The competent ecclesiastical authority to grant the *mandatum* is the bishop of the diocese in which the Catholic university is located; he may grant the *mandatum* personally or through a delegate.[42]

(2)   Without prejudice to the rights of the local bishop,[43] a *mandatum*, once granted, remains in effect wherever and as long as the professor teaches unless and until withdrawn by competent ecclesiastical authority.

---

41   "*Mandatum*" is a technical term referring to the juridical expression of the ecclesial relationship of communion that exists between the Church and the Catholic teacher of a theological discipline in the Catholic university. The prescription of canon 812 is grounded in the right and responsibility of bishops to safeguard the faithful teaching of Catholic doctrine to the people of God and to assure the authentic presentation of the Church's magisterium. Those with such a *mandatum* are not agents of the magisterium; they teach in their own name, not in the name of the bishop. Nonetheless, they are not separate from the Church's teaching mission. Responding to their baptismal call, their ecclesial task is to teach, write and research for the benefit of the Church and within its communion. The *mandatum* is essentially the recognition of an ecclesial relationship between the professor and the Church (see canon 229, §3). Moreover, it is not the responsibility of a Catholic university to seek the *mandatum*; this is a personal obligation of each professor. If a particular professor lacks a *mandatum* and continues to teach a theological discipline, the university must determine what further action may be taken in accordance with its own mission and statutes (see canon 810, §1).

42   The attestation or declaration of the professor that he or she will teach in communion with the Church can be expressed by the profession of faith and oath of fidelity or in any other reasonable manner acceptable to the one issuing the *mandatum*.

43   Although the general principle is that, once granted, there is no need for the *mandatum* to be granted again by another diocesan bishop, every diocesan bishop has the right to require otherwise in his own diocese.

(3) The *mandatum* should be given in writing. The reasons for denying or removing a *mandatum* should also be in writing.[44]

5. *Students.* With due regard for the principles of religious liberty and freedom of conscience, students should have the opportunity to be educated in the Church's moral and religious principles and social teachings and to participate in the life of faith.[45]

a. Catholic students have a right to receive from a university instruction in authentic Catholic doctrine and practice, especially from those who teach the theological disciplines. They also have a right to be provided with opportunities to practice the faith through participation in Mass, the sacraments, religious devotions and other authentic forms of Catholic spirituality.

b. Courses in Catholic doctrine and practice should be made available to all students.

c. Catholic teaching should have a place, if appropriate to the subject matter, in the various disciplines taught in the university.[46] Students should be provided with adequate instruction on professional ethics and moral issues related to their profession and the secular disciplines.

ART. 5. THE CATHOLIC UNIVERSITY IN THE CHURCH

1. *The Universal Church*

a. The university shall develop and maintain a plan for fulfilling its mission that communicates and develops the Catholic intellectual tradition, is of service to the Church and society, and encourages the members of the university community to grow in the practice of the faith.[47]

b. The university plan should address intellectual and pastoral contributions to the mission of communicating Gospel values,[48] service to the poor, social justice initiatives, and ecumenical and inter-religious activities.

---

44 Administrative acts in the external forum must be in writing (c. 37). The writing not only demonstrates the fulfillment of canon 812, but, in cases of denial or removal, it permits the person who considers his or her rights to have been injured to seek recourse. See canons 1732-1739.

45 In *Gravissimum Educationis* no. 10, the Vatican Council expressed the hope that students in Catholic institutions of higher learning will become "truly outstanding in learning, ready to shoulder society's heavier burdens and to witness the faith to the world."

46 See above footnotes 27 and 37.

47 See ECE, I, no. 38 ff. and footnote 44.

48 See ECE, I, nos. 48-49.

2. The Local Church

a. In accordance with Church teaching and the universal law of the Church, the local Bishop has a responsibility to promote the welfare of the Catholic universities in his diocese and to watch over the preservation and strengthening of their Catholic character.[49]

b. Bishops should, when appropriate, acknowledge publicly the service of Catholic universities to the Church and support the institution's Catholic identity if it is unjustifiably challenged.

c. Diocesan and university authorities should commit themselves mutually to regular dialogues to achieve the goals of *Ex corde Ecclesiae* according to local needs and circumstances.

d. University authorities and the local diocesan bishop should develop practical methods of collaboration that are harmonious with the university's structure and statutes. Similar forms of collaboration should also exist between the university and the religious institute to which it is related by establishment or tradition.[50]

e. *Doctrinal Responsibilities: Approaches to Promoting Cooperation and Resolving Misunderstandings between Bishops and Theologians*, approved and published by the National Conference of Catholic Bishops, June 17, 1989, can serve as a useful guide for diocesan bishops, professors of the theological disciplines and administrators of universities to promote informal cooperation and collaboration in the Church's teaching mission and the faithful observance within Catholic universities of the principles of Catholic doctrine.

f. Disputes about Church doctrine should be resolved, whenever possible, in an informal manner. At times, the resolution of such matters

---

49 See ECE, II, Art. 5, §2. See also the responsibilities of the diocesan bishop set forth in canons 392, §1; 394, §1; 756, §2; 810, §2; 813.

50 The following are some suggestions for collaboration:

a) Arranging for the diocesan bishop or his delegate and members of the religious institute to be involved in the university's governance, perhaps through representation on the board of trustees or in some other appropriate manner.

b) Sharing the university's annual report with the diocesan bishop and the religious institute, especially in regard to matters affecting Catholic identity and the religious institute's charism.

c) Scheduling regular pastoral visits to the university on the part of the diocesan bishop and the religious institute's leadership and involving the members of the diocese and the institute in campus ministry.

d) Collaborating on evangelization and on the special works of the religious institute.

e) Conducting dialogues on matters of doctrine and pastoral practice and on the development of spirituality in accordance with the religious institute's charism.

f) Resolving issues affecting the university's Catholic identity in accordance with established procedures. (See ECE, II, Art. 5, §2 and ECE footnote 51.)

g) Participating together in ecumenical and inter-faith endeavors.

h) Contributing to the diocesan process of formulating the quinquennial report to the Holy See.

may benefit from formal doctrinal dialogue as proposed by *Doctrinal Responsibilities* and adapted by the parties in question.[51]

g.   The National Conference of Catholic Bishops, through an appropriate committee structure, should continue to dialogue and collaborate with the Catholic academic community and its representative associations about ways of safeguarding and promoting the ideals, principles and norms expressed in *Ex corde Ecclesiae*.

ART. 6. PASTORAL MINISTRY

1. The diocesan bishop has overall responsibility for the pastoral care of the university's students, faculty, administration and staff.[52]

2. The university, in cooperation with the diocesan bishop, shall make provision for effective campus ministry programs, including the celebration of the sacraments, especially the Eucharist and penance, other liturgical celebrations, and opportunities for prayer and spiritual reflection.[53]

3. When selecting pastoral ministers—priests, deacons, religious and lay persons—to carry on the work of campus ministry, the university authorities should work closely with the diocesan bishop and interested religious institutes. Without prejudice to the provision of canon 969, §2, priests and deacons must enjoy pastoral faculties from the local ordinary in order to exercise their ministry on campus.

4. With due regard for religious liberty and freedom of conscience, the university, in cooperation with the diocesan bishop, should collaborate in ecumenical and interfaith efforts to care for the pastoral needs of students, faculty and other university personnel who are not Catholic.

5. In these pastoral efforts, the university and the diocesan bishop should take account of the prescriptions and recommendations issued by the Holy See and the guidance and pastoral statements of the National Conference of Catholic Bishops.[54]

---

51   See National Conference of Catholic Bishops, *Doctrinal Responsibilities: Approaches to Promoting Cooperation and Resolving Misunderstandings between Bishops and Theologians*, June 17, 1989, Washington, D.C.: USCC, III, C, 16-22. When such disputes are not resolved within the limits of informal or formal dialogue, they should be addressed in a timely manner by the competent ecclesiastical authority through appropriate doctrinal and administrative actions, taking into account the requirements of the common good and the rights of the individuals and institutions involved.

52   See canon 813.

53   See ECE, II, Art. 6, §2.

54   See ECE, II, Art. 7, §1; National Conference of Catholic Bishops, "Sons and Daughters of the Light: A Pastoral Plan for Ministry with Young Adults," *Origins*, November 28, 1996, 384-402, especially 398-401; "Letter to College Students," *Origins*, December 7, 1995, 429-430; *Empowered by the Spirit*, Washington, D.C.: USCC, 1985.

ART. 7. COOPERATION

1. Catholic universities should commit themselves to cooperate in a special way with other Catholic universities, institutions and professional associations, in the United States and abroad, in order to build up the entire Catholic academic community.[55]

2. In collaborating with governmental agencies, regional associations, and other universities, whether public or private, Catholic universities should give corporate witness to and promote the Church's social teaching and its moral principles in areas such as the fostering of peace and justice, respect for all human life, the eradication of poverty and unjust discrimination, the development of all peoples and the growth of human culture.[56]

CONCLUSION

This Application will become effective one year after its *recognitio* by the Holy See.

During the five years following the effective date of this Application, the National Conference of Catholic Bishops in collaboration with representatives of Catholic universities should develop a mutually agreeable process to review and evaluate the implementation of *Ex corde Ecclesiae* and this Application, particularly regarding the nature, mission and Catholic identity of the universities.

Ten years after the effective date of this Application, the National Conference of Catholic Bishops will review this Application of *Ex corde Ecclesiae* for the United States.

The Bishops of the United States, in offering this application of *Ex corde Ecclesiae*, join in sentiments expressed by Pope John Paul II:

> I turn to the whole Church, convinced that Catholic universities are essential to her growth and to the development of Christian culture and human progress. For this reason, the entire ecclesial community is invited to give its support to Catholic institutions of higher education and to assist them in their process of development and renewal. . . .[57]

---

55   See ECE, I, no. 35 and ECE, II, Art. 7, §2.

56   See ECE, I, nos. 32-35.

57   Ibid., Introduction, no. 11.

Guidelines Concerning the Academic *Mandatum* in Catholic Universities

(*Canon 812*)

2001

In December 2000 the NCCB Ad Hoc Committee on the *Mandatum* sent a draft copy of these guidelines to all Bishops for their use in conversations on the local level with theologians. The final draft entitled *Guidelines Concerning the Academic* Mandatum *in Catholic Universities* was discussed and accepted for publication by the general membership at its June 2001 General Meeting. The guidelines have been authorized for publication by the undersigned.

> Msgr. William P. Fay
> General Secretary
> USCCB

PREFACE

On November 17, 1999, the Catholic Bishops of the United States approved *The Application of Ex corde Ecclesiae for the United States*, implementing the apostolic constitution *Ex corde Ecclesiae*. This action received the *recognitio* from the Congregation for Bishops on May 3, 2000. Bishop Joseph A. Fiorenza, President of the United States Conference of Catholic Bishops (USCCB) (formerly the National Conference of Catholic Bishops [NCCB]), decreed that the *Application* would have the force of particular law for the United States on May 3, 2001.

GUIDELINES

Pope John Paul II's constitution *Ex corde Ecclesiae* of 1990 fostered a productive dialogue between the Bishops of the United States and the leaders of Catholic colleges and universities. It is anticipated that this recently approved *Application of Ex corde Ecclesiae for the United States* will further that conversation and build a community of trust and dialogue between Bishops and theologians. Without ongoing and respectful communication, the implementation of the *mandatum* might appear to be only a juridical constriction of the work of theologians. Both Bishops and theologians are engaged in a necessary though complementary service to the Church that requires ongoing and mutually respectful dialogue.

Article 4, 4, e, iv, of the *Application* states that "a detailed procedure will be developed outlining the process of requesting and granting (or withdrawing) the *mandatum*." These guidelines are intended to explain and serve as a resource for the conferral of the *mandatum*. Only those guidelines herein that repeat a norm of the *Application* have the force of particular law. They were accepted for distribution to the members of the USCCB on June 15, 2001, by the Conference's general membership.

1. Nature of the mandatum

   a. The *mandatum* is fundamentally an acknowledgment by church authority that a Catholic professor of a theological discipline is teaching within the full communion of the Catholic Church (*Application*: Article 4, 4, e, i).

   b. The object of the *mandatum* is the content of the professor's teaching, and thus the *mandatum* recognizes both the professor's "lawful freedom of inquiry" (*Application*: Article 2, 2) and the professor's commitment and responsibility to teach authentic Catholic doctrine and to refrain from putting forth as Catholic teaching anything contrary to the Church's magisterium (cf. *Application*: Article 4, 4, e, iii).

   c. The *mandatum* should not be construed as an appointment, authorization, delegation, or approbation of one's teaching by church authorities. Theologians who have received a *mandatum* are not catechists; they teach in their own name in virtue of their baptism and their academic and professional competence, not in the name of the Bishop or of the Church's magisterium (*Application*: Article 4, 4, e, ii).

2. Who is required to have the *mandatum*?

   a. All Catholics who teach theological disciplines in a Catholic university are required to have a *mandatum* (canon 812 and *Application*: Article 4, 4, e).

   b. In accord with canon 812, the *mandatum* is an obligation of the professor, not of the university.

   c. "Teaching" in this context signifies regular presentation (by full-time or part-time professors) of academic material in an academic institution. Occasional lectures as well as preaching and counseling are not within the meaning of the *Application* and these guidelines.

   d. "Theological disciplines" in this context signifies Sacred Scripture, dogmatic theology, moral theology, pastoral theology, canon law, liturgy, and church history (cf. canon 252).

   e. "University" in this context signifies not only institutions that bear the title "university" but also Catholic colleges and other institutions of higher learning.

3. Who is to grant the *mandatum*?

    a.   The *mandatum* is to be granted by the diocesan Bishop of the diocese in which the Catholic university is located, generally understood to be where the president and central administration offices are located (cf. *Application*: Article 4, 4, e , iv, [1]).

    b.   The competent ecclesiastical authority may grant the *mandatum* personally or through a delegate (*Application*: Article 4, 4, e, iv, [1]).

4. How is the *mandatum* to be granted?

    a.   A request for a *mandatum* by a professor of a Catholic theological discipline should be in writing and should include a declaration that the teacher will teach in full communion with the Church.

    b.   The ecclesiastical authority should respond in writing (*Application*: Article 4, 4, e, iv, [3]) (see Appendix for samples).

    c.   An ecclesiastical authority has the right to offer the *mandatum* on his own initiative (which requires an acceptance), provided that the commitment to teach in full communion with the Church is clear.

    d.   A professor already hired by the effective date (May 3, 2001) of the *Application* is required to obtain the *mandatum* by June 1, 2002.

           A professor hired after the effective date of the *Application* is required to obtain the *mandatum* within the academic year or within six months of the date of being hired, whichever is longer.

           If the professor does not obtain the *mandatum* within the time period given above, the competent ecclesiastical authority should notify the appropriate authority in the college or university.

    e.   Without prejudice to the rights of the diocesan Bishop, a *mandatum*, once granted, remains in effect wherever and as long as the professor teaches unless and until it is withdrawn by the competent ecclesiastical authority (*Application*: Article 4, 4, e, iv, [2]). Although there is no need for the *mandatum*, once granted, to be granted again by another diocesan Bishop, every diocesan Bishop has the right to require otherwise in his own diocese (*Application*: footnote 43).

    f.   If the Bishop is contemplating the denial or withdrawal of the *mandatum*, he should discuss this informally with the theologian, listing the reasons and identifying the sources, and allowing the theologian to make all appropriate responses.

5. Grounds and process for withholding or withdrawing the *mandatum*

    a. If all the conditions for granting the *mandatum* are fulfilled, the professor has a right to receive it and ecclesiastical authority has an obligation in justice to grant it.

    b. Right intentions and right conduct are to be presumed until the contrary is proven. Hence the ecclesiastical authority should presume, until the contrary is proven, that those who attest that they teach in full communion with the Church actually do so.

    c. Ecclesiastical authorities who, after discussion with the professor in question, withhold or withdraw the *mandatum* must state their reasons in writing and otherwise enable the person who believes that his or her rights have been violated to seek recourse (*Application*: Article 4, 4, e, [3]; footnote 44). Such withholding or withdrawal should be based on specific and detailed evidence that the teacher does not fulfill the conditions of the *mandatum* (these guidelines: 1, b, and c, supra; *Application*: Article 4, 4, e, iii; NCCB, *Doctrinal Responsibilities: Approaches to Promoting Cooperation and Resolving Misunderstandings Between Bishops and Theologians* [Washington, D.C.: United States Catholic Conference, 1989], III, C, 4).

    d. Any negative judgment concerning an objectionable portion of a professor's work should be assessed at three levels: (1) the significance of that portion of the professor's work within the context of his or her overall theological contribution; (2) its relationship to the larger Catholic tradition; (3) its implications for the life of the Church (cf. *Doctrinal Responsibilities*, III, C, 4).

6. Appeals and resolution of disputes

    a. Because the decision to withhold or withdraw the *mandatum* touches on the rights of theologians, the general principles of canon law should be adhered to in seeking recourse and in the process of appeal.

    b. In the resolution of disputes about the withholding or withdrawal of the *mandatum*, it is important for both parties to have competent canonical and theological counsel.

    c. For the resolution of disputes about the withholding or withdrawal of the *mandatum*, there should be that contact between the Bishop and the professor as urged in canon 1733 § 1. The process set forth in *Doctrinal Responsibilities* should be followed. The right of all parties to good reputation must always be honored (cf. canon 220).

    d. Other means for conflict resolution on the diocesan, regional, or provincial levels (not excluding local mediation procedures) can also be invoked (cf. canon 1733).

    e. While the use of informal procedures is preferable, the aggrieved party always has the right to formal recourse against the denial or withdrawal of a *mandatum* in accordance with the canonical norms for "Recourse Against Administrative Decrees" (canons 1732-1739).

7. Diocesan Bishops who have Catholic colleges or universities in their dioceses are encouraged to be available to meet with professors of Catholic theological disciplines to review concrete procedures for the granting, withholding, or withdrawal of the *mandatum* and to discuss other matters of common interest.

8. The members of the USCCB Committee for Bishops and Catholic Colleges and University Presidents and its staff will serve as resource personnel for information and guidance on matters connected with the *mandatum*.

9. These guidelines are to be reviewed after five years by a committee appointed by the Conference President.

APPENDIX

Sample *Mandatum* Draft

Attestation of the Professor of Catholic Theological Disciplines

I hereby declare my role and responsibility as a professor of a Catholic theological discipline within the full communion of the Church.

As a professor of a Catholic theological discipline, therefore, I am committed to teach authentic Catholic doctrine and to refrain from putting forth as Catholic teaching anything contrary to the Church's magisterium.

Signature: _____

Date: _____

Place:_____

Acknowledgement of the Diocesan Bishop

I hereby acknowledge your declaration to remain within the full communion of the Catholic Church in fulfillment of your role and responsibility as a professor of Catholic theological disciplines.

I recognize your commitment as a professor of Catholic theological disciplines to teach authentic Catholic doctrine and to refrain from putting forth as Catholic teaching anything contrary to the Church's magisterium.

While the *mandatum* does not constitute you as an agent of the magisterium, it does affirm that your work as a professor of Catholic theological disciplines is an important part of the Church's mission.

This *mandatum* remains in effect as long as you are engaged in the teaching of theology or until it is withdrawn by competent ecclesiastical authority for a just cause.

Signature:_____

Date:_____

Place: _____

SAMPLE *MANDATUM* DRAFT

Offered by the Bishop on his own Initiative

MEMORANDUM

TO: Professor Thomas Bellarmine

FROM: Most Reverend Angelo Buonpastore

RE: *MANDATUM*

DATE:

This memorandum constitutes the *mandatum* that you are required to have in order to be in compliance with canon 812. The purpose of the *mandatum* is to recognize the mutual ecclesial relationship that exists between the Church and Catholic professors of theology. It also constitutes my grateful response to your participation in the Church's mission.

I hereby acknowledge your role and responsibility as a professor of Catholic theology within the full communion of the Catholic Church.

As a professor of Catholic theology you are committed to teach authentic Catholic doctrine and to refrain from putting forth as Catholic teaching anything contrary to the Church's magisterium.

While this *mandatum* does not constitute you as an agent of the magisterium, it does affirm that your work as a professor of theology is an important part of the Church's mission.

This *mandatum* remains in effect as long as you are engaged in the teaching of Catholic theology or until it is withdrawn by appropriate authority for a just cause.

This *mandatum* takes effect upon my receipt of the enclosed statement of your understanding and acceptance of its terms.

Acknowledgement

I, **Thomas Bellarmine,** have reviewed the *mandatum* conferred on me by Bishop Angelo Buonpastore and, by means of my signature, express my understanding and acceptance of its terms.

Signature: _____

Date: _____

Place:_____

Resource Companion

This protocol was developed by USCCB staff in consultation with the Ad Hoc Committee on the Mandatum *to assist diocesan bishops, Catholic professors of Catholic theological disciplines, and presidents of Catholic colleges and universities in the implementation of the* Guidelines Concerning the Academic Mandatum *in Catholic Universities. This protocol was not subject to a vote by the bishops.*

Professors of Catholic Theological Disciplines and the *Mandatum*

1. Catholic professor of Catholic theological disciplines requests a *mandatum*

    a. The Catholic professor of Catholic theological disciplines writes to the Bishop of the diocese where the university is located (if there are branches, the diocese where the central administrative offices are located) requesting the *mandatum* and stating that s/he will teach in communion with the Church.

    b. When the professor receives notification that the *mandatum* has been granted, s/he may wish to inform the chair of the Theology Department and/or the president of the university.

    c. If the professor is notified that conditions for granting the *mandatum* may not be fulfilled for reasons given in writing, the professor should

    (1) meet with the Bishop, if s/he has not already done so, to discuss the action, the evidence, and the reasons for the Bishop's decision, and/or
    (2) be accompanied by theological and canonical counsel when meeting with the Bishop.

    d. Following the meeting, the Bishop

    (1) notifies the professor in writing and grants the *mandatum*, or
    (2) notifies the professor in writing that he will not grant the *mandatum* giving his reasons in the written notification.

    e. If the professor does not receive the mandatum, and s/he believes his or her rights have been violated, the professor has a right to

    (1) seek resolution through the formal process described in *Doctrinal Responsibilities*,
    (2) seek resolution through other means for conflict resolution that exist in the diocese, and/or
    (3) seek formal recourse in accord with canons 1732-1739, "Recourse Against Administrative Decrees."

    f.   If the professor decides to seek resolution of the dispute, s/he should obtain theological and canonical counsel throughout the process.

    g.   If the professor decides to seek resolution of the dispute, the Bishop should participate in the process, whether the process is informal or formal.

    h.   The Bishop notifies the president of the college/university of the granting/denial of the *mandatum* to the professor(s) of theological disciplines.

    i.   Public acknowledgment of the granting, refusal by the Bishop or the professor, withdrawing of the *mandatum* for professors of Catholic theological disciplines, and responses to inquiries regarding these matters should be made in accord with a procedure worked out, with appropriate counsel, by the Bishop and college/university presidents within a diocese.

2.   Catholic professor of Catholic theological disciplines receives a mandatum from the Bishop offered on his own initiative

    a.   The *mandatum* is offered in writing at the initiative of the diocesan Bishop. A professor receives a *mandatum* from the Bishop of the diocese in which the college/university where s/he teaches is located. The professor is asked to respond within a specified time period indicating his or her commitment to teach in communion with the Church.

    b.   The professor accepts the *mandatum*,

        (1) acknowledges the *mandatum* in writing stating that s/he will teach in communion with the Church, and

        (2) may wish to inform the president of the college/university.

    c.   If the professor does not wish to accept the *mandatum*, s/he

        (1) notifies the Bishop in writing of the decision giving reasons for the non-acceptance, and

        (2) may wish to inform the president of the college/university.

    d.   The Bishop notifies the president of the college/university of the acceptance/non-acceptance of the *mandatum* by the professor(s) of Catholic theological disciplines.

    e.   If a professor chooses not to respond to the Bishop regarding acceptance or non-acceptance of the *mandatum* within the specified time period, the Bishop may wish to notify the president of the college/university of the non-response.

    f.   Public acknowledgment of the granting, refusal by the Bishop or the professor, withdrawing of the *mandatum* for professors of Catholic theological disciplines, and responses to inquiries regarding these matters should be made in accord with a procedure worked out, with appropriate counsel, by the Bishop and college/university presidents within a diocese.

Diocesan Bishop and the *Mandatum*

1. Diocesan Bishop grants *mandatum* upon request from Catholic professor of Catholic theological disciplines

    a. The diocesan Bishop determines whether he will delegate the authority to grant the *mandatum* and, if so, to whom.

    b. The diocesan Bishop receives a request from a Catholic professor teaching a Catholic theological discipline in a Catholic college or university in his diocese for a *mandatum*.

    (1) If he has delegated the authority to grant the *mandatum*, he forwards the request to the delegate.

    (2) If he has reserved the authority to grant the *mandatum* to himself, he reviews the request to confirm that the professor

    i. is teaching a Catholic theological discipline, and
    ii. has stated that s/he will teach in communion with the Church.

    (3) If the professor of Catholic theological disciplines teaches in a branch of the college/university located in another diocese, the Bishop may wish to consult the diocesan Bishop of the diocese in which the branch is located regarding the conditions for granting the *mandatum*.

    c. If the conditions for granting the *mandatum* are fulfilled in the request,

    (1) the Bishop grants the *mandatum*, and
    (2) notifies the president of the college/university.

    d. Public acknowledgment of the granting, refusal by the Bishop or the professor, withdrawing of the *mandatum* for professors of Catholic theological disciplines, and responses to inquiries regarding these matters should be made in accord with a procedure worked out, with appropriate counsel, by the Bishop and college/university presidents within a diocese.

2. Diocesan Bishop offers *mandatum* to Catholic professor of Catholic theological disciplines on his own initiative

    a.   The diocesan Bishop requests names of Catholic professors of Catholic theological disciplines teaching in Catholic colleges and universities in his diocese from the appropriate representatives of the respective institutions.

    b.   The diocesan Bishop determines whether he will delegate the authority to grant the *mandatum* and, if so, to whom.

    c.   The diocesan Bishop (or his delegate) sends a letter to each professor of Catholic theological disciplines teaching in Catholic colleges and universities in his diocese

        (1) offering the *mandatum*, and

        (2) requesting a response from the professor within a specified time period indicating the professor's commitment to teach in communion with the Church.

    d.   The Bishop receives

        (1) response of acceptance from professor,

            i. acknowledges the response, and
            ii. notifies the president of the college/university.

        (2) response of non-acceptance from professor,

            i. acknowledges the response, and
            ii. notifies the president of the college/university.

        (3) no response from professor after specified time period has lapsed and so may wish to notify the president of the college/university of the non-response.

    e.   Public acknowledgment of the granting, refusal by the Bishop or the professor, withdrawing of the *mandatum* for professors of Catholic theological disciplines, and responses to inquiries regarding these matters should be made in accord with a procedure worked out, with appropriate counsel, by the Bishop and college/university presidents within a diocese.

3. Diocesan Bishop denies *mandatum* for Catholic professor of Catholic theological disciplines

    a.   The diocesan Bishop determines whether he will delegate the authority to grant the *mandatum* and, if so, to whom.

b. The diocesan Bishop receives a request from a Catholic professor teaching a Catholic theological discipline in a Catholic college or university in his diocese for a *mandatum*.

   (1) If he has delegated the authority to grant the *mandatum*, he forwards the request to the delegate.
   (2) If he has reserved the authority to grant the *mandatum* to himself, he reviews the request to confirm that the professor

      i. is teaching a Catholic theological discipline, and
      ii. has stated that s/he will teach in communion with the Church.

   (3) If the professor of Catholic theological disciplines teaches in a branch of the college/university located in another diocese, the Bishop may wish to consult the diocesan Bishop of the diocese in which the branch is located regarding the conditions for granting the *mandatum*.

c. If the conditions for granting the *mandatum* are fulfilled in the request,

   (1) the Bishop grants the *mandatum*, and
   (2) notifies the president of the college/university.

d. If the conditions for granting the *mandatum* do not seem to be fulfilled, the Bishop, if he judges it appropriate, asks theological and canonical counsel to review the evidence and advise him.

e. If, after hearing counsel, the Bishop determines that the conditions for granting the *mandatum* are fulfilled, he responds to the professor in writing and grants the *mandatum*.

f. If, after hearing counsel, the Bishop determines that the conditions for granting the *mandatum* may not be fulfilled,

   (1) he notifies the professor in writing, and
   (2) requests a meeting with the professor to discuss the evidence, stating that s/he may be accompanied by theological and canonical counsel.

g. Following the meeting, the Bishop decides whether or not the conditions for granting the *mandatum* are fulfilled. The Bishop

   (1) notifies the professor in writing and grants the *mandatum*, or
   (2) notifies the professor in writing that he will not grant the *mandatum* giving his reasons in the written notification, and
   (3) notifies the president of the college/university of his decision.

    h.   If the professor does not receive the *mandatum*, and s/he believes his or her rights have been violated, the professor has a right to

        (1) seek resolution through the formal process described in *Doctrinal Responsibilities*,

        (2) seek resolution through other means for conflict resolution that exist in the diocese, and/or

        (3) seek formal recourse in accord with canons 1732-1739, "Recourse Against Administrative Decrees."

    i.   If the professor decides to seek resolution of the dispute, the Bishop should participate in the process, whether the process is informal or formal.

    j.   Public acknowledgment of the granting, refusal by the Bishop or the professor, withdrawing of the *mandatum* for professors of Catholic theological disciplines, and responses to inquiries regarding these matters should be made in accord with a procedure worked out, with appropriate counsel, by the Bishop and college/university presidents within a diocese.

4.   Diocesan Bishop withdraws *mandatum* from Catholic professor of Catholic theological disciplines

    a.   The diocesan Bishop is informed in writing that a Catholic professor of Catholic theological disciplines who possesses a *mandatum* is not fulfilling the condition of the *mandatum*, that is, the Catholic professor is alleged not to be teaching in communion with the Church or to be teaching contrary to the Church's magisterium. The allegation must be written, specific as to a particular writing or public lecture, and it must detail on what grounds the teaching is not in conformity with the magisterium.

    b.   The diocesan Bishop

        (1) reviews the allegation and the evidence,

        (2) seeks theological and canonical counsel,

        (3) consults other appropriate individuals, and

        (4) determines whether or not the allegation is reasonable and the evidence sufficient to support the allegation.

    c.   If the diocesan Bishop determines that the grounds for the allegation are neither reasonable nor sufficient, he communicates this to the one(s) making the allegation.

    d.   If the diocesan Bishop determines the allegation is reasonable and the evidence sufficient to support the allegation, he

        (1) notifies the professor of the allegation(s) and the source of the allegation(s) in writing, and

      (2) requests a meeting with the professor to discuss the evidence, stating that s/he may be accompanied by theological and canonical counsel.

e.   During the meeting with the professor, the diocesan Bishop, accompanied by theological and canonical counsel,

      (1) presents the allegation, identifying its source,

      (2) reviews the evidence alleging that the professor has violated the condition of the *mandatum*,

      (3) provides opportunity for defense by the professor, and

      (4) informs the professor of his or her right to seek recourse in the event that the professor believes his or her rights have been violated.

f.   Following the meeting, the diocesan Bishop, after hearing from counsel, decides whether or not he will withdraw the *mandatum*.

      (1) If the diocesan Bishop decides not to withdraw the *mandatum*, he

          i.   notifies the professor of his decision in writing,

          ii. notifies the one(s) making the allegation of his decision, and

          iii. may wish to notify the president of the college/ university of his decision.

      (2) If the diocesan Bishop decides to withdraw the *mandatum*, he

          i.   notifies the professor in writing that he is withdrawing the *mandatum* giving his reasons,

          ii. informs the professor of his or her right to recourse in the event that the professor believes his or her rights have been violated, and

          iii. notifies the president of the college/university of his decision.

g.   If the diocesan Bishop withdraws the *mandatum*, and the professor believes his or her rights have been violated, the professor has a right to

      (1) seek resolution through the formal process described in *Doctrinal Responsibilities*,

      (2) seek resolution through other means for conflict resolution that exist in the diocese, and/or

      (3) seek formal recourse in accord with canons 1732-1739, "Recourse Against Administrative Decrees."

h. If the professor decides to seek resolution of the dispute, the diocesan Bishop should participate in the process, whether the process is informal or formal.

i. Public acknowledgment of the granting, refusal by the Bishop or the professor, withdrawing of the *mandatum* for professors of Catholic theological disciplines, and responses to inquiries regarding these matters should be made in accord with a procedure worked out, with appropriate counsel, by the Bishop and college/university presidents within a diocese.

President of Catholic College/University and the *Mandatum*

A. Upon request of the diocesan Bishop or his delegate, the president or the appropriate representative of the Catholic college/university forwards a list of Catholic professors of Catholic theological disciplines teaching in the college/university.

B. Following notification of the president by the diocesan Bishop or his delegate of the names of Catholic professors of Catholic theological disciplines in the college/university who have received, been denied, or explicitly or implicitly not accepted the *mandatum*, the president may wish to inform appropriate college/university personnel in accord with college/university policy.

C. Public acknowledgment of the granting, refusal by the Bishop or the professor, withdrawing of the *mandatum* for Catholic professors of theological disciplines, and responses to inquiries regarding these matters should be made in accord with a procedure worked out, with appropriate counsel, by the Bishop and college/university presidents within a diocese.

(1) Possible points to consider in developing a procedure:

i. The *mandatum* is an acknowledgment by church authority that the professor teaches in communion with the Church.

ii. The acknowledgment takes place in the external forum.

iii. Neither the Bishop nor the college/university is obliged to publish a list of professors who have received *mandata*, though either may wish to do so after appropriate consultation.

iv. In the absence of a published list, and when asked about a particular professor and the *mandatum*, the president might

1. respond affirmatively or negatively without details,
2. refer the inquiry to the Bishop, or
3. respond in accord with a procedure determined in consultation with the diocesan Bishop and other appropriate persons.

    v.   Reasons why a particular professor does not have a *mandatum* should not be made public without prior knowledge of the professor.

(2)   The procedure should be communicated to professors of Catholic theological disciplines.

 Committee on Catholic Education

Final Report for the Ten Year Review of *The Application of Ex corde Ecclesiae for the United States*

June 11, 2012

As Chairman of the Committee on Catholic Education, I am pleased to offer this report regarding the ten year review of *The Application of Ex corde Ecclesiae for the United States*. In January 2011 bishops were asked to hold conversations with college and university presidents in their dioceses. With more than 100 bishops reporting on their conversations at regional meetings during the November 2011 General Assembly, the prevailing tone was positive and the news was good. Bishops reported that they believe our institutions of Catholic higher education have made definite progress in advancing Catholic identity. The relationship between bishops and presidents on the local level can be characterized as positive and engaged, demonstrating progress on courtesy and cooperation in the last ten years. Clarity about Catholic identity among college and university leadership has fostered substantive dialogues and cultivated greater mission driven practices across the university. In acknowledging that much progress has been made, we recognize there is still work to be done.

The robust discussion among bishops at the regional meetings in November 2011 generated some constructive suggestions. The Committee on Catholic Education, having reviewed the compilation of the regional discussions, offers the following recommendation for your consideration.

Under the auspices of the Committee on Catholic Education, a working group of bishops and presidents will be formed to continue the dialogue about strategic subjects on a national level. As they consider topics, they will gather information regarding best practices, offer suggestions for conversation at the local level, and as needed, develop resources. The subject areas to be addressed by the working group are as follows:

- Continuing dialogue between bishops and presidents toward greater cooperation in advancing the mission of the Church
- Hiring for mission
- Forming trustees, faculty, and staff regarding Catholic identity
- Addressing the need for improved, accurate, and deeper theological and catechetical knowledge through curricular and pastoral means

With this report, I officially conclude the ten year review of *The Application of Ex corde Ecclesiae for the United States*. The review process yielded fruitful and necessary dialogue. The Committee on Catholic Education echoes the attitude of Pope John Paul II: "I turn to the whole Church, convinced that Catholic universities are essential to her growth and to the development of Christian culture and human progress." The success of the ten year review provides a clear course for continued dialogue regarding Catholic higher education and its essential contribution to the Church and society.

Most Rev. Joseph P. McFadden, Bishop of Harrisburg
Chairman, Committee on Catholic Education

 **Committee on Catholic Education**

Final Report of the *Ex Corde Ecclesiae* Working Group

March 13, 2014

Following the 2011 ten year review of *The Application of Ex Corde Ecclesiae for the United States,* Bishop McFadden, Chairman of the Committee on Catholic Education, formed a Working Group of bishops and presidents. Their task was to continue the dialogue on a national level about several strategic subjects, which emerged from the ten year review, and as necessary, gather information regarding best practices, offer suggestions for conversation at the local level, and develop resources. The subject areas to be addressed were as follows:

- Continuing dialogue between bishops and presidents toward greater cooperation in advancing the mission of the Church
- Hiring for mission
- Forming trustees and faculty regarding Catholic identity
- Addressing the need for improved, accurate, and deeper theological and catechetical knowledge through curricular and pastoral means.

During the initial meeting, held November 11, 2012, the Working Group affirmed the long tradition, under the egis of the Bishops' Conference, of collaboration between bishops and presidents. They emphasized the need for on-going dialogue and the value of regular communication among bishops and presidents. The members recognized the interconnectedness of the strategic topics as well as the importance of close and consistent relationship between bishops and presidents in addressing the issues. The university was described as a privileged place for the Church to think strategically and to listen carefully toward a fruitful dialogue between Gospel and culture. The members expressed a desire to gather best practices from colleges, universities and dioceses regarding efforts to continue the dialogue.

The January 2013 meeting focused on continued dialogue between bishops and presidents. The importance of a trust relationship between the bishop and president was noted. The Working Group expressed interest in gathering best practices to serve as a model. Key issues discussed were: policies regarding speakers and awards, student organizations, particularly LGBT groups, and hiring for mission. There was a call to collectively champion a current issue like immigration reform or gun control.

The March 2013 meeting addressed hiring for mission. Much attention was given to campus and diocesan practices for effective means to incorporate Catholic identity and mission into the hiring process. Several challenges and needs were voiced related to the identification of candidates who are not only well prepared within their discipline, but are articulate, practicing Catholics. The members clarified the phrase "hiring for mission" recognizing that it does not exclusively mean hiring only Catholics. In an effort to promote respect for Catholic identity and to assist in appropriating the value of mission based hiring across campus, the group acknowledged a variety of procedures, protocols, and resources developed by individual institutions toward that goal. The group wanted to explore the topic further by engaging CARA to assist in the collection and analysis of data regarding mission based hiring practices.

Formation was the topic of the May 2013 meeting. Several national programs (i.e. Collegium, Rome Seminar, Institute for Administrators in Catholic Higher Education, and Association of Student Affairs at Catholic Colleges and Universities' annual conference) were acknowledged for their work with particular university members including faculty, staff, administrators, trustees and student life professionals. The Catholic intellectual tradition, Catholic social teaching and the Catholic approach to interfaith relations were lifted up as helpful ways to engage administrators, faculty and staff. Several topics were identified for further exploration including: the self-understanding of board members, the organization of the board, the development of an assessment tool for mission and the human and fiscal resources allocated in service to mission.

The November 2013 meeting addressed the keenly sensed need for improved, accurate, and deeper theological and catechetical knowledge through curricular and pastoral means. Working Group members discussed, with a representative from the Committee on Doctrine, initiatives aimed at ongoing conversations between bishops and theologians. Extensive conversation explored significant observations: a) the need to meet students where they are, b) to recognize that many students have a limited faith foundation while also demonstrating openness to the spiritual dimension of life, and c) to awaken or cultivate the student's interest in the faith at the levels of both mind and heart. The discussion reinforced the importance of relationship, characterized by mutual trust, close and consistent cooperation and continuing dialogue, between the diocese and the college.

Recommendations

Given the purpose of the 2012 *Ex Corde Ecclesiae* Working Group and the expectations to gather information regarding best practices, offer suggestions for conversation at the local level, and as needed, develop resources, the following two recommendations are put forward by the members.

+ We strongly recommend that the conversation between bishops and presidents continue in a structured and deliberate manner at the national level. We ask for the creation of a Working Group, within the Committee on Catholic Education, to continue the important work begun in 2012.

+ We request the allocation of resources for the collection of data regarding collaboration between bishops and presidents, best practices and their results related to hiring for mission, formation of trustees, faculty and staff in Catholic identity, and the cultivation of curricular and pastoral means to improve and deepen theological and catechetical knowledge.

Members of the Working Group included: Bishop Walter Edyvean, Chairman, Archbishop John Vlazny, Bishop Richard Malone, Bishop John Noonan, Bishop David O'Connell, CM, Bishop George Thomas, President Michael Garanzini, SJ, President Margaret Carney, OSF, President John Garvey, President Thomas Keefe, President Rosalie Mirenda, President Stephen Minnis, Dr. Michael Galligan-Stierle, and Barbara H. McCrabb.

The activity of the *Ex Corde Ecclesiae* Working Group was scheduled to conclude in November of 2014. Due to the untimely death of Bishop McFadden, who was Chairman of the Committee on Catholic Education, and the decision of USCCB leadership to elect an immediate replacement for the Committee on Catholic Education, the Working Group ended its term a year earlier than anticipated. With the submission of this, their final report, to Archbishop George Lucas, Chairman of the Committee on Catholic Education, the Working Group concludes its task. The members wish to express their deep appreciation and gratitude for Bishop McFadden and his commitment to continuing the dialogue of Catholic higher education in the United States.

Bishop Walter Edyvean
Auxiliary Bishop of the Archdiocese of Boston
Chairman, *Ex Corde Ecclesiae* Working Group
February 26, 2014

* The Committee on Catholic Education approved this report on March 13, 2014.